Word for *Word*

Word for *Word*

A Translator's Memoir of Literature, Politics, and Survival in Soviet Russia

Lilianna Lungina

as told to
OLEG DORMAN

Translated from the Russian by
Polly Gannon and Ast A. Moore

OVERLOOK DUCKWORTH
NEW YORK · LONDON

This edition first published in hardcover in the United States and the United Kingdom
in 2014 by Overlook Duckworth, Peter Mayer Publishers, Inc.

NEW YORK
141 Wooster Street
New York, NY 10012
www.overlookpress.com

For bulk and special sales, please contact sales@overlookny.com,
or write us at the address above.

LONDON
30 Calvin Street
London E1 6NW
info@duckworth-publishers.co.uk
www.ducknet.co.uk

For bulk and special sales, please contact sales@duckworth-publishers.co.uk,
or write us at the above address.

Cataloging-in-Publication Data is available from the Library of Congress
A catalogue record for this book is available from the British Library

Book design and type formatting by Bernard Schleifer
Manufactured in the United States of America
ISBN: 978-1-4683-0732-0 (US)
ISBN 978-0-7156-4922-0 (UK)
FIRST EDITION
2 4 6 8 10 9 7 5 3 1

Word for *Word*

Preface

BY OLEG DORMAN

THIS BOOK IS THE TRANSCRIPT OF AN ORAL ACCOUNT BY LILIANNA Zinovievna Lungina of her own life, which was presented in a documentary series called *Word for Word*. I've added the most minor corrections, which are standard in the publication of any transcript, and have added those parts of the stories that could not, for various reasons, make it into the film, so the book is about a third longer than the series.

Lilianna Lungina (1920–1998) was a celebrated literary translator—it was through her translations that Russian readers discovered Astrid Lindgren's *Karlsson on the Roof* and the novels of Knut Hamsun, August Strindberg, Max Frisch, Heinrich Böll, Michael Ende, Colette, Alexandre Dumas, Georges Simenon, Boris Vian, and Romain Gary. She translated the plays of Friedrich Schiller, Gerhart Hauptmann, and Henrik Ibsen, and stories by E. T. A. Hoffmann and Hans Christian Andersen.

At the very beginning of the 1990s, a memoir by Lilianna Lungina, *Les saisons de Moscou* (*The Seasons of Moscow*), was published in France; it became a bestseller, and in an annual poll conducted by *Elle*, it was named by French readers as the best nonfiction book of the year. But Lungina was determined not to publish the book in Russia. She believed that her compatriots needed a completely different book, entirely rewritten from cover to cover. With one's own people, she explained, one can and must discuss the things that outsiders cannot understand.

And at a certain point, she agreed to take on this challenge in front of a television camera. I think that the French book was some-

thing like a first draft for her story, which stretched over many days.
In February of 1997, over the span of a week, I came to Lungina's
apartment on Novinsky Boulevard with the cinematographer
Vadim Yusov and a small camera crew to listen to and film an oral
novel, which would become the film *Word for Word*.

In her long life, Lilianna Lungina lived in many countries and
captured the twentieth century with an extraordinary depth and
clarity. This was a century that confirmed that there is no such thing
as a collective life—only the lives of individuals. A century that confirmed that one is the only soldier on the field—that, indeed, that
one is, himself, that field. That a person isn't the plaything of circumstances, nor life's victim, but a boundless and impregnable
source of good.

Few people in the world get the chance to meet people like
Lungina and her husband, the famous screenwriter Simon Lvovich
Lungin. And yet it's possible that other people—the people one
meets—are the most important thing in our lives. It is through
other people that we can take stock of life, of what human capabil-
ity, of what love can be, of whether loyalty, bravery, and truth truly
resemble what is written about them in books.

I was lucky enough to know and love such people. It is an
honor for me to present this book to you.

Introduction

My name is Lilya Lungina. From age five to ten, when I lived in Germany, I was called Lili Markovich, stress on the first syllable. Then, from age ten to fourteen, in France, they called me Lily Markovich—stress on the last syllable. And when I performed in my mother's puppet theater, I was called Lily Imali. Imali is my mother's pseudonym. It is an ancient Hebrew word that means "my mama." That's how many different names I've had. I studied in as many schools as I had names. I was enrolled in twelve schools, all told. After such a long life—on the 16th of June, 1997, I will be 77 years old; even thinking about it sends shivers down my spine! I never thought I would live to such a venerable age—after such a long life, I have still never learned to refer to myself by my name and patronymic. Maybe this is a mark of our generation. We have always thought of ourselves as young, and so avoided formal forms of address.

Still, seventy-seven is a ripe age, and it's time to start drawing conclusions about what has happened during my time. And not just provisional conclusions, as my husband Sima called the last chapter of his book *Seen and Believed*, but final ones. On the other hand, though, what kinds of conclusions can you draw about an activity, about a vocation? What kinds of conclusions are there to be drawn about life? The results of life are life itself, I think. The entire sum of happy, trying, unhappy, bright, and bland moments you live through is the essence of life. That is the conclusion, the only one that matters. That's why I now want to look back and reminisce. That's why I feel drawn to old photographs.

I remember very clearly the moment I realized that I was "myself," separate from the rest of the world.

I have a photograph in which I'm sitting on my father's lap—that was the very moment I'm talking about. I loved my father dearly and was terribly spoiled by him. Up to that very second, I had felt I was fused with him and the whole world. Suddenly I had the sensation that I stood apart from him and from everything around me. I think it was the consciousness of being a person in my own right. Until that moment I grew willy-nilly, programmed by my genes, by what was already innate in me from birth. But once I realized that I was separate from the world, it began to influence me, to act upon me. And what was innate in me began to undergo changes, to be refashioned and refined, to be subjected to the larger life that surrounded me. In other words, my experiences, the situations I found myself in, the choices I made, the relationships I formed with others—in all of this, the world that raged around me became ever more palpable. This is why I thought that when telling about my life I would be talking not so much about myself, but . . . It seemed rather presumptuous at first—why should I start talking about myself? I don't consider myself to be smarter or wiser than the next person. It just didn't make sense to talk about myself. But to talk about myself as some sort of organism that absorbed elements of the external world, the complex, very contradictory life of the world outside—maybe it's worth a try. Then you would end up with the experience of that larger life filtered through one person, something more objective within the personal. And that may turn out to be worthwhile.

It seems to me that now, at the end of the century, when our country is in the midst of such confusion and so rudderless—it feels like it's headed toward an abyss at an ever-increasing pace—that it may truly be important and valuable to salvage as many of the pieces of what we have lived through as possible. The whole twentieth century, and even, through our parents, the nineteenth. Perhaps the more people there are who bear witness to their own experience, the easier it will be to preserve it. Ultimately, it will be possible to piece together a more or less coherent picture of a humane life, of life with a human face, as they like to say nowadays.

And perhaps this may have something to offer to the twenty-first century. I'm speaking about a composite of voices, of course, in which mine is but a drop, even a fraction of a drop. Keeping this in mind, I can attempt to talk about myself, about what and how I have lived.

If we accept the premise (this is what I believe, anyway) that a work of art, a book or film, must bear some "message," some appeal to mankind, I would like to formulate this right off. What I wish to convey most strongly is that one must hope and believe that even the worst of situations can unexpectedly turn into something quite different and lead to something good. I will show how many misfortunes in my own life, and then in my life together with Sima, led to surprising and improbable happiness and richness. I'll stress this in order to show that one must not despair. Because I know that despair has taken root in the lives of many, many people. So one has to believe, to keep hoping, and then little by little things will take on a different meaning.

1

IT HAS BEEN MY EXPERIENCE—AND I OBSERVE THAT IT IS TRUE FOR others, as well—that interest in one's parents awakens later in life. At first you resist them and push them away, trying to affirm your own personality out of a desire to lead your own independent existence. You're so wrapped up in your own life that you have no use for your parents. You love them, of course, but they don't take part in the life of your heart. But with time, you become increasingly interested in where you came from, and you want to understand what the sources of your own life are, to learn what your parents did, who your grandmother and grandfather really were, and so forth, as far back as it goes. This happens later on in life. I see this in my own children, who at a mature age are beginning to take an interest in their mother and father—a father who is no longer with them . . . I went through the same thing, with the difference that I had already begun asking my mother these serious questions when I was still young. So almost everything that I will say about my grandfather and grandmother is not from my own recollection, but from recollections about what others have said.

My mother and father were both from Poltava, Ukraine. I always wanted to go there. Many times I asked my aunt, my mother's cousin who was married to Alexander Frumkin, a well-known academic, to take me to Poltava. I wanted her to show me their house. This never happened. Finally, after Sima and I had been married some thirty-five years, Fate itself arranged for us to visit there. Sima had been recovering from several serious bouts of pneumonia, and the doctors told him that he needed to convalesce in a mild, temperate climate. My friend Flora Litvinova, mother of the famous dissident Pavlik Litvinov, advised us to go to Shishaki, forty-four miles down from Poltava. The beautiful Psel River flows through the region, there are pine woods, and it's a lovely place. Without a lot of deliberation—I make decisions like that very quickly—I asked Flora to rent a cottage for us, and we set out.

Strangely enough, and completely by chance, we ended up in Poltava.

It was a very sweet provincial town with a few elegant stone buildings in the center. The outskirts, however, looked as though they were suspended in time. The houses and cottages were an unusual style of daubed clay structure. Unlike the ordinary rural dwellings—wattle and mud huts—these had visible wooden beams and supports, which made them seem more solid. Still, they were squat, one-story dwellings with little windows, and they looked more like barns than houses where people lived. I think that in the years that Mama and Papa lived there, the whole of Poltava, except for the very center, looked like that. And I imagine that in just such a small white cottage—they are all white, daubed and whitewashed twice a year, in spring and in autumn, so that everything gleamed and sparkled—lived my mother, Maria Danilovna Liberson. Her family called her Manya.

I know they had a two-story house. The first story was wooden, and the second was wattle and daub. The first floor was occupied by a drugstore. This was not an ordinary drugstore, because for some reason my grandfather sold toys there, as well. The drugstore had a large toy department.

My grandfather not only owned the drugstore, he was the

chemist. He spent time making experiments and discoveries in a little lab. And he adored toys. He ordered the latest toys from Europe and the US. They say people came all the way from Kiev to buy his toys. The latest top-of-the-line toys. He loved mechanical toys. Many years later, when the first Toy Exhibit opened in Moscow, our then six-year-old son Pavlik said, "I'm not interested in mechanical toys." But my grandfather was fascinated by them.

My grandfather also had a medal for rescuing someone from drowning. He had thrown himself into the water and then plucked someone out. In addition, he had been chief of the Jewish self-defense militia during the Pogroms.

My father was called Zyama—Zinovy Yakovlevich Markovich. He came from a poor Jewish family with eight or nine kids. He was the only one who received an education. Grandfather and Grandmother had nothing to do with it. His brother, a petty official, played a minor role in my life. We used to visit him in Moscow, and I remember endless dinners from those times. Later his son was arrested as a Trotskyite, and perished in prison. Those are the only things I know about my father's side of the family.

My mother and father had a high-school romance. Mother graduated from Poltava Gymnasium, and Father from the technical high school, with an engineering major. I have in my possession one of Mama's diaries, in which she describes how on the 6th of June 1907, they celebrated her graduation on the terrace of her home. There were three boys and three girls, and there is a record of the wonderful, romantic plans they had for the rest of their lives.

I'll tell more about Papa and Mama, and about Mama's friend Rebecca, a true beauty, as well, but first I want to mention three of their friends.

Milya Ulman moved to Moscow, went to university, and became a history teacher in a Soviet Worker's College.

Papa's friend Sunya left for Palestine, where he became a professor of chemistry and head of the department at the University of Jerusalem.

Papa's friend Misha became a socialist, and when World War I started he wrote to Plekhanov, asking whether a social-democrat should enlist to fight or not. Plekhanov, who, unlike Lenin, was convinced that Russia should be defended, answered: absolutely. Misha volunteered, and died in the war.

Mama and Papa were separated. After the Pogroms of 1907, Mama's family fled from Poltava to Germany. They spent two or three years there, then moved to Palestine. But Mother couldn't bear the separation from Father. She left her parents in Jaffa and returned to Russia to look for my father. He, in the meantime, had managed to graduate from the St. Petersburg Mining Institute.

2

IN 1907 OR 1908, SOON AFTER THE FAILURE OF THE FIRST RUSSIAN revolution of 1905, the youth—primarily urban young people, and especially in St. Petersburg—were overwhelmed by a sense of bitter disappointment. There was a spate of suicides, almost an epidemic. Mass suicides. Young people didn't know what to do with their lives. It seemed that all prospects for the future, all hope for change, for movement forward in this country, was lost. And it was just at this moment that Mama, who was a student in the Higher Women's Courses, published an open letter simultaneously in two or three newspapers: "Young men and women who feel lonely and alone, come to a gathering at my place. Every Thursday at five o'clock, I will hold an open house. Let us have tea and coffee together, discuss things, make friends. Maybe it will become easier for us to live a life in common than it is for each of us individually."

According to the customs of the time this was quite a daring and unusual venture, and it did not go unnoticed. In those days a little book called *The Society of the Solitary* came out. Recently, when I was reading Blok's correspondence, I discovered completely by chance a reference to the "strong and courageous act of the student Maria Liberson." I was fascinated. Reading this I realized that Mama had begun very early to take an active part in the life around her. She didn't confine herself to her small circle of acquaintances, but opened herself up to other people in the larger world. I was very happy to learn this.

From the letter of Maria Liberson to Alexander Blok:

> *Yesterday's presentation revealed to me yet again how profound the problem of loneliness is in our society.*
> *Alexander Alexandrovich, perhaps the fateful boundary between the intelligentsia and the people is so insurmountable*

precisely because an even higher barrier exists among people of
the intelligentsia themselves? Perhaps someone from the intelli-
gentsia can't find a path to the people because each person is so
alone? Perhaps the only path to the soul of the people is the strug-
gle against the solitude and alienation, the disconnectedness, of
the intelligentsia?

Yesterday you yourself brought up the subject of suicide,
which confirms your assumption that living this way is difficult,
almost impossible.

No matter what the reasons for which someone takes his own
life, at the moment that person does it he is undoubtedly pro-
foundly lonely and alone.

My mother and father were by this time already deeply in love.
Then World War I broke out, and my father went to fight as a "volunteer"—but in fact recruitment was mandatory. He was drafted.
He was captured by the Germans and remained a prisoner of war
in Germany for nearly four years, which is why he spoke German
so well. I have postcards that he wrote from prison.

During the war Mama organized a
kindergarten for Jewish children whose
fathers had been mobilized. The first
Jewish kindergarten was a "five-day"—
in other words, children lived and slept
there, and went home only on weekends.
In her diaries she describes these little
boys and girls with unusual tenderness
and love. She talks about how hard it
was to get hold of the children, how
their mothers, hungry and poor, nevertheless feared giving them up for day-
care, and how she tried to talk them
into it. She describes the story of the
kindergarten day after day and writes
something about each child. It was so
touching, I could hardly read it without crying, because Mama wrote with

such love about those—abstract for me—little Moishes and Judiths, who then became so real in the pages of the diary. She talked about how he said such-and-such a word today for the first time, and how she made a little donkey out of clay. Mama recorded all of this, nothing was insignificant to her. This made her job in the kindergarten (she also found two helpers) appear as an exceptionally poetic undertaking. It was as though she were raising rare flowers. Each of them was a precious specimen. Each of them was watered with a special formula and on a particular schedule. Gradually, as I read the diary, these children bloomed for me: one of them soon learned to sing, another to dance, yet another could sculpt in clay or recite poetry. Absolutely crushed and broken at first, they were transformed into lovingly cultivated little plants.

This captivated me, of course. I began to see Mama in a different light when I read the diary. Not in a mundane light—she wasn't the mother who asked when I was coming home, or whether I had tied my scarf or eaten my meat patty. Truth be told, Mama wasn't a very good housekeeper in ordinary circumstances. She only knew how to rise to the occasion on holidays—to prepare an unusual meal, to come up with a menu in verse. There was no end of that sort of thing. She simply wasn't interested in run-of-the-mill activities, in "dailiness." She was a person who flourished during holidays.

Papa returned from captivity, like any other POW, at the end of the war in 1919. Evidently, Papa and Mama joined their lives together once and for all at that point. Since Papa had become a member of some Jewish workers' party—not the Bund, but another one that had merged with the Communist party when they came to power—he was automatically accepted as a member of the party of the Bolsheviks. He received his first appointment: head of the Municipal Public Education Authority in the city of Smolensk. Papa and Mama moved there, and were lodged in a room—a cell in the Smolensk Monastery, converted into a dormitory for business travelers. This was the room I was born in, on 16 June 1920.

3

Papa was one of the few Bolsheviks with a higher education, and was also somehow acquainted with Anatoly Lunacharsky. When I was six months old, Papa was summoned to Moscow and appointed as one of Lunacharsky's deputies in the Commissariat of Public Education. We settled into an enormous building on Sretensky Boulevard. The apartment was divided into fifteen or twenty rooms with a family occupying each room, and a kitchen shared by twenty women. In our room we had a gigantic fireplace, over which, as far as I remember, heads made from black bread were always drying—puppet heads. During the entire Moscow period, and afterward as well, I was surrounded by puppets. Mama loved puppetry with a deep passion and wanted to start her own puppet theater. The black bread was inedible. It was soggy and sticky, and Mama used it as modeling clay.

I must say that Mama had a penchant for theater arts. She started her first puppet theater in Petersburg, in the kindergarten. Later, in Moscow, she got to know Ivan Efimov, the wonderful puppeteer and sculptor. Together with his wife he wrote an excellent book called *Petrushka*. He was an animal sculptor—his work is exhibited to this day. He was a superb artist, ruined by his student Sergei Obraztsov. In some sense, Obraztsov was also Mama's student, since she started working with Efimov first. Then Obraztsov ruined everyone. He threatened

people by saying, "You either work with me, for me—or I'll strangle you." Which he succeeded in doing.

When I was two years old, Mama took me to Berlin, to a German pension, where we met up with my grandmother. I don't remember much, but judging from my mother's letters to my father, my grandmother constantly reproached my mother for not dressing me, or combing my hair, properly.

Here are a few excerpts from the letters my mother wrote to my father from Birkenwerder Pension in September 1922:

My relations with Mama remain very cool. Somehow we seem to have a different approach to everything. She doesn't know how to deal with Lilith, either. Here is an example of her pedagogical method. "Lucy," (that's the name she usually calls her) "Lucy, do you want a chocolate?" "Want a tsocolate!" Lilith pipes up. "No, you may not have a chocolate. I don't have any more now, we'll buy some tomorrow." "Want a tsocolate!" Lilith screams. "Why do you offer her some if there isn't any?" I ask, surprised. "Can't I just ask? She must be a well-behaved girl and understand what it means when someone says 'you may not.'" Then follows a two-hour lecture about raising Lilith. Besides that, Lilith is not allowed to raise her voice, which is an absolute necessity for such little creatures. She isn't even allowed to laugh out loud. She is called to order immediately for it: "Shush, don't make noise, you will bother other people." She has to be on her best behavior at all times, like a well-brought-up young lady. In spite of my protests, Deborah Solomonovna engages Lilith in conversations about theology. Today Lilith said to me, "Oh, Mommy, that's all right, God is with you." I asked what she meant by the word "God." "What is this 'God'? I don't understand." "God is . . . well, I know, but I can't explain it," Lilith told me. "Wait a minute." Then she thought about it. "God is the name of what no one sees. It's just a name that we can pray to." I have written her words verbatim. Lilith asks about you every day: "Where's my daddy?" That's the first thing she asks as she opens her eyes in the morning. "Do you want me to give you a chocolate?" I said. "Give me Daddy," she answered. It's remarkable that such a small child has such a long memory.

One more tidbit:

Zyamochka, my dear friend. Today it is exactly two months since we left Moscow, and it seems it was already long, long ago. Now it is fall, and I'm a bit sad, as I always am in the fall. But the thought that I will soon see my dear one makes my heart beat faster from joy. I am saving up many sweet words for him, and sweet kisses, and, strangely enough, I have to admit that I think about him not so much as my husband, whom I've known for an eternity already, but as the sweetheart I am deeply in love with. I only tell him this in secret, though. It's awkward confessing your love to someone with such a grown-up daughter—in six days she'll be two years and four months. The little beauty is also in love with her Papa, and every day she asks, "When are we going to see Papa Zyama?"

At the end of 1924, Mama and I left for Palestine from Odessa by steamship to visit Grandmother. I can remember only two amusing incidents, and nothing more.

Egypt is famous for its unusually beautiful and high-quality glazed fruits. Mama bought two huge boxes of these glazed fruits as presents. When we arrived, the boxes turned out to be empty.

During the one day we were sailing from Egypt to Jaffa, termites—enormous ants—devoured every last bit of these fruits. This is the first thing I remember. The other thing I remember is that when we arrived in Jaffa, where everyone disembarked, there was no ladder for some reason. They simply grabbed hold of the luggage, then the passengers, and tossed them down. There were large boats that came up to the ship to pick up the passengers and their belongings—there simply wasn't a proper loading berth. So they grabbed me, then Mama, too, and threw us overboard, and the Arab who stood in the boat caught us in midair. I remember that very vividly.

By this time, Grandfather had died, and my grandmother lived with her sister, Aunt Antka, in what they considered a small (but for me very big) six-bedroom villa. They called it Villa Lili, after their granddaughter. They had six banana trees and twelve orange trees—an orchard.

When Grandfather settled in Jaffa, he earned a living by devising a method for removing salt from seawater. He first built a small laboratory, and then a factory. He was able to buy the house on the money he made.

It was spring. I remember the pungent smell of the oranges and mandarins, of lemon rind—that's what the trees smell like when they blossom. It was very beautiful, as I recall. I also remember the wooden sidewalks. In those days Tel Aviv was still half-marshland, and to dry it out they planted eucalyptus everywhere. Small wooden gangways, like sidewalks, ran between them. Eucalyptus sucks up water with a furious passion . . .

That's really all I remember of the journey. I don't even remember how we returned to Russia, whether by steamer or not . . . My memory is just a blank.

When I was three or four years old, Father bought me a goat. We had gone to the market for cabbage. It was a large market by the Belorussky Train Station. I caught a glimpse of a white goat and fell in love with it. I hugged it, I remember putting my small arms around it very clearly, and begged my father to get it for me. He couldn't resist my entreaties. So we went home to Mother with a white goat.

The first night the goat stayed under Papa's desk, and I demanded to be able to sleep next to her in a loving embrace right under that very desk. Much to the consternation of the neighbors in our apartment, she wandered through all the rooms for three or four days. Our building was full of enormous, splendid apartments that had obviously belonged to wealthy pre-Revolutionary families, and had been turned into horrible communal apartments for officials of the Public Education Commissariat. So there were fifteen or twenty rooms, with a single bathroom, a single toilet, and a common kitchen. Then, to liven things up even more, a goat appeared. On the fourth night it began to gnaw at books. I remember how I sobbed when Mama and Papa took it away to some kindergarten. I remember that very vividly.

I also remember that in the mornings Papa would sing while he was shaving, and Mama told him, "Please stop! I can't concentrate." At that time Mama worked in some preschool program and wrote reports for it in the morning. And Papa answered her—strange, how one remembers such things—he said, "Okay, I'll stop, but someday you'll think: how sad that he doesn't sing anymore. How nice it would be if he would start singing again." That phrase has stayed in my mind: "How nice it would be if he would start singing again." I also remember how we rode in a sleigh along Sretensky Boulevard. I remember Moscow under a blanket of snow, because later I didn't see snow anymore. There was no snow in Berlin.

4

In 1925 THE AUTHORITIES ANNOUNCED THE ADvent of a new policy. Russia had to trade with the West, buy cars, and industrialize the country. Many members of the party with a higher education were sent abroad to work. Papa, with his degree in engineering and fluent German, was instructed to leave his post in the Commissariat of Public Education and go to Berlin. He was the deputy of Nikolay Krestinsky, who was ambassador plenipotentiary at the time, and later deputy minister of foreign affairs. In 1937 Krestinsky was arrested and executed. His wife, Chief Physician of the Filatovsky Hospital, spent many years in the labor camps. Krestinsky's daughter, who also was later arrested, studied with me in the Russian school organized by the embassy. My mother was appointed headmistress and taught one grade. She also gave drawing lessons and organized a puppet theater.

I have a single vivid memory from the first grade. Once, Maxim Gorky came to visit us. He had emigrated from Russia already in 1921, and was living in Sorrento. He was very tall, hunched over, with bright blue eyes and shaggy brows. We each recited to him one of his poems. Gorky kissed each of us on the forehead, and was so moved (as he often was) that he shed some tears.

In my memory, Germany appears as one long children's holiday. It was childhood. I played with dolls and longed to have a baby stroller for them. Papa was adamant about not getting it: he had bought a goat, but a baby stroller, he thought, was improper for a little Soviet girl. It was too bourgeois. Still, I longed for it; it was the dream that never came true.

My grandmother visited us twice. She took me to a café and bought me some special candy—chocolate-covered pineapple, which no one ever bought for me after that for some reason.

During our time in Germany, I became a little German girl. I went to the embassy school only for the first year. After that I went to the regular German gymnasium. I learned to write in Gothic letters and eagerly read children's books printed in the Gothic script. It's something quite unusual, and I thought I had forgotten it completely. But recently I picked up a book printed in Gothic letters and was surprised to find I could still read it.

We kept albums, and wrote silly poems to each other. I still have one of those albums. Here is a poem (in German, of course): "If you think that I don't love you and am only toying with you, turn on a flashlight and shine it on my heart." Or: "If after many, many years you read this album, remember how little and happy we once were, and how we skipped lightly to school." All that sort of thing.

We had to sit with our hands placed on the desks. It was a strict German school. A girl's school—back then boys and girls studied separately. We had recess, we played the games girls usually play. I liked school. I experienced no negative emotions there. Everybody liked school. Back then I wanted to be like everyone else there, to fit in. This desire stayed with me, and I'll talk more about it. But back then it was especially easy to fit in.

Every summer we took a trip somewhere. Twice we went to Salzburg, to Switzerland, to Paris—I visited Paris for the first time when I was seven.

I remember that Papa left for Nice from Paris, while Mama and I went to Biarritz, on the southern coast. Mama wrote Papa a little poem in the post office:

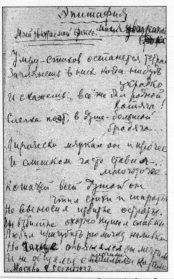

From Moscow to Biarritz
Lilya flew like a little bird,
And when she came to Biarritz,
She fell down from joy and did the splits.
The tail of the tomtit can't compare
with the firebird's plumage so fair,
And the beauty of Biarritz shines brighter
by far than the sun of your Nice.
Take my advice, I'm speaking my piece.
It's time to part ways with your second-rate
   Nice.
Buy your ticket and return
To your loving, longing Lili-Bird.

How can I describe my mother? Mother was full of jokes and pranks, she loved games. In the wink of an eye she could turn a dreary rented room in some hotel into something completely unique and magical: here she would spread out her silk kerchief, there she would place something eye-catching; she would move things around, buy a little vase with flowers, and everything came to life. She had a flair for interior arranging and decorating, a need to surround herself with lovely things—and to joke. From childhood she had loved to compose little ditties and rhymes. Here, for example is an epitaph she came up with:

> *I will die, and leave behind a notebook of my poems.*
> *You'll look at them furtively one day*
> *and say, "Yes, that dear old tomcat*

(I called Mama "kitty" one day, "tomcat" the next)

> *was a bit of a poet, wanderlust in the soul,*
> *who meowed lyrically and preferred an ellipsis*
> *to a period. A feline inside out, who loved verse*
> *and sardines, who shunned cant phrases*
> *and devoured whipped cream, and was*
> *partial to a drop of brandy of an evening,*
> *though drunk on dreams betimes, and lofty*
> *in the company of other felines."*

Things like that. She dashed them off without lifting up her pen from the paper.

I also remember how we went to the station to meet Father when he came to Biarritz. We were overjoyed. The sea, cliffs, a splendid, carefree, happy life. It was life as everyone else lived it. Everyone went off on holiday in the summer, then told everyone else about it when they returned home.

Then it ended. We always traveled on holiday either to Switzerland, or to France. Somewhere or other. Suddenly, Papa decided to go Russia for his vacation, to check on how the machinery he bought was operating.

Mama tried to dissuade him. She was fearful somehow. Mama had always feared Soviet Russia, and her fears would eventually prove to have been justified in our lives. One day the telephone rang, and some stranger on the other end asked to meet with Papa. Papa wanted to know who it was, but the person answered, "I must remain anonymous." Papa refused to meet with him. Two days later he called again and said that "it concerned the life and welfare of our family." So Papa agreed to meet him in a café. That person, a Russian Papa had never seen before, who wouldn't give his name, said, "Do not go to Russia. They won't let you out again."

When Papa returned home, he recounted the conversation to Mama, as I recall. He believed it was a provocation, that the Communists were testing his reliability and trustworthiness. Then he said, "Now I'm definitely going." And he did.

When Papa was due to return from his holiday, we went to meet him at the station. He wasn't on the train. The following day he called and said, "Don't wait for me." Two days later we received a letter that he had entrusted to someone to pass on to us. It was a letter that said, "I won't be coming to Berlin anymore, you must come back here to me."

They had taken Papa off the train. He had already arranged his luggage and sat down when two people came up to him to check his documents. They led him away. This was the favorite tactic of the secret police (the GPU)—seizing a person at the last minute, and in plain sight. A blow to the psyche of the victim, and at the same time to the witnesses. Papa was certain that he was being arrested. They didn't arrest him, however. They merely confiscated his travel passport and said that from now on he would be working in Russia.

He had no place to live. He stayed with his brother, whom I've already mentioned, in a single small room—eight square meters. He shared it with his brother, his brother's wife, and their son, until the son was arrested. There was no room for an extra bed, or even for a mattress, so Papa slept on a desk for almost four years. They spread out a blanket on top of it, and Papa slept. There would have been no room for me and Mama there, naturally; but that was only part of the problem. Mama was afraid to return.

5

We rented an apartment on Hohenzollernplatz. At that time it was a huge park. It was a small two-story house, and our four rooms were on the first floor, with windows overlooking a garden. Once a thief broke in. I woke up and heard Mama talking to someone. I looked up and saw a young fellow with his back to the bed. He had climbed into our room through the balcony door, and Mama engaged him in conversation.

A year and a half ago, when Sima and I were in Berlin, we visited that place. Everything had disappeared—no park, no gardens; there were eight- or nine-story buildings on that spot. I couldn't find a single trace of my German childhood.

Until the last year of my life there I lived some sort of somnolent childhood existence. My soul was still dormant. Then I found my first soul mate, my first "best friend"—a German-Jewish girl. Her name was Ursula Hoos, and she was from a very wealthy family. When I went over to her house for a visit, I discovered that Ursula had her own suite of rooms—a bedroom, a schoolroom, and a playroom. We were called to dinner, and it was all very grand and imposing, as one might see only in Germany: heavy draperies, chandeliers, a dining table where everyone sat three feet apart. The table itself was about forty feet long. Her father was a Junker of pure Aryan extraction; her mother, and her mother's parents, were Jewish. (Hoos is a German Junker surname.)

I remember that when she introduced me to her parents, Ursula's mother said, "Lilya comes from the Soviet Union, but she is Jewish, and a very sweet and smart little girl." That was the first time I felt that being Jewish was something special, but I didn't know whether it was bad or good.

I loved Ursula, or Ulya, dearly. This was most likely my first experience of the search for friendship, for a friend, which would later play such an important role in my life.

I also began to read. Until that moment I read little, and not very well. I remember Ulya saying to me, "Why should I give you books? You won't manage to read them anyway." But suddenly I had a breakthrough. I remember the very book I was reading—a German translation of a wonderful Danish writer, whom I later translated and edited myself. Her name was Karin Michaëlis. She wrote a two-volume children's book called *Bibi*. This was the book that helped me learn to read quickly and eagerly.

I took Karin Michaëlis' *Bibi* with me to Moscow, and I have never parted with this book, over—what is it?—sixty-five years now, I suppose. It has always been with me. The book is about a young girl's journey (a beloved form in those days). The girl travels from one province to another. It is a sort of geographical tale about Denmark and at the same time about various customs. Perhaps this book played a role in awakening my love of travel, of change, of seeking out the new and untried. An excellent book, and an excellent writer, Karin Michaëlis.

And so my soul began to live by reading, as well as by friendship. The second book I read, after which there was no going back, was *Doctor Dolittle*, a translation from the English. The English version is in fact a multi-volume novel. It's fascinating when you are nine or ten.

These two books expanded my entire world.

There was one other reason that I woke up. I want to talk about it, because it had a great influence on who I eventually became. I said in the beginning that the outside world shaped me in important ways. The year was 1930. There were demonstrations on the streets of Berlin—Communists and Hitler supporters. They were small groups of fifty to a hundred people, marching with flags and banners. The demonstrations often ended in scuffles or brawls. Nothing terribly serious, I remember that well, but they created a sense of alarm. The streets were no longer peaceful, something was always going on there. Mama realized that it was no longer safe for us to stay in Berlin. The Russian émigré community was moving en masse to Paris. Mama decided first to move to my grandmother's in Palestine. But we didn't go alone.

The owner of the house in which we rented our apartment had

a son named Ludwig. At first he struck up a friendship with me. He was a very handsome young man, younger than Mama by some five years, and he paid a great deal of attention to me. He invited me to children's cafés, to the puppet theater, to the movies . . . Every two or three days Ludwig would take me somewhere, and I grew to love him. Suddenly, he was having meals with us, and so on and so forth. Then Mama told me that she was leaving for Hamburg for a few days, and Ludwig disappeared with her. When Mama returned she said that she and Ludwig were getting married, that she had divorced Papa, and that from now on he was my new father. From that moment I did an about-face. I hated him.

Mama was angry that Papa had gone to Moscow in spite of the warning he had received. She felt he had neglected the family, her, and myself. She was afraid to go back to Russia—and, indeed, there was no place to live if we returned. And then a handsome, young journalist, a charming young man, appeared. He turned her head. Later she would pay a heavy price for this.

6

So together, we—Mama, Ludwig, and I—left for Palestine. This was the only period in my life, I think, when I behaved not like a good girl, but a bad boy. I did all I could to spite everyone. I remember that I was possessed with a kind of fury.

On one side there was Ludwig; on the other side Ursula Hoos. I was in despair that we had been separated, that I had lost her. During the entire journey on the steamship I wrote her endless letters in my idiotic Gothic handwriting.

Later, after Mama and I had moved to Paris, I tried to find Ulya; but the entire family had perished when the Nazis came to power. We couldn't find a single trace of them. This caused me terrible grief.

When we arrived in Palestine, I behaved so abominably toward Ludwig that Mama didn't want to live with Grandmother and me. She and Ludwig moved into an apartment of their own.

Tel Aviv's eucalyptus plants had already grown into mature trees that shaded the streets and offered refuge from the heat.

I had only one goal: to get rid of Ludwig. It's curious, since for the most part I'm a very mild-mannered and unassuming person. But this was a real crisis for me. The only truly pleasant recollection I have of that trip was a sandcastle-building contest. Tel Aviv has a broad and sandy beach that's remarkable. This was where the contests were held. I suddenly demonstrated outstanding architectural skills and placed third in the contest. It was stupendous. This was my first experience of joy stemming from a creative act. It gave me the sense of being capable of something, of doing something that others considered interesting and good. Against the background of my deep negativity toward Ludwig, this was very valuable.

I vaguely remember going to school. The classes were in Hebrew, a language I didn't understand. I managed to pick up just a few words. I was enrolled for a month—we arrived in spring, then it was summer vacation. And in the fall Mama decided to leave. Tel

Aviv bored her, and there was nothing for her to do. She decided to go to Paris. Ludwig thought that he wouldn't be able to find work in Paris, and left for the US. Mama promised that we would come to New York after he had settled down there.

My grandmother, Dora Solomonovna, was very displeased with Mama. Certain things she said have remained in my mind since that time. "She always tries to be different from other people. If only she could live here peacefully, in Palestine, if only she could live with Ludwig, such a levelheaded, handsome young man. But, no, he isn't good enough for her. He has to go to America, and she sends him packing; she doesn't want to go herself. She has to go to Paris. I know how this is all going to end: she'll return to her Zyama, back to Russia."

Our departure was fixed for a Saturday. This was a very serious matter in Palestine, because one isn't allowed to do anything on the Sabbath, including riding in a cab. Grandmother was not observant, and it wasn't religious considerations that held her back: she feared the condemnation of the neighbors. She was very agitated, and said, "We're saying goodbye, who knows when we'll see each other again? I must see you off." At the same time, she didn't dare flout the conventions of this small community and come with us in the cab. She produced some sort of veil out a drawer, thinking maybe they wouldn't recognize her if she covered herself with it. In the end, she didn't see us off. This fact—that the opinion of the neighbors influenced her so strongly that she was tormented by it, and that she couldn't accompany us to say goodbye—made a great impression on me. I was ten—I understood everything. Mama is right, I thought, one can't live like this, in this place. You can't live where you don't dare do what you want to do, what feels right and good to you. This was one of my first lessons about society. And we left.

I think I matured fairly late. It happened then, when I was nine or ten. Of course, already at the age of five I seemed to see myself in opposition to the world, but the life of the spirit—this involves suffering. The soul awakens with the first experience of suffering, I'm sure of this. When a person is happy, the soul simply floats along, it doesn't wake up; it isn't fully aware of itself. But once it has known suffering, it understands happiness as well. Awareness is connected to pain. This is the way it appears to me, this is what I think—this is how I experienced it, in any case. The pain I felt about my father, my indignation about this new person who appeared to take his place, a person who had been wonderful as a friend, but not in the role to which he aspired . . . He liked to lecture me . . . He was a rather amusing person, he wrote poetry, he and Mama corresponded in rhyming German. Still and all, this did not comfort me in the least, and I remained hurt and indignant. Everything about him troubled me, from the very moment that he tried to occupy a place he did not belong.

This first taste of misery caused by love, the hurt I felt for my father, the separation from Ursula—this was the turning point. I became conscious of these changes in me when we sailed on the boat to Marseille. The journey was a long one in those days: four, five, or even six days. I felt sharpened by the grief of parting and by hatred toward my companion. I remember undergoing a profound inner struggle, lying in a chaise longue on the deck.

In the midst of this pain, something shifted in me, and I seemed to make a turn toward adult life. I arrived in Paris a grown-up girl.

7

On the boat to Marseille I remember that Mama only taught me five French words. I learned *madame*, I knew *pardon*, and I knew the phrase that was written on every French coin: *Liberté, Égalité, Fraternité*. The slogan of the French revolution. With this linguistic baggage of five French words we arrived in Paris.

13 Boulevard Pasteur—I've remembered the address my whole life. This was Rebecca's address, the Rebecca who was my mother's high-school friend. She married the son of a well-known professor of psychiatry in Russia at the time, Professor Minor. They moved to Paris, and she worked in the Soviet Embassy. In 1930, when Stalin issued a decree stating that everyone who did not return immediately would be deemed "unreturnable" and lose Soviet citizenship, Rebecca stayed on in Paris with her two children.

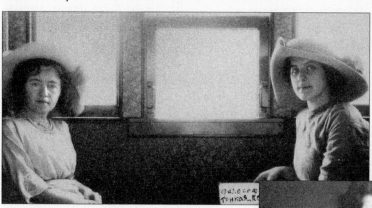

On our first night in Paris, Mama and Rebecca went out—evidently to enjoy the Paris nightlife—and left us children alone. The boy, Lyalya, was three years older than me, and Zina, the girl, a real beauty, with a head of blonde locks, was five years older than me.

They put me to bed in an armchair, since there was no place else to sleep. Lyalya made paper airplanes, which he sent flying out the open window. Then he would run down to the street in his pajamas, down onto Boulevard Pasteur, to fetch them. These are my first Paris memories, and they have stayed with me my whole life.

Soon, Mama found a studio—a one-room apartment with a bath but no standalone kitchen. She wanted to be close to Rebecca, and this was not far from where she lived—at 32-bis, rue du Cotentin, next to the Montparnasse train station. Two new buildings stood side by side. In the neighboring one, the one without the bis, lived Ilya Ehrenburg. Every morning, as I set out for school, I would run into him. He walked two black dogs, small ones, perhaps terriers, on a leash, and under his arm he carried a three-foot-long baguette and some newspapers. It was Mama who told me that this was Ilya Ehrenburg, the famous Russian writer.

At first I went to an ordinary local French school for children from the most unprivileged backgrounds. Now imagine a ten-year-old girl who already knew a thing or two, who had had the experience of parting, and had undergone loss. Suddenly I found myself in a class of thirty-five, knowing only five words in French. I had to sit there for five or six hours a day. No one could talk to me, nor could I talk to anyone else. The first days were awful. The first word in French I added to my supply was *allumette*—"match." In the arithmetic class they taught counting with the aid of matches. Each pupil brought a box of matches and arranged them on the desk: five matches plus three matches equals eight matches. They kept repeating the word "match": *allumette, allumette*. That was my first new word. I was a stranger to them, they called me *l'étrangère*. They didn't even call me by my name, and I felt very uncomfortable there.

Very soon, after two months or so (I was already speaking French by then), Mama enrolled me in a new school. It was very privileged, the Alsatian School. Ehrenburg's daughter wrote a book about it under the pseudonym Irina Erburg. She was five or six years older than me and was also enrolled there. I finished one year of that school, but Mama couldn't afford to send me there any more after that. It was very expensive, a school for the children of ministers, the upper bourgeoisie, children of academics.

We had no real means for survival. Grandmother sent us a little bit in the beginning. Then Mama organized a puppet theater. She called it by the Russian name of Petrushka. She made puppets from *papier mâché*. She no longer made the molds from brown bread, as she had in Russia, where the bread was inedible, but from modeling clay. However much we might have wanted it, there was no brown bread to be had in France. She made fifteen or twenty of these heads and assembled a group of kids, the children of friends. Rebecca had a circle of acquaintances that included Soviet people who had gone into emigration. They spoke French poorly, for the most part; but their children were already fluent in French, naturally. Children learn a language within a few months. Mama invited these people to act in her puppet theater. I was also part of the troupe, which was called, as I've already noted, Lili Imali—Mama's theatrical pseudonym. The puppet theater was very simple: puppets and a backdrop or screen. A backdrop in one hand, a suitcase with puppets in the other, and you can travel the world with it. A few props and decorations, and you're ready to roll.

Marie Imali
DIRECTRICE DU THÉÂTRE
« PÉTROUCHKA » MARIONNETTES D'ART

32 bis, Rue du Cotentin   Tél. Invalides 04-53

Mama rented a space in the Latin Quarter on rue Campagne-Première and put on plays four or five days a week. We needed to advertise it. It was expensive to take out an ad in the newspapers, so we printed flyers instead. One of my jobs was to pass them out on the street. It wasn't very pleasant work, but all the other children who performed in the theater passed them out, too.

We were also invited to perform at children's parties in rich people's homes. There I received my first lessons in social inequality. In these houses, where there were servants wearing white gloves, maids in starched uniforms, where a boisterous, cheerful group of children was gathered, we were never invited to the dining table. They brought us our food in another room. The children, noblemen's children, ate separately. This hurt me; I felt it keenly as unjust discrimination. Since we had just performed a play, it would have been fair if we had stayed after to play with these children—but nothing doing. We were prevented from coming into contact with them. Apparently our blood was insufficiently blue. I disliked these outings in the homes of the rich intensely, but they were a help to Mama. They gave her more money than the pittance that the performances in our own little theater brought in.

France has a folk tradition of puppet theater called Guignol. It takes place only outside or in parks. There are stock plays and stock characters. Mama tried creating a puppet theater of an entirely different kind—playful, creative, modern, the kind of puppet theater created by Efimov, the first Russian puppeteer.

Mama's first play was *The Turnip*. She translated the Russian folktale into French, which she had been able to speak fluently since her youth, and we performed it.

In the winter we performed in Paris, and in the summer we took trips to the sea, to Saint-Jean-de-Luz, a small town near Biarritz. Mama rented a space for our theater, and there were wealthy villas, as well, where we were invited to perform.

The theater provided us with a livelihood, albeit a modest one. We didn't starve. Still, enrolling me in the Alsatian School was beyond our means. I now realize that even for very affluent French families, the children of prominent journalists, for example, the expense was too great. Mama transferred me to the Victor Duruy

Lyceum. It was nearby, also in the Latin Quarter, and I went there every morning by foot. It was there that I found my beloved French best friend. She was from the family of Nakhimovich, the Russian Social Revolutionary, a fairly well-known figure. He was exiled, along with several other SRs, to Ryazan—back then they sent them not to Siberia, but to Ryazan.

In Ryazan he was thrown in jail, where he died. His widow and two daughters, aged ten and seven, were given permission to emigrate to Paris. The younger daughter, Lida, became my best friend.

She was a few years older than me and went to the same Victor Duruy Lyceum. Her older sister Gulia had a beautiful voice and was the star performer in Mama's little theater—she sang Russian romances with puppets. This was a hit. I saved quite a few reviews from French newspapers: the Petrushka Puppet Theater was the hit of the seasons for two years running.

« Petrouchka »

Les marionnettes de Mme Marie Imali ont été présentées jeudi après-midi, à Gure-Etchea, à un très nombreux public, dans lequel on pouvait constater la présence de plus de trois cents enfants. Une suite de scènes très bien conçues et réglées mettaient en valeur les jolies poupées, aux mouvements bien coordonnés, et le dialogue autant que les gestes était bien fait pour intéresser les tout petits qui ont suivi la représentation avec une attention passionnée. On en avait la preuve dans l'ensemble et l'ardeur avec lesquels les enfants répondaient aux questions que leur posaient par moments les minuscules acteurs.

Nous ne pouvons entrer dans le détail des nombreuses scènes, parlées et chantées par les marionnettes de Marie Imali. Costumées à ravir, manœuvrées avec exactitude et précision par d'invisibles mains, elles offraient un spectacle du plus grand intérêt non seulement pour les tout petits, mais même pour les grandes personnes qui les accompagnaient.

Nous enregistrons avec plaisir ce nouveau succès de Gure-Etchea. En organisant de véritables fêtes de famille, il comble une lacune et rend un service signalé aussi bien à la population luzienne qu'aux étrangers qui nous honorent de leur présence. Il n'est que juste d'en féliciter les dévoués organisateurs.

Finding Lida and her circle of friends played an important part in my development. They were all older than me: I was twelve, they were fifteen or sixteen. Because of them I began reading different kinds of books than my peers were reading. I read to keep up with my older friends. I began reading French classics very early on—so as not to be left behind, to be "in the know," and this was a great stimulus to accelerated development. It also distracted me from my routine schoolwork, however. I was nearly the worst pupil in the Lyceum until spring. In that system, when they passed back your tests, they not only gave you a grade, but they gave you a class ranking, as well: you were the eighth, you were the tenth, etc. There were twenty-eight people in my class, and I was either twenty-seventh or twenty-eighth. In other words, I did not participate at all in what was going on around me in school. I read books under my desk, which I was determined to finish as quickly as possible. My older friends read not only the classics, but also contemporary French authors. That was when I read Mauriac, du Gard, and André Gide. I read all of them at a very young age. Naturally, I had no time for my French history, or Greek and Roman history classes. No time for that—I had other, more important matters to attend to. Sometimes I just daydreamed away the hours.

At some point Mama became desperate: why was I such a bad pupil, what was wrong with me? One of Mama's friends was Eliane Tayar—an actress in the movies. Extremely beautiful, with enormous green eyes—I adored her. She sometimes took me to the film studio with her, and told everyone that I was her daughter. Once Eliane Tayar took me to a café, to the Rotunda, and said, "You know what? If you don't want to study, you don't have to go to the Lyceum. There are other options. You can go to a vocational school, for example. Graduating from the Lyceum is not for everybody."

This gave me a jolt. Did that mean I was incapable of learning, that I was deficient in some way? In two days I had a test in Greek and Roman history. I grabbed the textbook for the first time in my life and began poring over it. What the rest of the class had spent an entire semester learning, I mastered in two days. I took the test and placed third in the class. The class "inspector," as she was called, began passing back the tests. She started by saying, "And Markovich

is third in the class. So she is capable of learning, she just hasn't wanted to before; but when she studies hard, she can. I noticed long ago what an intelligent girl she was." And this was so flattering to me. I'll never forget how I felt. It committed me to something. I must say I believe that it is helpful to praise children sometimes. That remark, "I noticed long ago what an intelligent girl she was," was a stimulus for me. I realized it was very easy to study well. You simply have to join in the process, that's all. After this I had no problems in school. I caught up in one fell swoop.

The Victor Duruy Lyceum was a girls' school. We were not allowed to leave by ourselves without special permission, a note from home with a stamp from the director's office; because the girls longed to break out and skip school. There were two supervisors who stood at the doors and checked whether anyone leaving had permission to do so. Still, I didn't make friends with my classmates. My peers seemed too childish to me. I felt like I belonged to a different age group. There was only one girl, Jeanne, whom I visited in her home a few times. I liked going to her house because her mother owned a flower shop. There was a glorious flower arrangement in their entrance hall, as they like to have in Paris, and the whole courtyard was filled with buckets and pots with cut flowers that seemed to be awaiting their "appearance" on stage. I loved it.

Generally speaking, a "girl from Russia" was rather a negative than a positive description. You didn't feel especially welcome in the homes of other children. Each time I heard this, however, there was an addendum, which became a kind of leitmotif: little Lilya, however, is a smart, well-behaved girl, and you can play with her. I didn't feel singled out in any way due to my ethnic background. I can't say that the French are not anti-Semitic; a certain kind of anti-Semitism does flourish there. But the French are brought up in such a way that this is well concealed. People may think it, but they are ashamed to show it openly, and only in the most extreme circumstances does it rise to the surface. Not in the circumstances I found myself in, of course. Perhaps the mother of this girl in the flower shop wanted to add, "Besides, she's Jewish," but would never dare say so. This was thought, but never said out loud. So I never experienced this. I was "the girl from Russia," and that was all.

This didn't faze me, though. I was interested in grown-up company. I was proud and happy that I had been accepted by them. Curiously enough, all the boys in our group were French, and all the girls were, for some reason, émigrés. The group included Lida, Zina, and one other girl, Nina, whom I was also very fond of, and who wrote in my album when we went our separate ways: "In memory of that moment that I realized you were open to me." I considered this to be a very important confession. Nina later perished, killed by the Nazis. She ended up in a concentration camp and was shot for having participated in the underground resistance. I found this out only forty years later.

Mother's friends also played an important role in my Paris life. They introduced me little by little to adult life. One was Eliane Tayar, whom I adored, as I have mentioned. She missed not having children, apparently, and felt very attached to me. She showered me with attention, perhaps won over by my adoration of her.

Then I received a letter from Eliane, in which she said that she couldn't see me anymore. She had met a man who demanded that she break with all her former relations. He wanted her to belong only to him. He was also a royalist and hated anything that had to do with the Soviet Union. I was devastated by this loss and wept inconsolably.

Then there was a wonderful dancer, a friend of Mama's, named Tony Gregory, whose performances we attended. He visited us at home, too, though more often we visited him at his house. Back then there was a practice of "open house" on certain days. Every Thursday the doors of his studio were open for visitation. Mama took me with her. She never isolated me from her own life; on the contrary, she drew me into it. There I met a woman who was a stage director. She invited me to perform in an adult play. I had a small part, but at least it was a role in a big production. The play was called *The Thought Merchant*. My name was on the program, I've managed to save it: Lili Imali.

All in all, I loved my life. We spent the summer in Saint-Jean-de-Luz. We performed a lot, but there was free time, too. All the young people in Lida's circle went there every summer. And in the summer I joined the world of these older friends. It was exhilarating for me. I learned to swim there, and to dive.

« Le Marchand d'idées » à la Comédie-Caumartin

(Photo G.-L. Manuel frères.)
M. Lucien Paris et Mlle Lily Imali

8

Saint-Jean-de-Luz is a famous and prestigious resort. Feodor Chaliapin lived there, by the way. He had a villa overlooking the village, and Mama and I went there to invite him to a performance of our puppet theater. Unfortunately, he was away; but his daughter came to our show.

We rented a room from a French family there. The landlord was a chef on a merchant ship. I was thrilled with the way he made pommes frites—one of the national dishes of France. He tossed them up, nearly as far as the ceiling; they turned over in midair and landed neatly back in the frying pan.

The windows of our room (it was an inexpensive garret) looked out on the backyard of some local family. There were two children, a boy and a girl about five and seven years old, and I was always astonished at how dirty they were, how they loved digging in the backyard dirt. The children resembled paupers. I don't know what their parents did, but when Sunday came around, I suddenly saw them all going to mass. The children had been scrubbed clean and were dressed like a little prince and princess. The little girl was dressed all in lace, and the boy wore a pressed blue suit. That was when I first came to realize the contrasts that existed in France: on ordinary days it was one thing; on holidays—it became a wholly different society. The memory of this realization has stayed with me my entire life. The ambiguity of life there, its dualism. It was an important moment for me, visually. Every Sunday these children would turn into a prince and princess again; but the rest of the week they wallowed in dirt.

In Saint-Jean-de-Luz we became acquainted with several young men who will later play a role in this narrative. One of them, strikingly handsome, was the son of a local rich man. He was also older than me. His name was Albert Élissalde, and his father owned a canning factory in Saint-Jean-de-Luz—the only enterprise of that scale. Albert was in love with the beautiful Zina, Rebecca's daughter. Another one was Jean-Pierre Vernant—in France, people named Jean-Pierre are called J.P., so he was J.P. Vernant—along with his brother Jacques. Both of them were already philosophy students. J.P. was, I think, eighteen, and Jacques twenty. They were both quite well-known in spite of their tender age. When a student graduates from a French lyceum and takes an achievement exam, he takes it not in the lyceum where he has studied, but in another one, before a national committee. All graduates in France took the exam, as well as children who lived in the colonies. It is a great nationwide event. After the exam, they post a single list: who earned first place, who earned second, third, etc. Many young people graduate every year, and each person knows the number of his or her exam ranking. In his year, Jacques earned first place, and three years later, his brother Jean-Pierre also won a first. So they were brilliant young men, and they finished university with as much success as they finished high school. They took an exam known as the *agrégation*, which gave them the right to teach in French colleges and lyceums. Jacques ranked first in his year, and three years later J.P. came in first, as well.

J.P. was in love with Lida, my best friend. In those days, young people didn't go beyond kissing—they held hands and walked in the moonlight . . . At that time they hadn't even kissed, because I remember that later I received a letter from Lida, in which she told me that they had kissed for the first time.

I remember rushing to every rendezvous we had; everything the others did was so interesting for me. We went to the movies, we went dancing—well, I didn't dance yet, I considered myself too young for that. So they danced and I just sat and looked on. We talked about books, which I hurried to read, trying to keep up with them. I thought that things were already settled, that it would be like this for the rest of our lives.

In this new phase of my existence, I missed Papa very much, and needed him. He wrote me a postcard every day. The postcards didn't arrive every day, though—they came in bunches of three or four. Every day on his way to work in Moscow, Papa would drop a postcard in the mailbox. Over time I amassed, let's see: 365 postcards a year times four years. He never missed a single day, no matter what. Whenever he took a leave, wherever he was, without fail, like shaving, he took the time to write his Lyalka, as he called me.

More often than not they were pictures of factories and power plants under construction. Papa described his trips to industrial plants, mines, and so forth, thinking most likely that it would be very interesting for a thirteen-year-old Parisian girl.

His postcards forced me to read Russian, because I wanted to read them myself. I began to read Russian books. I didn't read much,

Читай, Лилька!

Лиля, детка родная,
помни, что вера в
жизнь это самое важное
не теряй ее никогда

1933г.

Souvenir affectueux d'un
professeur qui n'oubliera pas
sa petite Lili, partie dans
sa patrie lointaine.
28 avril 1933

but I did read. I didn't know how to write, but I could read. I noticed that Mama had begun corresponding with Papa again. I knew that she had answered Ludwig's telegram invitations, saying that she no longer had any intention of going to New York. He had found a job, and wished for us to join him there, but Mama refused. She was completely infatuated with her life in France. Her theater was making a name for itself, her circle of friends was growing . . . But I saw that she missed Papa more and more. The French newspapers wrote about famine in Russia, and Mama was very much afraid. Nevertheless, in 1933 I could feel that the decision to return was taking root. Mama was driven by love and longing for my father. By that time he had been accommodated in an apartment, where we would all be able to live. I had very mixed feelings about all of this.

After spending the summer of 1933 in Saint-Jean-de-Luz, instead of going back to Paris, Mama and I traveled through the Pyrenees south to Nice. Her plan was to leave me in Nice for the winter, and go to Berlin herself to rustle up the paperwork necessary for her to go back to Moscow. Since she and my father had been divorced, and she had lost her Soviet citizenship, she couldn't return just like that, automatically. In Nice we stayed in several different boarding houses. I didn't like it one bit, and resisted staying there. Mama had some friends in Nice, and they advised her to find a nice French family with children that I could stay with through the winter. That was what she did. Mama found a widow, with three girls. The middle daughter, Simone, was my age. A second was three years younger than me, and the third three years older. I lived with this family for the year, and I must admit that it was a very happy year. I became friends with the elder daughter, Colette, and grew very fond of her. At night, instead of sleeping, we would sit on the window seat and talk. I was already in the habit of befriending people older than me. Besides, Simone, who was my age, studied in a ballet school and came home every day absolutely exhausted. Colette, Simone, and Jacqueline, the youngest. I attended the lyceum and spent a wonderful winter in their company. Then Mama came to fetch me in the spring, and I was sad to have to part with them. My life seemed to consist of partings, new affections and attachments, and again separations. We went back to Paris, and Mama told me in earnest that we were going to return to Russia. We were going back to Papa.

9

THERE WAS A SENSE OF RUPTURE IN THE FABRIC OF LIFE. ALL MAMA'S friends knew that this would be a final farewell, that we were parting with them forever. I remember going to say goodbye to Tony Gregory, the dancer, on one of his open-house Thursdays. He sat me on his knees and said, "So, going back to your homeland?" I was very ambivalent. On the one hand, of course, I had a strong desire to see my father, and a general curiosity. Like every young person, I had an interest in the unknown. On the other hand, I was frightened to lose everything I had grown to love there. "Yes," I said. Then he said something to me I have never forgotten. "You know that you'll go there, and the key will turn in the lock. You will never be able to come back."

My favorite teacher in the lyceum wrote in my album (I still have the album in which my German friends had written their verses and messages): "To my favorite pupil, Lilya, with fear that we will never meet again. She is going to her faraway Homeland, so inaccessible to us." All of this struck fear into my heart, naturally.

Mama's friend Rebecca wrote me a message that I couldn't understand at the time, but later grew to appreciate: "Dear Lilya, the most important thing is not to lose faith in life. Don't ever lose it."

Everything was ready for our departure. We had made the rounds of our friends, and they had visited us, saying goodbye. I called Eliane Tayar and begged her to meet me. She refused. She hurried to cut short the conversation. "I have to go, I have to go. My beloved is waiting for me." I asked whether I could write her. "No, never."

The story didn't end there, however. We had been living in Moscow for about a year, when I received a letter from her. Eliane wrote: "I am terribly unhappy, the person I loved has thrown me over. Could I not come to see you? Maybe I could begin a new life." I replied immediately, but I never heard from her again.

We spent the eve of our departure with Rebecca Minor, on 13 Pasteur Boulevard, with her and her two children—her beautiful daughter Zina and her son Lyalka. There was a fireplace in her home, as there was in nearly every old French house. It was a sad evening. Partings are always sad. Something was drawing me toward the future, though. This is one of my character traits: when something new beckons, I am always compelled to move forward, to seek out the unknown. Still, separations and departures are sad and difficult, all the more when everyone around you says it is forever.

After the evening at Rebecca's Mama wrote a poem. Mama's poems are, of course, somewhat awkward and naïve. But she wrote so easily, all in one go, as though the lines formed themselves. There was so much sincerity in them that they are still very meaningful to me, and dear to my heart. Mother had always been a surprising mixture of maturity and wisdom, and childish naïveté. She was very open and trusting. Very early on I began to feel older than she was: I felt wiser, less impulsive, more adept at envisioning the future. At the same time I envied her artistry, her ability to join any game, to create in an instant something out of nothing. Everything she did— the Society of Solitary People, the kindergarten, the Petrushka Puppet Theater, which won the heart of Paris (all the papers reviewed it, that must mean something)—she did with real talent. She had a childishly naïve, naturally endowed talent. This is how Mama remains in my memory, in my heart: not so much as a mother, but as a friend, with a childlike soul. I will recite her poem here. My memory won't falter—I remember every word.

> *How many years have passed, my friend?*
> *Twenty? Twenty-five?*
> *Life has made a circle*
> *And now we drink wine together*
> *With toasts and speeches*
> *As it was then—long ago,*
> *Remember? Behind our shoulders*
> *Like wings, our youth evoked dreams,*
> *Over the mountains and valleys*
> *A star shone for us.*
>
> *You remember, my friend, the narrow terrace*
> *And that boundless world that followed?*
> *Did happiness wear a mask then, or now,*
> *And where is that wreath of former fires?*
> *Your eyes are the same as they used to be,*
> *Though now they are kinder, I see.*
> *You sit before me dressed in black,*
> *And we are drinking wine, the two of us.*
>
> *We see young faces before us.*
> *They are like ours once were, my friend.*
> *Or am I only dreaming all of this?*
> *And we are still the same, and the years did not pass?*
> *But this girl with charming features and*
> *The grace of the seventeenth spring—*
> *Who reincarnated you in her*
> *With magical fingers, reality into dream?*
> *I saw that girl once, I saw her then—*
> *The sixth of June, at night—*
> *The date remains with us,*
> *And it is strange to me that it's your daughter.*
>
> *Well then, my friend, let the wine in the goblets froth,*
> *We had a wonderful time together,*

And the roses were scarlet for us,
And we were once seventeen ourselves.

Such a touching, naïve, poem.

Hitler was already in power in Germany, so it was impossible to travel through it. We were forced to make a detour, through Austria and Italy.

I remember the train, at first so cheerful and happy. It was the beginning of May, and people were still doing downhill skiing. There were skiers in their ski suits, suntanned and bubbling with energy. The farther eastward we traveled, the more despondent the train seemed. Already there were no skiers, just downcast faces— and then we were in Warsaw.

We stopped there and stayed for a few days with Mama's friends. After Paris, Warsaw seemed like a city from another part of the world—half-Asiatic, overpopulated, untidy, crammed with fiacres and antediluvian cars. Mama's friends turned out to be very sweet and cordial people. There were five children in the house, and it was constantly full of guests and neighbors. We were immediately seated at the table. I had never seen so much sausage and cured meat in my life. Everyone said the same thing over and over, "Why are you going there? How can you go to such a terrible place? There is a famine! Everyone is trying to get out, and you go there voluntarily. They'll never let you out again, you'll be locked in it's a cage!" My heart felt heavier and heavier at this prospect, but Mama said, "The decision has been made. My husband is waiting for us." Inspired by these conversations, she bought mountains of sausage and stuffed them into our suitcases. Then we got on the train again.

At that time the border station between Russia and Poland was not Brest-Litovsk, as it is now, but the Negoreloe Station. Mama wanted to send a telegram to my father, and we got out onto the platform. The train stood for several hours in Negoreloe, and the post office, they told us, was on the square. Exiting the station onto the platform wasn't allowed, we were told, but it was possible to enter it from the platform. We went into the waiting room, and I saw a terrifying spectacle. The entire floor was covered with people. Some of them were sleeping, it seemed, others were sick and listless;

I couldn't understand what was wrong with them. Children were crying . . . In short, it was like a vision of half-living, half-dead people. And when we went out into the city, the whole square was covered with them. They were people trying to escape the famine, people dying of hunger. I stood there in my blue coat with silver or gold buttons and karakul collar, and before me was a mass of rags, all blackened. I felt such a sense of horror, and such a sense of dislocation. I was filled with fear. I remember that I cried and said, "Mama, I don't want to go. Let's go back, I'm afraid. I don't want to go any further." And Mama answered, "It's too late, sweetie, we've already crossed the border. We're in the Soviet Union now. There's no going back."

My life in Paris remained in my memory as a sense of flight. I was rushing headlong into the unknown. I didn't walk, I didn't sit, I ran; I was running to meet something head-on. Then suddenly, I was knocked off course and began moving in an entirely different direction.

10

We arrived in Moscow on the 4th of May 1934. First impressions. The apartment. A famous house: 5 Kalyaevka St., built on the money of people working abroad. Papa received an apartment in exchange for the foreign currency he earned in Berlin. Apartment 215, on the seventh floor. The stairs hadn't been built yet, not to mention an elevator. There was just planking and ramps, and we had to ascend to the seventh floor using these. That was my first lasting impression. I had never seen apartments you had to reach not by stairs, but by ramps hanging over the edge of a precipice. The gas and water had also not been hooked up. We had to go down to the courtyard to get water.

There were three rooms; we each had our own. Mine, the smallest, looked out onto the courtyard, so it was very quiet. My parents each had one of the larger ones. To me this seemed unbelievably impoverished, of course. There was hardly any furniture, only the bare necessities: a divan and a small desk for me, a larger desk and divan for Papa; Mama also had a dining table, four chairs, and some sort of cupboard. This was the only furniture we had in this "chic" apartment. From conversations I overheard I learned that this was considered the ultimate in luxury, that it was the envy of everyone, and that we were incredibly fortunate to have been able to get it.

The second impression, much stronger than the ramps instead of stairs, were the vats for boiling tar that sat on the corner of Kalyaevka and the Garden Ring. Homeless children were living in them. The entire neighborhood was covered with asphalt rather than paving stones. There were fires burning under the vats during the day, and a thick smoke billowed from them, spreading an acrid odor through the air. In the evening the workers stopped their labor and dispersed, and hordes of little boys began swarming around the huge vats. Fierce battles to secure the best spots ensued. They were sometimes bloody. The victors clung to the vats and slept until morning, pressing against the warm, cast iron sides. During the first days, I didn't dare go out alone. In the fall, on my way to school every morning, dozens of little faces covered with tar poked out of the vats and watched me mockingly. I was afraid of running into them one day, all the more since my blue Parisian coat with gold buttons stood out starkly against the background of the drab clothes of the Moscow children. I was very embarrassed by the coat, and grew to hate it.

Father wanted to bring me up in the spirit of communism right away, so the first day that we arrived he took me to Red Square. It was still sporting its May Day decorations. I was, of course, taken aback by all these red banners with the slogans "Socialism Will Be Victorious," "Workers of the World Unite," and so forth, but what surprised me most of all was something else: next to the Lobnoye Mesto ("execution place") hung a huge effigy of Austen Chamberlain. People kept setting fire to this effigy and dancing around it in a circle, holding hands. For a young girl who had just arrived from Europe, this looked absolutely barbaric, like some sort of cannibalistic ritual. They were burning what looked like a living person and dancing around it in ecstasy! Here Papa had miscalculated. My first impression was horribly negative.

The most relevant issue, however, was school. As I already mentioned, I couldn't write in Russian. I knew how to read, but not to write. I was fourteen years old. I should have been in the sixth or seventh grade. How could I do the sixth grade if I couldn't write? For some reason, my parents first decided to send me to a ballet school, and they took me to the Bolshoi Theater to audition. I suppose the idea was that there you wrote with your feet. They thought I would be able to get by at a ballet school. The Bolshoi rejected me out of hand, however. As a result, after many inquiries and much searching, they decided to enroll me in a German school. This was a school for the children of Communists, refugees from Hitler, and experts who were helping to build the new Socialist power by pro-

viding it with industrialization. And there they did, indeed, enroll me in the sixth grade. The school was relatively large, with parallel grades. It stood next to the Sukharev Tower. At that time, streetcars ran along the Garden Ring; it was the fourth stop from Kalyaevka.

For four years I had had no experience whatsoever of the German language. Furthermore, in this school they wrote not in Gothic script, but in the regular Latin alphabet. On the one hand, this was easier, because it resembled French, but on the other, it was visually unfamiliar to me. I still only knew how to read German in Gothic script, and that was also the only way I could write. I adapted fairly easily, however.

This was my introduction into the Soviet system. The schoolchildren were unusually politicized. (They were, after all, primarily children of political refugees.) The majority of them lived in the de Luxe, a hotel on Gorky Street, now reverted to its original name, Tverskaya Street. One felt the intense romanticism of revolution, the building of a new world, much more strongly there than in any ordinary school.

What surprised me was the degree to which all the kids thought in an identical manner about things, the coincidence of all their interests. I was surprised by the conformism, the unanimity, the absence of individual traits in them. In Paris everyone had been different. Perhaps that was because I had been friends with people older than me. Here everyone seemed cut from the same piece of cloth. The Communist ardor was incredibly strong.

I wanted very much to be like everyone else. The wish to be like others, to be at one with them, and the realization that this was impossible due to certain notions and ways of seeing the world that were deeply ingrained in me, made my school years very difficult. And not just the school years. The monolith of political unity that reigned in the country in those days, it can't be denied, was something incomprehensible for a person, even a child, newly arrived from another world. At the same time, it seemed very desirable. Somehow it seemed, when they were singing, marching in demonstrations, and so on, that they were happy and united—but I saw things otherwise. I felt like Kai from the fairytale *The Snow Queen*: I had a splinter from a troll's mirror in my eye, and I saw what no one else could see. I saw the ambiguity, the duality, of every situation, I saw things from another perspective, in another light, than others did. This troubled me. I thought that my vision of the world must be impaired in some way.

You would read a story, a book—everyone would express the same opinion about it. You write an essay—they give you a plan, an outline, and you have to write according to this outline. I was very preoccupied with how to become a member of the Pioneers, how to write the application. It turned out that there was nothing to worry about. There was a formula. I thought that I was supposed to express something—my feelings, my attitudes. Nothing of the sort. There were readymade formulas for everything; you just had to copy the text from the board. This simplified existence lulled me and drew me in, and at the same time aroused a sense of protest in me. From the first months there was something in me that balked at the system, which was imposed on the behavior of children—who were nevertheless already human beings.

By that time I already felt myself to be a person, a personality, and I didn't like it that everything was decided for me beforehand, that my path was already marked out for me. I wanted to unlearn this in myself—and could not.

There was one girl in that school I liked very much. She was in the other grade, parallel to mine. I liked her because I could not detect in her this enthusiasm for activity—to be like everyone else and to participate. She seemed very sad, with enormous, beautiful gray eyes. She was small, thin, and quiet. Most of the kids in school were boisterous. They were demonstrative and self-aggrandizing. They all wanted to be *päpstlicher als der Papst*, as they say in German— "holier than the Pope." That is, they wanted to be the most active, determined, trustworthy young Communists. This girl, however, seemed to shun all that, which immediately sparked my sympathy for her. Her name was Lucy—Lucy Tovalev. A Russian name—why was she studying in a German school?

It turned out that Tovalev was her stepfather's name. She came from Hamburg. I saw her mother one day when she came to pick her up from school. She was an attractive young woman, very chic, dressed in clothes that were beyond the means of someone from Moscow in those days. After I had seen her mother, Lucy's downtrodden and generally unhappy appearance touched me still more. I felt sorry for her. Soon I grew fond of her, and we became good friends.

I found out that she didn't live with her mother, but with various acquaintances. Her mother, a Lithuanian Jew, had run away with a Prussian officer when she was seventeen. He abandoned her soon after. Lucy was born out of this affair. Her mother, who adored society, neglected the child. She changed lovers often, and Lucy spent most of her life living with strangers. This continued until her mother met a man in Berlin who worked in the Soviet Department of Foreign Affairs. This was Tovalev. They got married.

At the beginning of the 1930s, Tovalev, like most Soviet citizens living abroad, was recalled to Moscow. At first they lived a life of luxury in a hotel, but just a few months after his return, he was arrested. Lucy's mother was a translator; she translated books and films. She very quickly found herself a Russian boyfriend, and the girl got in the way. The mother was young and pretty, and she was determined to continue living a life of amusement. She didn't realize that after Tovalev's arrest, she herself was doomed. No one understood these things yet, of course. This was 1934 or 1935. The first wave of arrests had begun, albeit not on such a massive scale as those of 1937.

In the summer I convinced my parents to let me go to a Pioneer camp near Kaluga, on the Oka River. I loved all of that, and I loved our camp leaders. They were young members of the Schutzbund who had emigrated from Austria. We had very cordial relations with them, not like those between adults and children, but similar to those among young people in a sports training camp. At the same time I noticed that they were much more involved in their own personal lives and affairs. I observed some romances, and so forth, and yet again I became convinced that the showy facade, all these pioneer campfires, gatherings and assemblies, were one thing, but that real life was something else altogether. Even in the Pioneer camp, they were more interested in each other, than in us. But the freedom we had there, the freedom in which we lived, was very pleasant.

When I came home from camp, Papa wouldn't let me go back to the German school. I was shattered. I cried inconsolably, begging him to let me go back for at least one year; but he, always so indulgent with me, was adamant in this matter. Soon I understood that his decision had been a wise one. In 1936, nearly everyone in the school was arrested: all the teachers, many of the parents, and quite a few students, as well. Soon the school itself was closed down.

11

In the seventh grade I started attending the school from which I graduated. It was my twelfth school. The most important one, the one I loved most. It had a very grand name: The First Experimental Model School of the Committee for Public Education. The headmistress was a remarkable woman, a pedagogue of the old stamp, Klavdia Poltavskaya. She had worked with the famous Russian pedagogue Stanislav Shatsky.

The school was housed in a beautiful building from the 1920s, with turrets and passageways—not a standard, but a completely unique and individualized school. There were no parallel grades. One class per grade, and in each class no more than twenty pupils.

About twenty years ago I felt I had to reunite the people from my class, those who were still alive. We were all long past fifty. Life had scattered us about. We met only very irregularly, two or three at a time. I decided it would be great to meet as a group, to compare notes and draw some conclusions about the paths we had taken, the lives we had lived thus far. We had been so close in our schooldays, and even long afterward. The reunion of the remains of our class gathered at my place. There were still quite a few of us around, about fifteen. After that, very quickly, people began to pass away. So that it wouldn't just be about dinner, but a more festive and solemn occasion, I said, "Look, let's be honest: let's all, one by one, tell each other about the most important thing that has happened to us over the past years."

Just imagine, these grown-up people, most of them already

graying or bald, began to talk about the past, very openly, in great detail and at length. It was an absolutely surprising and unforgettable evening. I should have recorded it, of course, at least on a tape recorder. It should have been preserved for posterity. It was such a testament to the times, an act of witness, yet I failed to do this, with my typical lighthearted optimism that there would still be time. What you don't do now, you never manage to do later.

The stories of the lives of my friends remained for me a sort of summary. Life didn't just slip through the fingers. It poured out in stories that I remember. I understood that I had given each of them a way, a path, through stories. It was a very important evening for all of us.

Two years later I organized another reunion. Our ranks had already shrunk. Two of us had died in the interim. We assigned ourselves a difficult task—each of us was to describe the most worthy, and the most unworthy, deed in our lives, and to talk about what the next step in our lives would be. Again, we were all very frank. This opportunity to talk openly about serious and painful matters after not seeing each other for many years testifies to the closeness we had once had.

We had a truly remarkable class, and it produced many interesting people.

In the eighth grade a boy by the name of Dezik Kaufman joined our class. We had met him before through Zhora Kostretsov, our class monitor, a very upright young man. We had gathered at my house, and Zhora brought a buddy of his along, someone who lived in his building. We liked him immediately. He had a flair for the dramatic, was a wonderful storyteller. There was a broken chair in the room, and he picked it up and started doing stunts with it, using it as a prop. First it was a guitar, then a machine gun, then something else. In later years the boy became well-known throughout the country. I believe he was the best poet of our generation: David Samoylov. He studied with us, beginning in the eighth grade.

Tolya Chernyaev looked like Gorky. He had a typical "Russian" physiognomy, short cropped hair, and a clear, direct gaze. In a photograph I have of him he's wearing a white shirt with a black tie and a green jacket, fashioned out of a formal military uniform that had belonged to his grandfather, an officer in the Czarist army. Tolya lived in Maryina Roshcha, a very impoverished neighborhood back then. They had two rooms in a decrepit wooden house. He was assiduous in his studies and wanted to be the top student in the class, and played piano beautifully. He was shy, and his voice often gave way when it began changing. He was very principled and incapable of telling lies. Much later, when Tolya was about to graduate from the history department, he married a fellow student, who was Jewish— for love, and out of protest. He was given to understand that if he wanted to make a career for himself, he had to break off his relations with this girl. A few days later they got married. Today Tolya—Anatoly

—is one of Gorbachev's closest advisors, and we are still friends.

Lev Bezymensky was the son of a Komsomol poet of the 1920s and 30s. He always wore a suit and tie (the other kids dressed any which way). During the war he was an interpreter and interrogated Friedrich Paulus. Later, he served for a long time as a correspondent in Western Germany, as a head of the news bureau there. Now he works for the *New Times*. His area of expertise is Hitlerism.

At the second reunion Lev said something that I believe speaks volumes about him, and so I record his words here: "I must repent." He probably had changed his attitude toward the work he did during the war and post-war years, when he was a foreign correspondent (and, evidently, carried out other functions).

Ilya Pinsker, a boy from a very poor Jewish family, had an infectious laugh. He always seemed to be daydreaming and not paying attention in class. When he was called to the board, however, he always performed brilliantly, especially in mathematics. We were all convinced he would one day win the Nobel Prize. And that might easily have been the case, if Ilya had not been the victim of the struggle against "cosmopolitanism."

Felix Siegel was passionate about astronomy and became one of the best-known ufologists, the first in the Soviet Union. He had no doubts that there was life on other planets. At the same time, he was also a very religious person.

Nina Gegechkori was hotheaded, ardent, and forthright. I will have more to say about her later.

The prettiest girl was Natasha Stankevich. She came from a prominent family and was the granddaughter of Vasily Vatagin, an animal sculptor famous in the 1920s. All the boys in our class were in love with her. In the end her life was not in any way out of the ordinary, however.

That was our class.

Staying home from school was a form of punishment. When we had a temperature, we shook down the thermometer. We had excellent teachers, and I will talk about them presently, but the most important thing for us was our interaction with one another. It consumed us completely; we stayed together as long as we could each day, and walked each other home. Life followed its intense and unpredictable path.

12

WE WOKE UP TO A SPECIAL SOUND, A KIND OF SCRAPING: THE YARD-keepers were breaking up the ice. This was the background "melody" of my Moscow childhood. The climate in Moscow has changed dramatically. In those days, winters were still very cold and snowy, and this sound of scraping and of splintering ice accompanied the start of every day. It was very poetic. I would describe it in this way: it was the sound of old Moscow, of ancient, patriarchal Moscow, which then disappeared altogether. At the end of the day, when we returned home from school, the yard-keepers would have scraped this ice together in piles, after which they dragged it into the courtyards on sleds. In the courtyards there were big vats in which they melted the ice. The streets were always very clean back then. There was none of the machinery, none of the new street-cleaning technology that we have nowadays. And now the streets and sidewalks are impassable in winter! The streets were clean, and there was always this scraping sound against a background of winter ice and snow. That is all gone now.

Just like the boys and girls who all carried their ice skates around, we had a special way of carrying them. It was considered very cool to wear the skate-guards flung over your shoulder. During my university days, everyone skied on Saturdays and Sundays. I hardly ever see any young people on skates or skis anymore. But in those days, as soon as you went out the door you'd see crowds of people on skis, on their way to the parks or to open country outside of town.

In the morning the streets were full of milkmaids, who were also part of this picture of old Moscow. They came from the nearby towns and settlements with two milk cans strapped on their backs and a sack of potatoes in front. Every day they made the rounds of particular neighborhoods. Everyone had a milkmaid back then. Sometimes they traded milk for bread. The government used to requisition all the flour from the countryside and bring it to the city, so that the villages often had no bread. Sometimes they traded the milk for rags, which were difficult to come by there. Sometimes they just sold the milk. This was our daily life—the rattling of milk cans, milk pouring out, potatoes they brought us, still smelling of snow. Our cozy, homegrown, patriarchal Moscow.

Moscow was still very much a nineteenth century city, with a multitude of ancient mansions with classical blue or yellow façades. All kinds of local Party committees—the raikoms—and other organizations called by their Soviet abbreviations, organizations no less secretive than their activities, had taken them over. There were thousands of one- or two-story wooden houses with picket fences. In the endless mazes of interconnected courtyards and alleyways worked the last of the artisans and skilled laborers.

I can also still remember the cabbies and draymen. In 1934 and 1935 they still drove sledges and carriages through the streets. It was very expensive to take one. They addressed the passengers as barin and barynya ("mister" and "ma'am"). They disappeared soon after, and the only form of public transportation was the streetcar. It was a struggle to get on, and a struggle to get off. The cars were full to bursting. People hung off the footboards and grabbed onto the first thing that came to hand. Traveling was real torture. It was always accompanied by the deafening sound of the clattering wheels, and you were packed in like sardines, to the great delight of dexterous pickpockets.

I remember another Moscow that was not homey and patriarchal, but horrific. There were people who went from house to house, apparently fleeing the collective farms (*kolkhozy*), primarily women, begging for alms. They never asked for money, though. They asked for bread and household necessities. I'll never forget one such woman who came to our door, saying, "Give me something, in the name of Christ, anything." She tore open her ragged, filthy coat to reveal her complete nakedness underneath. She didn't even have a shirt on. I've never forgotten it. People like that came to our door nearly every day, newly arrived from somewhere, refugees, people fleeing something, searching for something, most often with children. We always tried to give them something. I remember giving them bed linens, and sometimes our own clothes.

Juxtaposed to this desperate poverty was the TORGSIN—literally, "Trade with Foreigners," where you could buy almost anything, but only with foreign currency, gold, or silver. The TORGSIN was established with the goal of taking away the valuables that remained to the few descendants of the nobility and merchant families who had not emigrated or been arrested. One day my parents and I were visiting friends, and the hostess apologized for the knives with only iron pegs instead of handles. The silver handles had been "taken to TORGSIN."

My family lived quite well. We were poor by western standards, but very comfortable by Soviet, Moscow standards. At the time there was a distribution system, by cards. Papa had a "closed distribution" card. He was designated as TE-A, which stood for Technical Engineer of the top level. The distribution center was located in the House on the Embankment, described by Yuri Trifonov in his eponymous novel. One could visit it once or twice a week and pick up a ration packet stamped with the letter A. So we were never lacking the basic necessities, though we lived very modestly.

My classmates lived quite differently, however. I was friends with one girl named Nina Popova. She was the daughter of a seamstress in a textile atelier. She lived with her mother and her sister in Maryina Roshcha, like many of my classmates. The first time I visited her home, I was astonished—here you must make allowances for my naïveté and foolishness—to discover that not every family made dinner. I had never suspected this before. This came as a great surprise to me. I still remember it. At their house they had tea, and they were lucky if they had sugar; sometimes there wasn't any. And they ate bread—with salt and vegetable oil. That was dinner in Nina Popova's family.

I went home with friends who lived in communal apartments in which a large, extended family—say, a grandmother, grandfather, father, mother, and two children—lived in a 170- or 180-square-foot room, and that was considered not so bad. Many lived in rooms partitioned off by screens, or sheets sewn together and hung from the ceiling. If, say, the oldest son got married and brought home a young wife to live in the room, they curtained off a corner with these sheets, and that was where they lived. I saw many living quarters like this.

Another strong impression that remains from those years was my father's friendship with Emanuel Lasker, the famous chess player. On

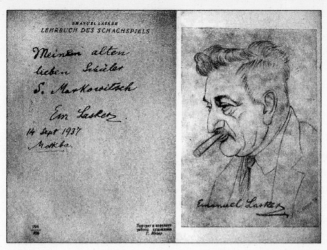

Sundays, two or three times a month, our whole family went to have dinner at his home. He was Jewish, and he lived here as a refugee, having fled Hitler's Germany. He did not feel at home here, knew few people, and was quite attached to Papa. They often played chess after dinner. It was 1936. Lasker was completely preoccupied with the war in Spain. His entire room was crammed with bookshelves and books, and a huge map of Spain took up one whole wall. There were red flags pinned on it, which he moved as the troops progressed. In those days, everyone followed the news from Spain. There was a great deal of discussion about it, and everyone felt involved. In later years, when I was in college, the first Spanish children arrived. They were placed in boarding schools. But at that time the war was still going on.

Then the wave of arrests began.

One of the first prominent officials to be arrested was Nikolai Krylenko. Krylenko was a People's Commissar. He loved chess, and ran a Chess Society. He was someone Lasker could turn to for assistance or advice, and someone who often visited him on those Sunday dinners when we were present. I remember very clearly how Lasker panicked. At first he couldn't understand why he couldn't get through to Krylenko by phone. Evidently, it was harder for westerners to grasp the rapid changes that were already underway in our lives. It wasn't until several weeks later that he realized that Krylenko had been arrested. Soon after, other friends of Lasker's were arrested, too. Finally, at one of our regular Sunday dinners, he said, "That's it. We've requested visas to go to the United States. We're afraid to stay here any longer."

13

It would be wrong to suggest, however, that there were only negative moments in my life, that all my experience back then boiled down to a rejection of the Soviet System. This was not the case. There was much that broadened my worldview, that allowed me to ascend in my path of development. One very important experience—I would even call it decisive—was a visit my mother and I made to Koktebel, on the Black Sea, in 1935.

Mama was head of a puppet theater group at the Union of Writers. Through them she obtained a voucher for a vacation at a writer's retreat (the House of Writers) in Koktebel. When we arrived, I was immediately captivated by the beauty of the place. It is on the eastern coast of the Crimea, and very different from the southern part of it. It is far wilder and more severe. I felt I had arrived in ancient Greece. That was the way I imagined it. The craggy surface, the astonishing beauty of the outline of one of Europe's oldest mountain ranges—the Kara Dag; it was mesmerizing. The epitome of all this beauty, harmonious and lyrical, was the Poet's House, the home of Maximilian Voloshin.

Voloshin had at one point chosen this Greco-Bulgarian set-tlement, where he bought a piece of land and built a house ac-cording to his own unique vision and design. From Egypt he brought a statue, a marble bust of the goddess Taiakh, which he placed in the low, spacious salon, the center that united the entire structure of the house. All around stood bookshelves containing a remarkable French library, which for me was very important; I plunged into reading French books there. There was also a col-lection of poetry of the Silver Age. I first read Mandelstam and Tsvetaeva there. I can say with great certainty that this signaled a new departure in my understanding of poetry, literature, of life itself.

It was there, too, that I met someone who remained a friend through all the years of my life thus far: Ilya Nusinov, or Elka, as everyone called him. He had also come to Koktebel with his mother. His father was a well-known literary critic and theorist.

My mother became friends with Maria Voloshin, which is how I had the opportunity to attend the remarkable soirées that she held in her home. Some-times they were concerts, sometimes poetry readings with young poets. I first heard Sergey Mikhalkov there, for example. He was still a rather sweet young man. He read "Uncle Styopa," which he had just written, and there was as yet nothing that pointed to the sellout he would eventually become. Maria Voloshin was very gracious to him and accepted him into her home with-out hesitation.

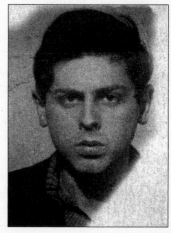

Voloshin had died in 1932. The memory of him was still very fresh. His spirit filled the house—that of an unusually broad-minded, poetic, and deeply humane man. On the anniversary of his death, they braided wreaths and walked to his grave. He had chosen a spot on the crown of a hill, from which the entire valley of Kok-tebel was visible. We ascended the hillside, and when we reached the top, all of life seemed transfigured by poetry. This could not but make a deep and lasting impression on a fifteen-year-old girl.

When our vacation was ending, Maria Voloshin suggested to Mama that I stay on and live in her attic with several other children of her friends. I was sure that Mama would refuse—but, to my amazement, she agreed. She was charmed by Maria Voloshin, who was indeed a fascinating woman, very original.

She was poorly educated. She had worked as a nurse, but she had very broad interests and notions. At the beginning of the 1920s, when the Crimea changed hands between the Bolsheviks and several other splinter groups, then was conquered by the Whites, and who knows who else, she would shelter three or four members of hostile parties in her home at the same time. In one room there would be a Bolshevik, in another a member of some splinter organization, in a third someone else. She was a devout Christian, and believed that the task of people on earth was to help one another. This was why she had gone to this Bulgarian village—it was for the most part Bulgarian; there were still some Greeks, but they were resettled at the beginning of the war—to tend to the villagers, to feed them, to embrace and care for as many people as she could. This outlook on life, of course, made a deep and lasting impression on me. The idea that one had to help others first, and try to sort out everything else later. That you could not refuse other people, you had to trust them and help them. That was her modus operandi. An excellent example for a fifteen-year-old girl to be exposed to.

Among the young people in this attic was one boy I noticed immediately. His name was Yura Shakhovsky; he was the son of Prince Shakhovsky. Yura's father was executed even before Yura was born, when his mother, baroness von Timoroth, a maid-of-honor to the empress, was in her fourth month of pregnancy. When I met Yura, his mother worked as a babysitter and washed floors at the Tropical Institute. He was eighteen years old and studied in a school for workers' children. He already worked as a driver, because he and his mother could hardly make ends meet. He was a very interesting boy, and knew many verses by heart. This friendship that I formed in Koktebel also lasted for many years to come.

This, I believe, points to something that characterizes my bonds with others. It has usually been the case that someone who comes within my circle of acquaintances remains there. People have rarely arrived within my circle and then abandoned it. And when people become dear to me I do not let go of them (nor do they want to escape, it seems). Relationships with people always had some kind of continuity. I have often observed that people who have a diverse group of friends and acquaintances try to avoid merging them. They prefer to keep them apart in separate groups. I, on the contrary, always had the urge—however idiotic, or even destructive—to unite them, to bring them all together under one roof. And that is just what I did. This is why I introduced my friends from my first trip to Koktebel (and there were dozens of trips to Koktebel after that) to my classmates in Moscow, and we all became one large group of friends.

These friends, these books, the poetry of the Silver Age, all of this engrossed me deeply and sheltered me both from over-politicization, and from the negation of Soviet reality, from the life that would later absorb me completely. It somehow broadened the dimensions of my inner life, the life inside me.

14

Fᴿᴏᴍ 1936 ᴛᴏ 1938, ᴅᴜʀɪɴɢ ᴛʜᴇ ᴡᴏʀsᴛ ᴏғ ᴛʜᴇ Tᴇʀʀᴏʀ, ᴅᴀɪʟʏ ʟɪғᴇ seemed to improve, however strange it may seem. After years of food scarcity and hunger, after collectivization, which drove people to the brink of starvation and misery, there was a lull in the hardship. Stalin himself gave the signal. He pronounced the infamous words: "Life has become better, life has become happier." All the newspapers repeated it in chorus. In 1935, ration cards were finally abolished. Little by little the grocery stores filled up with goods. Smoked fish, caviar, and four or five kinds of cheese suddenly appeared. Spanish oranges were widely available. Cafés opened, such as the Cocktail Bar on Gorky Street. You could have a drink there, sitting in semidarkness on a bar stool. This was considered to be the height of chic and luxury. In the Artistic across from the Moscow Art Theater, you could have a cup of coffee before or after a play, or eat an omelette.

People were better groomed. Women began to go to the hairdresser and to get manicures—manicures were even offered at the factories. They wore red lipstick and plucked their eyebrows. Before, everyone had dressed in identically nondescript ways, and equally unattractively, but now it became possible to dress with elegance. Fashion magazines were published. Comrade Zhemchuzhina, the wife of Vyacheslav Molotov, was charged with the task of manufacturing perfumes, lotions, and creams.

Stalin gave his blessing to the joys of life. Love was legalized, along with family happiness (divorce was difficult to achieve) and paternal duty. Poetry was permitted, one could openly discuss humanism, and rouge and jewelry were allowed. The tango and the foxtrot made a comeback, and Leonid Utesov created Soviet jazz. He had a song that expressed the spirit of the new era:

In the allies of Central Park
grows mignonette on a May morning.
You can wear a shocking tie
and be a hero of labor in a mine.
How is that—mignonette and
a hero of labor?
I don't get it, explain it to me.
Because where we live
everyone is young now
in our youthful, wonderful country.

And it went without saying that "I know no other country where a person breathes so freely." This song blared nonstop from loudspeakers on the streets and in P.A. systems in apartments, and God forbid you should ask to turn it down in the kitchen or hallways of communal apartments. Someone would turn you in to the authorities without a second's notice; there was never a dearth of stool pigeons. There was no way to close yourself off from the deluge of propaganda. Virtually every room had a photograph of Lenin and Stalin hanging on the wall, titled *A Great Friendship*. Later, under Khrushchev, it was revealed to have been a photomontage: two different photographs, one of Lenin and another of Stalin, had been joined together to canonize Stalin during his lifetime.

Until 1936 everyone lived for the "common cause," and no one thought about private life. There was hardly enough of it to make children. Suddenly, after Stalin uttered the words "Life has become happier," everything changed. The people obeyed. Communists began promptly to fall in love and to start families. At the same time, a new literature came into being. Lyrical poetry reappeared in the form of poems by Konstantin Simonov and Yevgeniy Dolmatovsky, who spoke of love under the cloudless skies of the Homeland. It was even permitted to mention Dostoevsky and Esenin, for which you could have been thrown in jail not long before. In 1937, with a great deal of pomp and ceremony, the hundredth anniversary of Pushkin's death was celebrated. Two editions of the *Complete Works* were printed in millions of copies. Films were made and musical comedies were staged. The theater was more successful than it had ever been before. People waited in line through the night for tickets to watch a performance at the Moscow Art Theater to see actors like Vasily Kachalov, Anatoly Moskvin, and Olga Knipper-Chekhova. The most popular play was *Anna Karenina*. It even traveled to Paris. Bulgakov's *The Days of the Turbins* was wildly successful. I personally knew people who went to see it thirty-two times. Bulgakov demonstrated that even the White officers had feelings of self-worth and honor. They said that Stalin himself saw the play many times, and would sit in the depths of a box seat, hidden from view.

He never appeared to the people. He was invisible, like God. Sometimes he phoned people in the middle of the night. In Moscow, many rumors of his conversations with Pasternak, Ehrenburg, and Stanislavsky made the rounds. He invited actors to perform in the Kremlin. Ordinary people, however, could only see him two or three times a year: at the Mausoleum during May Day parades, or on November 7th (the day the October 25th Revolution was celebrated). It is impossible to describe the excitement and trepidation people felt in his presence. Especially the youth. They woke up at six o'clock in anticipation of happiness, then waited for hours in their ranks and columns . . . Impatient and joyous, they played accordions, sang, waved flags, and couldn't believe that they would see Him at such close range. They marched in ranks. When it came time to march past the Mausoleum, the pace would speed up, and the guard would command: Mind your step! Look lively! People craned their necks so they could see more, so they could imprint the sight of the great teacher and leader on their memories.

People worshiped him. They cried out "Long live Stalin!" when they were being executed, convinced that he didn't know what was happening to them. Later, during World War II, soldiers would die with his name on their lips—Ehrenburg, Vasily Grossman, and Konstantin Paustovsky all describe this.

I never saw him. The only time I had the opportunity, I fell ill. In the evening, my friends, terribly excited, came to see me and tell me about it. I very much regretted that I couldn't have been there with them. I listened, and felt once again that I was a stranger.

15

In those days we went to school five days a week. Every fifth day we met at my house, because I was the only one in the class who had a room all to herself—this was an almost unthinkable luxury back then. We would write silly little plays that we later acted out, and made up hundreds of epigrams. No one wrote a word about me, though. Finally, Dezik rose to the challenge:

Why, when it comes to you,
is there a special policy?
No one pens you epigrams—
Are you above critique, or underneath?

In the eighth grade we started our own newspaper. We named it *The Class (Not)Pravda*—The Untruth. It used the same typefaces as the official Soviet newspaper, *Pravda*. Each of us wrote what we wished, all kinds of little observations and notes. The year was 1937, and the show trials had begun. We were foolish enough, or mad enough—I don't know how to characterize it; let's say we didn't understand the situation—to express our indignation at the way Gorky was being reviled, and things of that nature, in the pages of our newspaper. In our classroom there was a cupboard under lock and key, and there was a boy—the treasurer and keeper of the editorial archives—who always kept the key in his pocket. Once we came to school, opened this cupboard, and found it empty. We were canny enough to realize that this was very worrying, very dangerous. We rushed to find Klavdia Poltavskaya, the headmistress. We trusted her so implicitly that she was the one we sought out, saying, "What do we do? Someone has taken hold of our archive!" She said, "Children"—she always called us "children," which in the Soviet era was an absolutely inadmissible form of address—"children, I took it. I took it home and burned it in my bathroom last night.

I was afraid. Afraid that it would fall into the hands of someone else. I wanted to save both myself and all of you."

Her fear was not misplaced. A week later a Komsomol organizer by the name of Misha was sent to us. We quickly figured out that his function was to keep an eye not only on us, but also on Mrs. Poltavskaya.

The day began with a lineup in the school auditorium. Before we dispersed to our classrooms, Klavdia Poltavskaya called us together for five or six minutes and made some announcements. We saw him sitting behind her and writing down all her words. And we were afraid. We began to see that she was in danger. It gradually dawned on us that Poltavskaya was not completely in step with the times. When she spoke to us she did not use the term "Communist Party" or mention Stalin. We understood by her choice of words, her diction, that she differed from others. We were such bumbling idiots that we marched over to the local Komsomol office to defend her and to lodge a complaint about this Misha, the Komsomol organizer. We felt called upon to protect her. At that point it was still possible to call things into question, things were still open to discussion, and several times at our meetings he allowed himself to say, "I cannot agree with Mrs. Poltavskaya when she says this or that." We thought that this signaled a terrible danger. If he said such things in her presence, here in school, what did he say in other places behind her back? Needless to say, our actions put her in a far worse position.

When we were in the eighth grade, the fathers of two of our classmates were arrested. One of them was the well-known journalist Lev Sosnovsky. In every issue of *Izvestia* he wrote a column called "Underground." During the Spanish Civil War he traveled to Spain and sent reports from the front. His son Volodya studied with us. Another girl who went to my school was Galya Lifshitz, the daughter of the First Deputy Grigory Ordzhonikidze. Both Volodya's and Galya's fathers were arrested. Later their mothers were arrested, too; but at first it was only their fathers. At the school, a Komsomol meeting was immediately called to expel Volodya and Galya from the ranks, on some charge that appeared utterly awkward and idiotic to me. If young people today are reading this, I hope it will be useful to them to hear about the horrific absurdities of life during that period. Modern-day Communists walk around at demonstrations filled with nostalgia for the old times, and yet back then they expelled a fifteen-year-old boy and girl from the Komsomol because they had not managed to denounce their own parents before they were denounced by the KGB (then NKVD). How do you like that? Not used to keeping my mouth shut yet, at my paltry fifteen years of age, I stood up and said that it was stupid, absurd, and impossible to expel children. First, no one would denounce their own parents; and, second, how could they have done so, on what grounds? The meeting was adjourned for a time, and after it resumed they expelled me for having dared speak against their decision.

I have something to confess, and to repent, by the way. Only two of our classmates were Komsomol members. Unfortunately, I was one of the first to join, out of my still deep-seated desire to be part of the status quo. Myself and Lev Bezymensky. When I was expelled, he stood up for me. So the meeting adjourned a second time, and when it was called again, he was expelled, too. It was older members who expelled us, and Misha, the Komsomol organizer, was chairing the meeting.

Lev and I were still foolish and naïve enough to think that when we went to the local Komsomol office to clarify our positions, we would be immediately reinstated. They did not even allow us to explain ourselves. Why we had been expelled didn't interest anyone in the least. The expulsions of Galya Lifshitz and Volodya Sosnovsky didn't interest them, either. They simply voted and affirmed that the expulsions had taken place. That was it. They hardly allowed us to open our mouths.

I think this was the definitive moment in my disenchantment with the system, and my final rejection of it. I realized that it was rotten to the core. I saw that it was all performance, staged theatrics. I remember this very clearly—my eighth-grade class, the visit to the local Komsomol office, the degree of apathy we met with, the lack of any desire even to pretend that they wanted to listen to us. This produced a very strong impression on a young, unprejudiced person. I realized that I simply couldn't accept such a system. Later, when my peers, my fellow students, especially during my studies at the Institute for Philosophy, Literature, and History, began to think critically about these matters, and to become disillusioned, it seemed that I was the wise one, that I had seen it all coming much earlier. But I want to stress that it wasn't really so. I had simply learned to exercise freedom of thought during my childhood abroad; and that faculty stayed with me. I wasn't better, or smarter, or more prescient, than anyone else. It was just that certain notions had formed in me early on, and had become so deep-rooted in my soul that even the mind-numbing stupefaction that was inculcated in all of us was powerless against them. This was why I didn't believe in the trials of the "enemies of the people" for a single minute. I was absolutely convinced that it was all staged; there wasn't a drop of doubt in my mind about it.

Then the third wave of repressions and trials began. Every day the papers reported details of the court hearings. It was January 1937. This time, top party officials—Nikolai Bukharin, Alexei Rykov, and others, dubbed the "Trotskyists"—appeared before the state prosecutor Andrey Vyshinsky. All of them to a man, except, as I recall, Krestinsky, who had rejected the charges from the beginning, all of them confessed, and testified against themselves, saying that they had defected to foreign intelligence services and were involved in a conspiracy against the Party.

The people believed it. How could there be any doubt, when they had confessed themselves? But I couldn't believe it. I remember saying to one of my friends, "But they were all close comrades of Lenin's, they were the ones who carried out the revolution. Why would they betray it like that?" I think my father influenced me, as well. He had been close to Krestinsky during his time in Berlin, and I could see that he did not doubt for a second that Krestinsky was innocent. Nor did he doubt the innocence of the others. I understood perfectly that he didn't believe the confessions. Although he avoided open criticism of the matter, and always stopped Mama from expressing herself when she grew indignant about it, I could see he was suppressing rage when he read the newspaper accounts of the trials. But he was very wary of compromising me, of putting me in an awkward position, so he didn't want to let on about his consternation.

Several months later, Lev and I were reinstated in the Komsomol. Stalin had announced that the repressions had gone too far. This was a familiar tactic of his—to take on the role or appearance of a benefactor.

About forty years later I was standing in line for oranges on the Arbat. I noticed a stranger looking at me with a fixed expression. Very well dressed, wearing an expensive hat—such hats were only sold in exclusive distribution centers. The Arbat is near the Ministry of Foreign Affairs, so I immediately concluded he was a diplomat. Suddenly, he approached me.

"Are you Lilya?"

"Yes."

"Don't you recognize me? I'm Misha, your Komsomol organizer."

"You recognized me? You remember me?"

"How could I forget you? You're Lilya, 'Miss Opposition.'" That was what he called me during our school years. He seemed to be joking, but I always felt behind it some sort of threat. "You always had your own opinion."

He had become quite stout, as people who have the opportunity to be well fed always do. We studied each other, and, despite all the years that had passed, I knew we were still enemies.

Galya Lifshitz, who is also now seventy-seven years old, wrote a book about her life and phoned me a few days ago to say, "I recall that you were the only one who defended me. I'm writing about this. Wasn't it you who invited me over to your house after school? You know, when we all sat around the table, you and me and your parents?" I said, "Yes, that was me." Then she said, "I remember it so well. It was the only ray of hope throughout those terrible years."

It's remarkable, since so many years have passed. Volodya Sosnovsky was arrested and ended up in Siberia. He found me ten years ago, too; and he had not forgotten anything, either. It turns out that none of those memories of the past simply disappeared without a trace. We remember it all.

These events created a state of alarm for us at home. Papa was a perfect candidate for arrest in 1937–38. He had worked abroad for four years, then he had been prohibited from leaving the Soviet Union. These circumstances were all cause for suspicion.

All of his colleagues in the unit where he worked—it was called TechnoPromImport—had been arrested already. Fortunately Papa was ill, though it's terrible to say so, for it was only because of his illness that he was not arrested with them. He had been diagnosed with pernicious anemia, which can now be treated, but was not curable back then. This was what allowed him to die peacefully in his own bed, and not in a prison cell. But what happened in our building was simply beyond belief. The house had been built by employees of the embassies, trade delegations, and so on. It was an enormous building. Every day, dozens of lights went out. Our yard-keeper was always called upon as a witness, and several months later he ended up in an insane asylum from lack of sleep. In the daytime he broke up the ice and shoveled snow, and at night he went from apartment to apartment witnessing arrests.

I was aware that Papa didn't sleep, either. He was often hospitalized, but in between his visits to the hospital, when he came home, he paced up and down in his study instead of sleeping. He had a suitcase packed with shaving articles, sheets, and soap. Mama was also terrified. She dried bread for rations and stored it in sacks, and listened for every step on the stairs . . . The elevator going up . . . we finally got an elevator, by the way, in the second or third year we were living in Moscow. The sound insulation was so poor that you could hear every sound it made. It was terrifying. When it creaked into motion at nine or ten in the evening, everyone was on edge, everyone started shaking.

Ours was not the only family living in this sort of fear. All around me I could sense this warm, living fear, real, and not imagined, which formed the basis of our lives at that time. I remember walking through Moscow one night with Yura Shakhovsky. The streets were quiet and empty. There were hardly any cars, but now and then a huge truck drove past marked MEAT, FISH, or BREAD. We parted at dawn by my house. Sunk in thought, I entered my court-yard. Suddenly, coming toward me, swaying ever so slightly, I saw a friend of Papa's, accompanied by two strangers in plainclothes who were leading him away, gripping him under his arms. I rushed toward him, saying, "Where are you going at this hour?" They said to me, "Move along!" I realized that they were arresting him. When I turned around to look, I saw them shove him into a truck covered with a tarpaulin. Imagine a sixteen-year-old girl witnessing such a scene: an acquaintance being bundled into a vehicle, and not al-lowed to say a word . . . It is worth reminding people of these events, in case they have forgotten, and telling those who aren't aware that they took place. I would like to pass the memory of these things on to the young people. The feeling of fear is hard to imagine if you have never experienced it. Once you have known it, it never leaves you; but it is difficult to imagine. You have to have lived it. Not knowing what will become of you the next minute, the next hour, the next day, is perhaps the most intense kind of stress imaginable. At that time, it seemed to me that entire urban populations were gripped by this kind of fear. But—and I'll return to this part of the story later—when the war began, I saw that it wasn't only the urban citizens, but the rural dwellers, too.

16

I STARTED SPENDING TIME WITH YURA SHAKHOVSKY. HE AND HIS mother had a room in a miserable communal apartment full of proletarians. The proletarians despised them because they hailed from the nobility, even though Yura's mother, as I have already mentioned, worked as a babysitter and washed floors in the Tropical Institute for a living. Their room resembled a pencil box—so long and narrow was it. In that room she would recount for me how she danced at her first ball, showing me photographs of herself wearing all her finery when she was maid-of-honor to the empress. Yura introduced me to his girlfriend, who lived in the building I live in now, 23 Novinsky Boulevard. Her name was Alyona Ilsen. Alyona's mother was the head of the Latin Department at the university, and her father was a doctor who held a high position in the People's Commissariat of Health. They lived in the third entrance on the first floor of our building. Alyona had a great influence on a person whose existence I knew nothing of at the time, but who would one day be my husband: Sima. Alyona loved to recount novels, which she devoured greedily. She would gather the kids together in the courtyard and narrate the stories.

Sima, who was three years younger than she, was one of her most passionate listeners. He later told me that he would spend hours at a time standing in the courtyard and listening to her stories. He heard both Russian and world classics in the renditions of Alyona Ilsen.

Her parents were arrested within two weeks of each other: first her father, then her mother. She and her younger sister Lilika remained at home alone, in a small room of this apartment.

In my eagerness to connect everyone to one another, I introduced them to Lucy Tovalev, my classmate in the German school. By then her mother had also been arrested. Her stepfather hated Lucy, because he wanted to take away the room in the apartment in which she lived. So Lucy moved in to live with Alyona.

The apartment was clean and spacious. It hadn't yet been converted into communal living quarters. Kids began to gather there regularly, primarily kids whose parents had been arrested. There they chatted (sometimes saying things one would be better off keeping to himself), and also practiced spiritualism. Elka Nusinov, who spent time with them, told me with indignation that these girls had completely lost their minds. In addition they had quit school and gone to work in factories. Actually, Alyona had never gone to school, since her mother was a strong believer in home schooling. She was the one person I had ever met who hadn't gone to school.

Around the eve of the New Year of 1938, Lucy was arrested in Alyona's apartment.

In those years, Elka was still very loyal to the Komsomol, a "true believer." He understood nothing; he refused to see, and all my efforts to make him understand came to naught. I was very much at fault. I immediately suspected that Elka must have told some Komsomol meeting somewhere that he knew a place where they were practicing spiritualism—so incomprehensible was it to me that they would arrest a tenth-grade girl. This is how I explained it to myself. Filled with anger and indignation, at the New Year's celebration at Elka's house I told him, "Look what you've done, now Lucy has been arrested! I don't want to know you anymore, forget you ever knew me. I no longer exist for you." He didn't even try to defend himself, most likely because the accusation was so outlandish. We broke off relations until midway through the war. But he continued to send me huge bouquets of roses on my birthday and wrote me the same note: "We're still in the ninth grade forever." He had declared his love for me in the ninth grade.

I continued seeing Alyona. One day, after the arrest of Lucy and another girl of our acquaintance—in other words, when I already realized that they were not above arresting children—Alyona called me and said, "I need to talk to you. Let's meet up and take a walk."

We met on the Old Arbat, and walked up and down it—to Plotnikov Street and back. I couldn't figure out what she wanted to talk to me about. I said:

"Well? What's it about?"

She answered, "Wait a minute and I'll tell you."

She didn't have time to tell me anything; suddenly, a person approached us and asked, "Which of you is Alyona Ilsen?"

She said: "I am."

"Then you must come with me."

They took her to an automobile with its headlights off, stuffed her in, and drove off. What was I to think? The only thing I could conclude was that they had arrested her right in front of my eyes. That was when I was in tenth grade. I was horrified. I was afraid to go home; I had no idea what to do. But I thought about Alyona's fourteen-year-old sister Lilika, who had been left alone at home, and I began walking up and down the Arbat, to make sure no one was following me. Finally, I went to see Yura, who was already asleep, since it was around midnight by this time. I woke him up and said:

"Yura, listen, they just arrested Alyona right before my very eyes." I told him everything. "Let's go over to check on Lilika."

He got dressed, and we went over to their apartment. When we rang the doorbell, Alyona herself opened it. Laughing, she said that it was a prank to see what I would do—whether I would go to see her sister or not. Alyona was afraid of being arrested, and wanted to test me, so she arranged that strange scenario. I believe that this was a profound reflection of the times we lived in, when such jokes were possible.

For some time afterward, I didn't want to see her. Then it

passed. I was so shaken by this event, however, that I couldn't even go to school the next day. I had been so upset, so frightened about what would become of Lilika . . .

Later, during the war, Alyona Ilsen was arrested. She spent twelve years in a prison camp and survived only because she was so adept at relating novels to the inmates. They took care of her and fed her, and protected her, because she was such a gifted storyteller. This was a highly prized art in the camps.

17

WE GRADUATED FROM HIGH SCHOOL. I MUST SAY THAT WE HAD OUT-standing teachers. We were all steeped in the humanities. Our boys studied philosophy, reading Kant and Hegel already in the ninth grade; that was the sort of thing that interested them. Many of them wrote poetry—because of Dezik Kaufman. We had a fairly decent literature teacher, but the one who influenced us most strongly was our mathematics teacher. He came to teach us in the ninth grade. Before that we had also had a good math teacher. He always carried twenty pieces of colored chalk with him, and everything that he explained he drew and colored in with multihued chalk. We were terribly disappointed, of course, when the new teacher arrived. His name was Peter Dorf. He walked into the classroom, and we stood up to greet him very languidly and reluctantly, as though to register our displeasure that he was replacing our favorite teacher. He grew irate and broke a red pencil that he held in his hand, threw it on the desk, and left the room. That was how disgruntled he was by our first meeting.

Ultimately he became the teacher to whom we were most devoted. He was an extremely interesting, original, and deep human being. He worked at the university and agreed to teach our class as a kind of experiment. Would it be possible to teach higher mathematics to high-school students? For two years we studied with a kind of crazy enthusiasm, and he inspired everyone to want to study further at the Mathematics Department. We could talk about anything in the world with him. He often stayed after school for hours just to talk to us. He even talked politics. He wasn't afraid to talk about politics with us—within the bounds of what was admissible, naturally. I remember him even talking about the show trials, saying, "You know, it's still too early to judge the matter. Let's not make up our minds for now; but, of course, it's also hard to believe all of this." That's what he told us. For us it was an incredible demonstration of trust, a kind of openness and intellectual nonconformism.

I was so preoccupied with my complicated, multilayered life, my activities, the books I was reading, and we were so intensely involved with each other and spent so much time together, that I somehow lost sight of my parents. Even now, some sixty years later, I feel a bitter shame when I remember my seventeenth birthday party, for example. My friends came over to celebrate. My mother wasn't home for some reason, but Papa was. He was about to leave the room, but I could sense that he wanted to linger and stay with us at the table. I didn't suggest that he stay, though. The memory of this torments me to this day, all the more since he died soon after. I had reached the age at which self-awareness, burgeoning self-confidence, and personal development seem to go hand in hand with rejection of one's parents. With Peter Dorf, however, whom Dezik, inspired by our passionate interest in the classical world, had dubbed Petrocles, I was ready to babble on for hours and hours. It seemed there was never time for this at home. Or I didn't have the psychological and emotional maturity for it, perhaps. It was all the more problematic for me because I knew Papa was sick, and that he was very anxious—that he and Mama both feared arrest. The situation was extremely tense. Their personal relations, too, as far as I could understand them, were strained. They didn't go on vacation together, so I think they were experiencing difficulties together, although our family life was very peaceful at home. It seemed to me that Mama suffered because Papa couldn't forget or forgive her what had happened between them before. I didn't avoid these matters consciously, but rather unconsciously, during those years. And since they were together—not really together, but at least some sort of unit—I felt I had the right to have my own life. Now I think about this with horror, and with shame. Of course, I didn't give my father enough love or tenderness. I remember him saying to me once, when I went up to kiss him, during the time when the windows were all going dark in our building, "I want you to know that you are dearer to me than anything on earth." I couldn't respond in any meaningful way. Not then. Later I could, but then it was already too late. It often happens that way.

In the tenth grade, a new girl joined our class. Her name was Nina Gegechkori. Her father was an important party functionary. She lived next to the Butyrskaya Prison, where only the top brass lived, and they had a four or five-room apartment—an unimaginable luxury. In the middle of the tenth grade, before the New Year, her father was arrested. Two weeks later she stopped coming to school. We went to Butyrskaya Street, and saw that their apartment had been sealed off. That could mean only one thing in those days—the whole family had been arrested. We thought that maybe Nina had been taken to an orphanage, but Klavdia Poltavskaya made inquiries and confirmed our suspicion.

When we were writing our final compositions in the tenth grade, whom should we see walking into the schoolyard but Nina! We rushed out of the classroom and down the stairs to greet her. I think this was a unique case: she had been assigned to a wise investigator who set her free after she had spent six months in Butyrskaya Prison. She was released on the same day we were to write our final compositions. When she left the prison, which was in the vicinity, she didn't go home—she no longer had a home—but came to school. Mrs. Poltavskaya took her under her wing. She took her home to live with her, and she was able to graduate from school the following year. This was an extraordinary act of courage on Poltavskaya's part: she took in a girl whose father and mother had both been arrested. Her father was executed, and her mother returned only after ten years.

I will say something else about Klavdia Poltavskaya, to make it absolutely clear what a remarkable person she was. There was another young person, a homeless boy who was a year older than we were, living with her at the time. She had found him living in a tar vat somewhere. She was able to win his trust so fully that he agreed to live in her house and go to school. She told everyone that he was a distant relative—most likely out of modesty, so that there would be no gossip. But we knew, for he had told us, that Klavdia Poltavskaya had picked him up off the street. He wrote poetry. He enrolled in the Literature Institute, then went off to war and was killed in one of the first battles. I wish to honor his memory and his name: Boris Rozhdestvensky. I even remember several lines from one of his poems.

I don't remember the color of the rags
that barely covered her body,
I don't remember her hands,
my mother's hands.
But suddenly I realized
that once born, one must
live for roads that lead into the distance
along the crests of years.

Perhaps one of the happiest moments of my years at school was my graduation, when Mrs. Poltavskaya, who was usually very strict, allowed us to drink wine for the first time (which was forbidden in school), and when Peter Dorf gave me a red rose and kissed my hand. I was happy as only a seventeen-year-old girl can be.

Ultimately, my school years are yet another example of what I was trying to express at the beginning of this narrative. Sometimes a terrible event, one that seems will lead only to tragedy and devastation, leads to unhoped for joy. When Papa refused to let me return to the German school, I thought it was a disaster. In fact, it made possible the joy I experienced at my wonderful school, with its remarkable teachers—Klavdia Poltavskaya, Peter Dorf, dear Petrocles; but above all, my classmates and friends. More than through the efforts of our teachers, it was through one another that we were ground and polished, like little stones rubbing against each other. Naturally, it was a long and intense process of mutual shaping and becoming. One meeting with Dezik Samoilov alone was a significant event. And with Tolya, and with Zhorzhik, and with all the kids; with Esya Cherikover, who departed this life so young, and about whom Dezik wrote an epigram that so aptly summed up this person:

A soul of such fine cloth
can also catch a whale in a glass.

All of these people honed and polished each other, helping one another grow into his or her own personality. Each of them—it is simply not possible, and there is not time, to name them all—was a unique individual and carried something absolutely original inside. Without my beloved school, I would have lived my life, no doubt, completely differently. The school gave me so very much. Yet at first it seemed to me to be an utter disaster.

There will be other examples of this later in my story, and I want to stress it each time, because it is a comforting thought. When one encounters misfortune or difficulty, one need not immediately think that one is doomed. You never know how things will turn out. It is especially important for young people to remember this.

18

PETER DORF TOLD ME ONCE, "Lilya, you must enroll in the Mathematics Department." I was ready to obey, but fortunately, I didn't. Dezik took my hand in his, and we went to IPhLH (the Institute of Philosophy, Literature, and History). This was an elite institution, modeled loosely after Pushkin's lyceum, which the Soviet authorities had created at the moment it became clear that they needed highly educated and cultivated people to interact with foreign governments. When we began our studies in 1938, it had only existed for only two years. The competition ratio for admission was incredible: sixteen to one. One had to take exams in all the fields, not just in one's desired major. All the exams that we had had to pass in school we were expected to pass again to gain admission to the Institute: mathematics, physics, chemistry . . . I was lucky to have finished high school with excellent grades, the equivalent of what was later called a "gold medal," so I didn't have to sit for the written exams. An oral examination would suffice. Dezik had to take all the exams, however. Together we went to the admissions office.

I was surprised that the interview was conducted not by a professor or a teacher, but by a very young man. His name, as I later found out, was Yasha Dodzin, and he was at the same time (this I also found out later) head of the personnel department and head of the "special department" of the Institute of Philosophy, Literature, and History.

He screened all the applicants to the Institute. The interview did not proceed along the lines of a discussion of academic interests and strengths, but came down to why we wanted to gain admission. He spoke very kindly to me. I told him that I had lived in France, had always loved French literature and culture and wanted to study it further, and perhaps eventually teach. Because I hadn't written a C.V. containing my "political profile," I was afraid I might not be admitted. I had enough political acumen to understand the necessity of this. I didn't want to set out on a new path in life with insincere words, however. At that point, a very young man came out, someone my age, and said, "Don't worry, they'll take you." This young man was a student who had just completed his first year of studies. He was to become a very close friend of mine, and a brilliant translator (we worked together). His name was Noam Katzman.

They did, indeed, accept me. I left for Koktebel even before I received official notification of this. Our return ticket on the train to Moscow was for the first of September, and I was late for the first lecture. Yura Shakhovsky had gone with us, and he put me in a cab as soon as we arrived. Suntanned, with a red, peeling nose, in a

ПРОФЕССОР РАДЦИГ

ПРОФЕССОР РАДЦИГ

flimsy summer dress, I made it in time for the second lecture. The professor was an elderly man, completely gray, with a gray beard. His name was Professor Radzig. He recited a song about a horse in hexameter, and we loved it. Unfortunately, old Professor Radzig comported himself very poorly during the persecution campaign. He repented, spoke out publicly, denounced people. Still, our first impression of him was captivating. So my first class was classical literature. Greece, hexameters—after which, for some reason, we had Phys. Ed.

The IPhLH was located in Sokolniki. From the Sokolniki subway it was five stops by streetcar. The building stood in the middle of a wooded area. The autumn of 1938 was exceptionally colorful and warm; it was a true Indian Summer. From that first day, the most important dimension of our experience at the Institute (in addition to lectures and professors, naturally) had already begun: the mutual honing and shaping we underwent during our daily interactions with each other. It was a continuation of the process that had started in high school, though at a different level. We always walked home after classes through the woods. (In the morning, we always had to rush to make it in time for the first lectures, of course.) Sometimes we lingered for a long time after class and returned home only at six or seven. We strolled through those magical woods and found out everything there was to know about each other.

We started forming a group of friends during the first two or three days. One of the first members of the group was Yura Knabe. He later became the head of the department of foreign languages at the VGIK (National Institute of Cinematography) and taught several generations of film students.

Yura surprised us during one of our first days at the Institute, when we were all sitting around at the home of Anya Grishina (my dear friend to this day). He phoned the Lenin Library and ordered books in Latin—thus demonstrating that he already knew the language. He did eventually learn Greek and Latin—but that was later.

Mark Bershadsky studied in the Russian department. He was a year older than the rest of us, because he had completed a year at the Conservatory. He decided that it wasn't for him, and transferred to the IPhLH.

Zhenya Asterman studied in the English department. He evidently took notice of me immediately, because he gave me a wonderful New Year's gift that first year. What boys wouldn't do to make a girl like them! He managed to get hold of a book by Pasternak and one by Akhmatova, *From Seven Books*, and to present them to me. He also transcribed poems by Tsvetaeva (who knows how he managed to find them), and made a small book out of them to give me. He also vowed to find Lucy Tovalev.

I still have photographs of Mark and Zhenya, which by some miracle I acquired many years after the war.

These young people were remarkable in their purity of heart. They had a kind of deep spiritual charm. Zhenya would no doubt have become a writer. He already wrote prose and composed amusing little stories and descriptions . . . And they spoke rather eccentrically, whimsically. Recently, Arkady Belinkov's book *Rough Draft* was published. This book was the cause of his arrest, the book for which he was sentenced to so many years in prison. Echoes of this associative, image-rich, allusive language, resembling

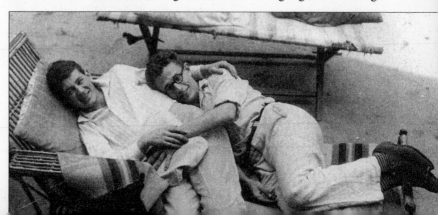

a kind of birdsong, resound through the book. They devoured Babel, and knew Yury Olesha by heart. They were searching for a new language of expression. These young people were determined to find a new approach to authorship, a new interiority.

The atmosphere at IPhLH was marked by an incessant quest for knowledge. This urge to study a subject as thoroughly as possible, to get down to the very essence of things, was something new in Soviet society. Very recently the slogans of Russian Association of Proletarian Writers (RAPP) and the Proletkult were still being loudly proclaimed: "Jettison the classics from the ship of modernity," and so forth. Our teachers encouraged this thirst for knowledge. Most of them were true scholars. Dzhivelegov and Gudzy, for example, were already well known before the Revolution; and there were others, who had managed to avoid exile, or had just returned.

We had many very young professors. The first year, we were taught by Mikhalchi, who was very scholarly. But the older students all said, "Just wait until the second year, when you have Vladimir Grib. You'll see what a real teacher is."

And we did.

Grib was about thirty-two years old. He sat on top of the desk, or on the edge of a chair. He smoked during lectures, and spoke beautifully, with extraordinary verve and inspiring energy. He showed us western albums of art, with huge reproductions. This was a first for us—we had never seen anything like it before. We were over the moon about him; but this came to an abrupt end. Professor Grib lectured us only twice, for four hours each session, on the "Introduction to the Renaissance." Then he fell ill. It was a blood disease, complicated by depression, which he had suffered from after he witnessed the collectivization and famine in the Ukrainian countryside, where he grew up and where his mother was a teacher. The whole IPhLH went to visit him in the hospital and took turns keeping watch at his bedside and giving him medicine. He died in October of 1941. A small collection of lectures, *The Spanish Baroque and French Classicism*, is the only book he had time to write.

After Grib ended up in the hospital, Professor Leonid Pinsky took over the lectures on the Renaissance. After the effervescent lecturing style of Grib, who engaged us directly, he seemed unbearably dull. He stood with his back to the auditorium by the window, twisting a lock of hair around his finger. He spoke very slowly and indistinctly, as though agonizing over every word. No one paid any attention to him. No one listened; we did whatever we felt like doing—played Battleship, read a book, chatted. The entire first lecture was like that, and the second. Then someone began listening to what he was saying, almost by chance, and word got around that it was kind of interesting . . . Within a month, we were hanging on to his every word, and second-year students started sitting in on the lectures, too. In short, despite his extreme lack of eloquence, he managed to hold the audience in thrall.

I'd never seen anything like it. Of course, he came to lectures completely prepared, but at the same time he put forth new ideas each time. His indistinct mumbling was a process of thought. For the first time in our lives we were able to witness and hear a person think, seeking new ways of formulating an idea, of refining an aesthetic conception. Attending this course on the Renaissance before the war, and then the sixteenth and seventeenth centuries, was a momentous event for all the people who began their studies the same year I did.

His was a completely new approach to literature. Professor Pinsky possessed a unique gift—the pleasure that he experienced was infectious. He delved into every detail of a text and gradually drew us into the very essence of the thought of an author. At the same time, he knew how to contextualize it within the era in which the author lived and worked. The result was such a broad and profound perspective on the epoch, on the essence of its art, that we threw ourselves with a vengeance into reading all we could, studied like we were

possessed (and feared exams), and dreamed of ways we could get closer to our brilliant teacher.

The erudition of our senior professors was exhilarating, but our encounters with Grib and Pinsky were earth-shattering. Each of them was brilliant in his own way, yet they were similar—equally passionate and committed, and wholeheartedly devoted to the subject. Grib, always eager to hear Pinsky's opinion, could seek him out in the middle of the night, walking through Moscow to reach his place so he could read him his student Grisha Pomerantz's essay on Dostoevsky, for example.

Much later, I learned that even then Professor Pinsky was already wracked by doubts. Yet, like other representatives of the intelligentsia, such as Pasternak, he made titanic efforts to find ways of justifying the party line. In his heart of hearts, he hadn't yet been able to break with Marxism or with the Soviet political system.

We hardly spent any time at home. We were either in classes in the IPhLH, taking long strolls, or studying in the library. We all preferred the Lenin Library—the famous Main Hall, which I dearly love because so many memories of that time are attached to it. A balcony runs all around the perimeter of the hall, and that was where we would meet to converse. We spent at least half our time on the balcony or in the smoking room. Our discussions never ceased.

I made a big mistake, of course, when I chose to major in French, since I knew French already. Two groups were formed, however: one with people who were just starting to learn the language, and the other with those of us who were more advanced. My spirit failed me—rather than studying English, which to this day I don't know, I chose the stronger French group. We all became very good friends. Here, too, we experienced several breakthroughs into another world. In our first year, there was a girl in our group who had arrived from the US. Her father and mother brought many albums of art with them. We hadn't seen anything at that time—our horizons were terribly limited. The degree of deafness, the wall that separated us from European culture, is hard for people nowadays to imagine. Contemporary western culture, western painting, had been banished already in the prewar years.

As we discovered later, Mira's father had been an ordinary Soviet spy. He lived in America and spied for the Soviet Union under the guise of a watchmaker. Before that he had worked in Spain, and Mira had a bottle of Spanish wine on her bookshelf that she planned to open on the day of the Republican victory. It was never opened, of course, since the Republicans never won.

In our second year at the Institute, the son of the Soviet ambassador to the United States came to study with us. He was a very sweet young man, and his name was Oleg Troyanovsky.

He spoke Russian poorly and didn't know all the words. I still remember a phrase we repeated to tease him. He once asked, "What's a karapuz (a chubby fellow)?" And this "karapooz" became a running joke in the IPhLH. Oleg later became a diplomat and was at one point our representative to the UN. When Ilf and Petrov traveled in the US to write their book *One-Story America*, Oleg had been their chauffeur, driving them around the country. He was a very sweet guy, and he drove us around in a car, too, since he had a driver's license (something that was absolutely unheard of for us). Just as we had once met at my house at the end of the week, now we gathered at his very comfortable, western-style apartment, which had upholstered furniture, armchairs, and, most important, music. We were introduced to the world of music there. They had brought a great deal of records with them from America. Art albums, records on Saturdays—we grew accustomed to this, grew familiar with this culture. These were pastimes of a different sort than we had known before.

19

My father died in November of 1938. He died in the hospital from pernicious anemia. At that moment it felt as though life simply broke off. Only when he died did I realize how unforgivable my behavior had been. Intoxicated with my life as an IPhLH student, I rarely visited him in the hospital. I did see him, but not as often as I should have. I failed to use these last months of his life to get closer to him, to get to know him better. I didn't realize, of course, that he was dying.

Mama went to the hospital all the time and took care of him. Naturally, they put all their differences and conflicts behind them.

I felt a profound and terrible dissatisfaction with myself. I was crushed by his death and my own bewilderment about what was happening. This was a very difficult period in my life. Zhenya Asterman helped me to emerge from this emotional turmoil and return to the Institute, but I have been haunted my whole life by a deep sense of remorse, by some kind of emotional chasm that opened up in me then. As long as I am talking about my life, about my experiences, I must speak about this, too. One should remember that things like this have a profound impact on the rest of one's life. The feeling never goes away. The sense of my inadequacy at a particular moment, in a particular circumstance, has never left me. It's with me for good. In 1938 I was a still a young girl. I was only eighteen. Now, in my advanced years, I remember this time with profound emotion; it is with me as I speak. Even during periods of the greatest enjoyment and self-discovery in your youth, you should never neglect your parents— not even so much out of moral considerations, but out of a sense of self-respect, in the interests of self-preservation. Otherwise, you will have to bear a burden of regret that won't diminish with the years.

Stalin's wave of terror raged all the way though 1938 and 1939. At the IPhLH a series of terrifying meetings were held. I remember that for some reason they chose to hold them in an auditorium at the Conservatory. Most likely there was not a hall large enough to accommodate the meetings in the IPhLH itself. There, with unbridled enthusiasm, the senior students indulged in self-flagellation, lambasted their parents, and made self-incriminating speeches. They repented before the Party and the country that their father or mother had been arrested, and they had not turned them in to the authorities in time. What rubbish these young people churned out in the guise of "repentance"! The same intelligent, thoughtful young people who had read all the Western classics, had listened to Grib and Pinsky, and who had a broad cultural perspective and an enlightened view of the world. They beat their breasts and repented that they had had not managed to expose their own parents' "wrongdoing" before the KGB did it for them.

I knew one of the girls who took part in this charade. She was two years ahead of me. The IPhLH had a system by which the senior Komsomol members guided the younger ones. This girl's father had also been arrested. I asked her, "Anya, why are you saying all this?" She said, "Well, that's what I sincerely believe. I have to come clean before the Party. It's my duty. I understand the need for it." She even challenged all of us: "You should all think about it, too. Maybe you've heard something? Overheard some unhealthy conversations? You need to say something about it, to put a stop to it before it's too late." In other words, she, one of our companions, someone we put our trust in, was exhorting us to inform on one another. A spirit of double-crossing prevailed and was passed down from the senior students to the junior students.

I believe the psychology of this era was a kind of religious psychosis. Confession, repentance . . . It was a kind of mysticism, beyond logic; a sincere, but appalling condition of the spirit. Evidently there is a hypnosis of repentance that is like an arrow let loose. Once it flies, there is no stopping it. But, I repeat, from the point of view of normal human reason, it's one of the most horrifying states of mass blindness imaginable. That is the only way to describe it.

As it happened (because in my narration everything is "as it happened"), much later, during the struggle against cosmopolitanism, the same fine, well-educated girls—young theater critics at the GITIS (the National Institute of Theater Arts and Cinema)—exhibited similar behavior. With the difference that this time they were denouncing not themselves and their families, but their adored professors. Also with great relish. I don't want to name names, because some of them are well-known critics nowadays; but it happened, and I remember it.

We were terribly indignant. We couldn't fathom what was going on. I discussed it most frequently with Zhenya Asterman. Yura expressed himself more vaguely, saying that maybe they really did feel that way, maybe they really did need to repent. Zhenya, however, partly through his own soul-searching, and partly through our conversations (for we were very close), eventually came to reject the system completely. By the way, we spoke very candidly in our group of friends about everything, as we had earlier in high school, and no one was arrested.

All these terrible meetings were held at the behest of the aforementioned Yasha Dodzin. I wish to say a few words about him in particular.

He was in the KGB, of course; a dyed-in-the-wool KGB agent. At the same time, he was exceptionally honest, with a noble soul, and saved many people in years to come. He even warned people to leave Moscow. He arranged a rendezvous outside somewhere, so no one would be listening, and said, "Clear out to another city if you can, go work in a factory for the time being, drop your studies. Try it that way to avoid arrest." We weren't aware of all this at the time, but word filtered through eventually. A friend of mine told me that many years afterward, she met a person in Abkhazia, an Abkhazian man who had also studied at the IPhLH. Yasha flew to Abkhazia just to warn him not to return to Moscow for his third year: they were planning to arrest him.

Yasha survived the war, but they expelled him from the Party, naturally. He was a thorn in the side of the authorities. One day I met him after the war had ended. "Why did you do it?" I asked. He said, "I was a true believer, so I thought everything should be just and humane. I considered these to be just anomalies, exaggerations. I knew those kids, knew they were honest and innocent of wrongdoing. I couldn't have acted otherwise."

I want to point out that there were people like that, too. For example, the investigator who let Nina Gegechkori, my classmate, out of prison after half a year; and Yasha Dodzin, who helped people to the best of his ability.

20

THE YEARS IN IPhLH FLEW BY. THEY WERE FILLED WITH SOCIALIZING and studies—we studied avidly, trying to read everything we could get our hands on. That included *Foreign Literature*, which published Aldington, Remarque, Hemingway. When Hemingway sided with the Republicans during the Spanish Civil War, he became a true hero for us. We knew his stories by heart, and after the war his photograph hung in the room of every young intellectual—sometimes next to a portrait of Stalin. Under the influence of Hemingway and the atmosphere in his novels, I believe, relations among young people changed. We became more uninhibited. We started smoking, we drank wine, danced the tango and the foxtrot, and played jazz on the piano.

At the end of the summer of 1939, Mama took me and my IPhLH friend Busya (Beatrice Olkina) to Teberda in the Caucasus Mountains. Zhenya Asterman and Mark Bershadsky joined us there, and we spent several days together.

We watched the dawns, watched the sun rise over the icy peaks of the mountains, listened to the rushing water of mountain streams, and somehow forgot about the preceding winter. Everyone was hoping that the purges had ended. We were all thinking, Maybe normal life will resume now? By that time, quite a few people were returning from prison; the father of one of my friends from the German school, Ruth Nagler, for example. She ran over to tell me about it the day he came back. They had released her father that morning. He didn't have a penny to his name, and he had to go on foot through the entire city to get home. He hadn't shaved for months, and had grown a full, gray beard. The whole way, boys cried after him, "Uncle Marx is coming! Here comes Uncle Marx!"

We spent a happy summer in Teberda. Then Mama stayed on, and we returned to Moscow, to the IPhLH.

The first thing we heard was that a German-Soviet Pact had been signed. On the front pages of all the newspapers there was a picture of Stalin shaking Ribbentrop's hand. Underneath was a caption that read: *I know how the German people love their Führer, and I drink to his health.* His toast. This was simply incomprehensible to us. So Hitler was our friend now? What about the Civil War in Spain? The antifascists who had fled to take refuge in our country? This union with Fascist Germany seemed like unadulterated betrayal to us. Hadn't they been beating it into our heads for years that Fascism was the greatest evil on Earth?

At around that time, Mama and I had begun renting out a room to make ends meet. One of the lodgers was a woman who had gone away for a time, and was subletting the room to her friend. I was home sick, with the flu. This lodger, whom I didn't really know— his name was Sasha; he was a journalist and spent the whole time banging away on the typewriter—looked in on me from time to time. We got to be friends. Every day after class at the IPhLH, the guys—Zhenya, Mark, Yura—would come to bring me food, and we spent the evening together. Mama was away. Suddenly, on the sixth or seventh day of my illness, I got a call from Yasha Dodzin.

"We need you to translate a text from French," he said. "Can you do it?"

I said, "Yes, probably, what kind of text is it?"

"I can't tell you exactly. Come to the IPhLH. Bring your passport, too."

I said, "You know, I'm still running a temperature. I probably shouldn't go outside."

"All right, we'll send a car for you."

This was the 4th of October, I'll remember that date my whole life. It was sunny. When he called I was reading a book by Pasternak.

After some time, a car did come to pick me up. A young man with an expressionless face came up to get me. We drove to the

IPhLH. I tried to engage him in conversation, but he refused to join in. We went up to see Yasha in the Cadres Department. I said:

"Let me see the text."

"Oh, but we can't do it here, we have to go somewhere else. I'll introduce you to a comrade of mine, he's the one who needs it."

Another young man appeared, also completely nondescript. He said:

"Okay, come with me."

We went downstairs and got into the same car that had just dropped me off. I said:

"Where are we going?"

"You'll see," he said.

And we went to the Lubyanka Prison. I realized that I was under arrest. How else could I have interpreted it?

We drove up to the building and got out of the car. He asked me for my passport, they issued me a pass—though not through the main gates, but through a side entrance. We took the elevator up to one of the higher floors—I can't remember whether it was the sixth, seventh, or eighth. I do remember the hallway, though. It was a hallway with many doors, which all looked the same and didn't have numbers. They didn't have any markings at all. A hallway, and doors, doors, doors, one after another. It was unnerving and strange.

He guided me into a room behind one of the doors, sat me down on a chair, and said, "Wait here, they'll be with you in a minute." Then he left.

A small room, a desk with an armchair; and on my side of the desk was a chair, a large wardrobe, and a window onto Lubyanka Square.

Where the other person came from, I didn't know. He seemed to come out of the wardrobe. Maybe it wasn't a wardrobe but another door. I didn't notice the moment when he arrived. I was gazing out the window, and the next thing I knew someone was sitting in the armchair in front of me—the same kind of person. That was another impression I'll never be able to shake: they all had the same kind of face. I couldn't remember what any of their faces looked like. I wouldn't even be able to recognize them if I were being tortured. They were all twenty-six to twenty-eight years old, they had the same haircut, they were in half-military uniform. At that time many people wore soldier's blouses—it wasn't full military dress, but half-military uniform. And they all had bland, featureless faces.

So this person, who had appeared mysteriously from the wardrobe and was now sitting opposite me, said:

"Well, let's get acquainted. What's your name?"

I said, "You know what it is. You have my pass right in front of you."

"No, I'll ask the questions, and you'll answer them. That's the way we do it here. Tell me who you are."

I told him. Then I said, "Pardon me, but Yasha told me I would need to translate something. Give me a job to do."

"Translating? That was just a pretext to get you over here," he said to me. "And why are you addressing me with the formal you? We're comrades, aren't we?"

"I'm unable to use the informal form of address with people I don't know."

I suddenly felt this was extremely important—to address him with the formal you. So as not to cultivate familiarity or to be on a casual footing.

"You don't want to?"

"No. I just can't."

"Well, tell me what kind of an environment you live in, who you see, what you talk about."

I said, "About literature, about art. We are very keen on paintings, and we listen to interesting lectures about them."

"And what sorts of lectures are they?"

"They all have to do with the remote past."

"And there are no allusions there?"

I said, "Allusions? What kinds of allusions could there be, when we're talking about the Renaissance, or the Baroque period?"

In fact Pinsky's whole course on the Baroque was organized around allusion. He taught us how to think. He never touched directly on politics, but posed questions in such a way that it was impossible not to draw parallels with what was happening around us. The reason we were so enthralled with his lectures—apart from the way he presented the material itself—was that they were lessons in thinking. It was there that I learned to draw analogies. Not so much in the spirit of the Renaissance as of the Baroque period. The disharmonies of the Baroque world were very much in keeping with our reality, and they were true lessons in revealing the social milieu in which we lived.

But of course I said, with an innocent expression: come now, what analogies? What kinds of analogies could there be? It was another epoch altogether, another time.

He asked about the editor of the IPhLH wall newspaper—it was called *Komsomolia*—Alexander Shelipin. That was easy to answer—Shelipin was the secretary of the Komsomol committee of our institute, and his nickname was Iron Shurik. When he was asked what he wanted to be in life, he didn't even have to think about it. He answered, "A Leader."

He didn't ask any concrete questions, but kept trying to pry more information out of me. The conversation was exhausting because I had to be very careful about what I was saying. I think I was very resourceful. He prodded and prodded some more, but I made vague generalizations and, I thought and hoped, didn't reveal anything bad.

"Who lives in your apartment now?"

Later I came to understand that this was not really about my IPhLH comrades, but about our lodger, because they arrested him a month later. Not at our house—he had already moved out—but we heard about it through the grapevine. And the woman we rented the apartment to, and who had taken him in—she was also arrested. So this was what it had all been about, apparently. But he kept coming back to the subject of IPhLH, to the kids there.

At a certain point he said, "You know what? You have such a busy social life, your cooperation will be very useful to us. Just sign this paper saying you agree to cooperate with us."

I said, "I won't sign."

"Why won't you sign it? Are you against the Soviet government?"

I said, "No. I'm not against the Soviet government, but I can't do this work. I'm not up to it. I'm a very impressionable person, very excitable, and I wouldn't be able to socialize with anyone under those circumstances."

"But what if you spot enemies?"

"Well, if I see that they are really enemies, I'll come to you myself, but I won't sign anything."

"Think about it before you refuse to help us. It's a serious move."

I said, "There's nothing to think about. I can't do it. I don't have the inner wherewithal."

"Is that your final decision?"

"Yes," I said. "It's my final decision. I can't do it."

Suddenly he said, "Fine then, let me sign your pass."

And then the feeling I had . . . There were two things that struck me. First, when I was going downstairs, I glanced into the elevator shaft next door. There were several elevators side by side, and the one next to mine had stopped somewhere on the upper floors. I looked down and saw, maybe, nine or ten floors. It was terrifying. There is a huge space underground in the Lubyanka. That was my first impression. Then the feeling when you come outside. It's impossible to describe. It's like intoxication and . . . real fear was what I experienced when I stepped outside. I remember that I just stood there and couldn't take another step. I couldn't process what had just happened.

And they did make me sign a nondisclosure statement. Naturally, despite signing the document, I told my friends everything. I have to admit, though, that I was already afraid to talk at home; I told them when we were outside. It was such a lesson in fear that I had become quite a bit more cautious.

When I told Yura Knabe about it, he said, "They called me up, too, you know. I didn't want to tell anyone, because I also signed a nondisclosure agreement; but you told me, so I'm telling you." It happened differently in his case. They approached him on the street, which was most likely even more frightening. They said, "Documents, please." Zhenya said it didn't surprise him at all. He had been expecting something like that to happen any time—he expected it to happen to himself, to me, to everyone. It was the logical unfolding of events. I said to him that for me it was unexpected, and he said, "I always thought about the possibility, and I wanted to tell you that it could happen so you would be prepared, but I just didn't get around to it." That was the reaction of my boys. Mother came two days later. She fully supported me, naturally. Her support was absolute. But she was very much afraid and kept saying, "Stop talking politics, you have to avoid this topic at all costs." But it wasn't possible anymore. It was too late.

If I wanted to weigh the significance of this meeting against that of the IPhLH lectures, they would come out even. Henceforth, I understood what a Kafkaesque reality was (although I knew nothing yet about Kafka). The mysterious appearance out of the wardrobe. The fact that Yasha Dodzin—who, I thought, helped everybody—had launched me into this terrible world. And that he didn't want to warn me; or, perhaps, couldn't. I don't know. I went up to him later and asked, "What was that all about?" "We're not going to talk about it," he said coldly and cruelly. "That was your coming of age."

That was a tremendous step for me in coming to grips with our reality—and, alas, it was a step forward, into the future.

21

THERE WAS A GROUP OF VERY TALENTED YOUNG POETS AT IPHLH. Pavel Kogan was the unofficial leader of the group. One couplet of his poetry conveys the essence of who he was:

> *Since childhood I've disliked ovals,*
> *Since childhood I've preferred to draw angles.*

He had a very sharp wit, and was angular and awkward, impassioned and hot-tempered. To us he represented the epitome of talent. Sergei Narovchatov also belonged to this group. After the war, unfortunately, he became an official poet, a "poet-for-hire." At the time, though, he was a young man of exceptional beauty—a blue-eyed Viking—and wrote very good poetry. Another member of this group was Savik Gudzenko. And, of course, our Dezik Kaufman, who became Samoilov, with his "Carpenters at the Executioner's Block"—that famous poem he wrote when he was only in the eighth grade, and which is now considered a classic—they accepted with open arms.

They set themselves against the poets of the older generation, who, in their view, wrote mundane verse. Sweet, innocuous ditties. In those days there was as yet no tension in the cultural sphere. But the guys somehow felt it approaching.

Профессор Гудзий.

Tvardovsky and Simonov were graduate students at the IPhLH at this time. And Dolmatovsky orbited around them.

These were the poets (primarily Simonov and Dolmatovsky—Tvardovsky was always a special case) that our IPhLH friends arrayed themselves against. Simonov, with his lyrical "Five Pages," was the most popular poet of the time. Everyone knew Dolmatovsky, as well. And our young IPhLH students challenged them to a contest. A face-off between the poets of these two generations was held one evening, for some reason, in the Law School. The auditorium was stuffed to the rafters with people. The young people felt that this was a momentous event, that they had to defend their positions, and that they were able to work much more seriously and profoundly within their system.

There was a much greater interest in poetry at that time than there was later. People knew and read Pasternak, Aseev, Kirsanov. I think that the Mayakovsky brigade, which in those days traveled from factory to factory performing verse, nurtured and ensured this interest in poetry, bringing it to the masses in a meaningful way. Many of these poems were about struggle, about the experiences of our day-to-day life at the time. I think if Brodsky arrived today to read poetry in the factories, there would not be as much interest as there was then. Perhaps the wall, the Iron Curtain separating us from the West, had something to do with it. There was absolutely no real influx of culture from the world outside at all. There was, of course, an interest in culture, in the expressions of the spirit, but in 1937–38 a sort of quietism reigned, and the IPhLH poets wanted to oppose that.

There was also a theater group, organized along the same lines, in the same spirit. The drama students felt that the theater world, too, was in the grip of stagnation, of an excess of complacency. Many classics were being staged. MKhAT, the Moscow Art Theater, was undergoing a crisis. For years it had been floundering in its own brand of academicism. Meyerhold's theater was closed because the authorities required a spineless verisimilitude in art that Meyerhold openly mocked. It must be remembered that Stanislavsky, in spite of his fear of Stalin, called Meyerhold on the very evening that they closed down his theater and invited him to come to work at the MKhAT. The whole of Moscow talked about it in hushed voices afterward.

Then a young actor named Pluchek, together with a young dramatist by the name of Alexey Arbuzov, established a drama studio.

They believed that professional actors, even those from acting schools, were no good, that a fresh influx of living life could originate only in young people who had no previous involvement in theater at all. With only their love for the theater, nothing more. They gave a shout, and the young people came running. Most of them worked at factories, and hurried to the studio in the evening, after a long, hard day of work.

At first, they were housed in some house manager's office; then they received permission to rehearse in the evenings in a school on Karetny Ryad Street. The kids wanted to write their own play and act in it. I think there was some desire to whip up Komsomol enthusiasm, which had obviously waned somewhat, lulled by the relative prosperity of the previous years. What they decided was that each person would think up an image of what he wanted to be, and submit a proposal. Then a group of more literary-minded kids gathered these proposals and joined them together into a single plot. Thus, a play by the name of *City at Dawn* was born. It was the story of a group of Komsomol members who went to the taiga and began to build a new city.

All the members of the troupe were hungry, all of them poorly dressed—and all were passionately devoted to the theater. Kolya Potemkin worked as a turner in a factory. He had light blue eyes and flaxen hair, and he performed in the role of a kulak son. He might have become a great actor, had he not perished in the war.

Sasha Ginzburg (who later became the famous poet Alexander Galich) quit his studies at the MKhAT to work with this troupe that no one had ever heard of. He was cast for the part of a construction crew foreman who made too many demands on his laborers—the implication was that he was a Trotskyite.

Seva Bagritsky was a small fellow with pitch-black eyes. He was long-haired and disheveled. His father, the poet Eduard Bargritsky, had died by then, and his mother had been arrested—her sister was Babel's wife. For Seva, who was left alone, the theater became a surrogate home. Together with Alexander Galich, he wrote the final script and the lyrics to the songs.

Anya Bogacheva was the daughter of a servant. An angular girl with large sad eyes, she wore black stockings full of holes. She played a young worker who had come from the boondocks to build the city of her dreams, and as a result got married to Alexey Arbuzov. There was also Isai Kuznetsov, a budding famous playwright, and Zinovy Gerdt who played a simultaneously romantic and comical character—rather in the spirit of Woody Allen.

When I found out about the studio, I visited them and said that I wanted to take a closer look at what they were doing. There were several other people with me. They allowed us to sit in on a rehearsal. They called us "the moochers." Then I took the IPhLH poets there to get to know them. I thought that they were kindred spirits; but there was no meeting of the minds. I think I even know why. The poets were on a higher level—they were concerned with more "elevated" matters than these kids, who were very down-to-earth, very sincere. Many of them lived outside of town. They hardly got any sleep, traveling back and forth on commuter trains—all so that they could be at the studio, which was holy to them. They had a true "cult of the drama studio."

The play was finally finished. When the announcements for the opening performances came out, crowds of people waited outside for tickets. It was a theatrical event of the first order. It was true "living theater." The rumor that these kids had created something on their own, had written it and performed it themselves, thrilled the young people of Moscow. They flocked to the theater in droves. And it was wonderful . . . Truly living performances—I can't think of a better description. An authentic, human word was uttered there on that stage.

I wanted others to know about it, and so I wrote my first articles. I marched right in to the editorial offices of *Moscow Komsomolets* and found an elderly gentleman by the name of Kronhaus sitting there. He said:

"And who sent you?"

"No one," I said.

"But who told you to come here?"

"No one told me to come here."

"How did you end up here, then?"

"I just walked right in."

"Have you written anything before?"

"No, I've never written anything before."

"But what makes you think that you know how to write?"

Then I said, "I'll write something, and you tell me whether I know how to write or not. Something new is happening, something so interesting and important that I felt I had to write about it. I'm offering the piece to you."

He looked at me astonished, and said, "Well, since you're such a risk-taker—let's give it a try."

That was how I wrote my first article. It was called "In the Cradle of the Theater." A trivial title. He published it without a single correction. Then I went to the *Komsomol Pravda* offices, every bit as determined as before. I thought that the readership of Moscow *Komsomolets* was too small for me, and that the news of this drama studio needed to reach a wider audience. The same thing happened there. They published my second article. Both papers offered to let me continue to write for them. I was very proud that I had started to earn a bit of money and could take it home to my mother. In addition, I had the pleasant feeling that I was doing something useful. A slew of other reviews about this play followed. In short, the drama studio took the Moscow theater world by storm.

Soon afterward, the war began. The best of these young people went off as soldiers and perished. Kolya, Seva . . . Kirill Arbuzov, a remarkable young man, Alexey Arbuzov's cousin—he was the protagonist in the production—was killed in the first month of the war.

Zinovy and Isai went through the war and survived by some miracle. Zinovy, who was seriously wounded in the leg, became one of the country's best actors.

The remaining members of the troupe formed a frontline theater; but it wasn't the same.

22

In the middle of the winter of 1941, a seminar of working journalists from the IPhLH was organized. The seminar was led by Kornely Zelinsky. He was a corrupt, mercenary literary critic, famous in those years.

He flirted with the kids, wanting to be liked by them—they were the most active members of IPhLH, those who were destined to become the cultural backbone of the country. He promoted an image of himself as liberal and interesting, and this and that. He was a well-educated man.

This was the moment when Marina Tsvetaeva and her family returned to Russia. Tsvetaeva compiled a group of poems and sent them to *Soviet Writer*, in the hope that they would be published. It was a question of extreme significance for the remainder of her life. This collection of poems ended up in the hands of Zelinsky as the reviewer. He was so devoid of insight into the mood of young people that he thought he could win them over by reading his own internal review, not meant to appear in print, in which he acknowledged Tsvetaeva as a talented poet. He was very proud of himself. But he wasn't telling us anything we didn't know already. Still, he dismissed the collection, claiming that ideologically it was impermissible in Soviet culture and that it could not be published.

This was when I realized for the first time that it was not only "anti-Soviet" ideas that were ideologically unacceptable, but also style and manner. He believed that writing like Tsvetaeva's, fraught with extreme tension, resorting to abstract imagery, contradicted the principles of Socialist Realism. Everything that fell outside the bounds of Socialist Realism was hostile to the Soviet system. He condemned the collection (because Tsvetaeva, naturally, did not include any poems on political subjects), both for the "triviality" of its thematics—in other words, too many personal sensations and experiences—and, most important, for its manner, its style, which contradicted the aesthetic principles of Socialist Realism.

Socialist Realism was established on a primitive representation of life. Complexity was by definition ambiguous, and everything should be unequivocal. This unequivocality of style was cultivated very carefully. This careful cultivation was necessary in order for the system to maintain its authority. In addition, it corresponded to the intellectual level of those who were in charge of ideology. The point was to preserve the simplest, most elementary form of clarity. The moment of interpretation was dangerous. In that sense, the generation of lyric poets which our IPhLH poets set themselves against—Simonov, Dolmatovsky, Margarita Aliger, Tvardovsky in some of his inferior manifestations (because he had gone down the peasant route at that point)—suited them to a tee, because they seemed to be both fresh and straightforward.

This was, of course, the reign of mediocrity. Mediocrity, shorn of any traces of darkness or mystery. I believe that the cultural authorities were hostile to Dostoevsky, not because he held reactionary views—no one really cared about that—but because he was not completely comprehensible. He was ambiguous and open to interpretation. It was never unequivocally clear who was "positive" and who was "negative" in his works. This was what they could not accept. What was positive and what was negative had to be beyond dispute; that is to say, guidance for the pen was every bit as strong in culture as it was in other spheres. This was a deeply paternalistic attitude and relationship: we are like your own parents, and we will show you how to think, so there is no possibility of misinterpretation. They didn't want misinterpretations or ambiguities. Even Alexander Blok was undesirable up to a point, because, like every great poet, he was insufficiently clear and transparent. He could be obscure. Tyutchev was suspect. But Pushkin was fine; although he was a great writer, he was also clear. Unequivocal. His relationship to his characters is always self-evident. For this reason, Pushkin was acceptable. Tolstoy was also acceptable. Tolstoy's moral sentiments are always uppermost his works. But as soon as one was required to delve into a text and untangle it, the moment it was possible for a reader to take it in different directions, it wouldn't pass muster. This is the way I saw it, in any case.

I spoke my piece during the seminar. I said, "An article like this is a disgrace. A person has come back home, she's a great poet, and you yourself realize this, since in the first part of the article you admit she is a great poet. How can you trip her up like this? It is a monstrous act of cowardice." I said that I refused to take part in the seminar anymore. Several other people stood up with me and walked out. We would no doubt have paid a steep price for this, but several months later war broke out.

Perhaps if that swine Zelinsky had not written such a review and had decided to publish her collection, Tsvetaeva would not have taken her own life in Elabuga. It might have been published! If it had fallen into other hands, hands that were not so soiled; if there had been two good reviews . . . For, indeed, all the people who approved or rejected the publication of something were not very strongly endowed intellectually. They needed to have things explained and interpreted to them. If someone had explained to them that Tsvetaeva had marked out a path and arrived at realism, at a truer Socialist Realism, and that our poetry needed only her collection to complete it—this was certainly within the realm of possibility at the time—then perhaps her life would not have ended so tragically.

She was very well received. Everyone in poetic circles realized that she was a great poet; they wanted to be close to her. She had been granted permission to return to the country, she was given a dacha in the suburb of Bolshevo, she put together a collection of poetry and submitted it to *Soviet Writer*—until that moment, there was still hope. But when the collection was killed, people deserted Tsvetaeva. If they had accepted her into this herd of Soviet writers, perhaps things would have turned out differently. For when the war began and writers were evacuated to Chistopol, they wouldn't allow her to live there. They sent her to Elabuga, where she was absolutely alone, and was unable cope with such a life. If her collection had been published, she could have stayed in Chistopol, and I am convinced that things would not have ended so tragically.

23

Starting in the winter of 1941, a literary debate unfolded in the press—in the *Literary Gazette* and the *Literary Critic*—which touched on questions of politics and worldview. It was popularly known as the discussion between the Despites and the Because Ofs. In other words, between the point of view that the writer, despite his reactionary worldview, can describe reality in a penetrating manner, and the point of view that grasping reality is only possible because of a revolutionary worldview. This debate developed primarily out of a comparative analysis of Balzac and Victor Hugo. Here is Hugo, who was progressive in his philosophy and outlook; his novels are thus—and here is Balzac, a Royalist and a reactionary; his novels are so. Two scholars were trying to breathe fresh life into Marxism. One was the Hungarian scholar Georg Lukács, a figure of global significance in Marxism. The other was Mikhail Lifshitz, a brilliant philosopher, very young—he was the teacher of Grib and Pinsky, but was only two or three years older than they were.

An anthology called *Marx and Engels on Art*, edited by Lifshitz, was published in 1937. This was a real event. People scoured the bookstores in search of it. The book settled accounts with vulgar sociology, which explained everything through the lens of class struggle.

Lifshitz and Lukács claimed that a reactionary worldview did not prevent, and often promoted, a deeper and fuller expression of reality, and that the work of Balzac was a hundred times more valuable in its grasp of the world than that of the romantic Victor Hugo. They insisted that in contemporary literature, for example, Céline, who held almost Fascist views, wrote very powerful narratives about the modern bourgeois world. They defended Dostoevsky, who was not being published at the time. Ideas aside, Lifshitz claimed, Dostoevsky had described the complexities of the Russian soul with incomparable depth and cogency. This was an attempt to ground Marxism in modern philosophical thought. Evgeny

Knipovich and Vladimir Ermilov, an unfortunately famous critic, were ideologists of the opposing camp.

The dispute, at the center of which was the problem of the relationship between revolutionary ideology and artistic freedom, raged primarily in articles and rejoinders in journals and newspapers. Then, around the beginning of April, they decided to hold a debate in an auditorium at the IPhLH. For a week, all of literary, intellectual Moscow and its entire student population descended on the IPhLH to listen to these people debate. The heat of passion was so intense that people whistled, clapped, and shouted. There was no place to sit, people crammed into the aisles of the largest amphitheater in the Institute. It was explosive. Naturally, we sided with Lifshitz and Lukács. Lukács spoke comically, with his Hungarian accent. His argument was weighty, but, ultimately, when the debate broke up, it was unclear who had won, and everyone awaited a verdict from *Pravda*. It was common knowledge that an article that would sum up the discussion was in the works. April came to an end, and even before the article appeared there was an announcement about the closure of *Literary Critic*. This was an answer of sorts, implying that the supporters of Ermilov and Knipovich had prevailed. Then a scathing article written by ideologist Lebedev came out in *Pravda*.

This failed attempt to rejuvenate Marxist thought took down our IPhLH with it. We had managed to complete three years of studies.

I think that it was at the IPhLH that I acquired a truer vision of the world, of people, of culture. I am very much indebted to my professors—even to those eight hours with Grib, and of course to Pinsky's remarkable course, and to my acquaintance and, later, my friendship with him. I was already oriented toward the humanities, and toward human experience, and my world expanded. This gave me access to world culture. I felt at home there. I learned to operate with different categories. It is possible that without the understanding I had acquired I would never have stood up to Zelinsky. I had understood that some things must be defended. Perhaps it was then that my fear subsided, too; I don't know.

24

In June we studied for our exams. We were preparing to take, among others, an exam in nineteenth century literature. We studied together in groups. Oleg Troyanovsky, who was taking part in our little group, and whom I was expecting to bring over some lecture notes to me at home, called me up and said:

"You know, Lili, I was listening to the radio last night . . ." Now, Troyanovsky's radio was not just some little black speaker, the kind that could be found in every household, but a huge, splendid, state-of-the-art apparatus that they had brought with them from America. It was a record player combined with a radio, which could pick up western radio broadcasts. Oleg said, "I'm not sure, Lili, it was hard for me to make it out, but I think war broke out last night. I think Hitler crossed over the border."

I said, "Come on, Oleg. You can't be serious!"

"Well, don't quote me, but that's what I gathered from it."

He brought me the lecture notes.

"Oleg, what were you saying over the phone?"

He said, "Well, I tried to tune to the broadcast again in the morning, but they jammed it all. Listen to the *Latest News* at noon."

At twelve we turned on the radio, and listened to the *Latest News*. There were reports that some kolkhoz members won a competition somewhere, a shock workers brigade turned in so-many tons of coal, and so on. We listened to all this, then wondered: What is Oleg up to? Why is he trying to scare us? Suddenly we heard: "In fifteen minutes, Molotov will address the nation." Molotov spoke, and told us that war had been declared.

We all rushed headlong over to the IPhLH. We gathered around our Latin teacher, Maria Grabar-Passek—she was a strict, dry, very no-nonsense person. She stood in the middle of the landing, surrounded by all of us, weeping openly. Tears streamed down her face. We were bewildered.

"Why are you crying?"

"Children"—she also addressed us as 'children'—"you have no idea what war is. I lived through World War I. It was horrific. It means that an era of horror is upon us."

We, of course, were all thinking, what's a little war? The Soviet Union is so powerful. In a week or two, or a month, it will all be over. Yet this image of Mrs. Grabar-Passek sobbing on the landing still remains my first image of the war.

No one knew why there was no word from Stalin. He kept silent. Now it's common knowledge, but I want to tell young people, who might not be aware of this, that less than two months prior to the outbreak of war, Stalin had destroyed the remaining top military commanders of the country. One of my friends lived in Lefortovo, next to the prison. It was the most dreadful of the Moscow prisons, and it was there they were holding the arrested officers. After the war, my friend told me that for two nights in the beginning of May 1941, no one had been able to sleep. Rounds of rifle fire rang out all night long. They were executing those who had been imprisoned, for the most part, in 1937, the year when Marshal Tukhachevsky, unjustly accused of being a traitor and working for Germany, had been executed.

Only at the beginning of July did Stalin make a speech over the radio. He addressed us then not as "comrades," but as "brothers and sisters."

Soon the bombardments began, and air raid alarms sounded all over Moscow. My mother was deathly afraid of them. She was absolutely terrified. Of the bombardments, of war itself. I was faced with a choice. I could enter the labor force to support the war effort, as most of my girlfriends had, since the boys had already volunteered to fight. Zhenya Asterman, Mark Bershadsky—they had signed up immediately. Girls were recruited to dig the trenches. The other option was to consider my mother. Though my friends greeted it with censure, I decided that I had an obligation to consider my mother. I felt I had to take her away. None of us believed, of course, that the war would last so long. We thought it was a question of a few summer months . . . I went to the *Moscow Komsomolets*, since I had begun writing for them, and said to Kronhaus, "I need to take my mother away." He said, "Fine, you can take our train." So he organized this. They were going to Kazan.

Mother and I did everything the worst way possible, without any foresight, of course. True, someone did persuade me to take a winter coat at the last minute; but, for the most part, we didn't take any warm things with us. We hardly took a thing. We locked up the apartment as if we were going on a picnic, and left. We had a single suitcase each. From the minute we got on the train, I felt that my mother was the child, and I was the full-grown adult who was responsible for her.

25

THE KAZAN TRAIN STATION WAS ALREADY FRIGHTENING AND CHAOTIC. I still cringe when I remember how crammed it was with people, this crowd that swayed to and fro like a wave, first to one side, then to the other. People were pushed up against each other as though they were in a packed bus. Mama was afraid to stay alone, but I had to leave her to find the local office of the Union of Journalists, as I had been instructed to do. I took whatever assignment they gave me, naturally. They appointed me senior correspondent (which was absurd, since there were only two of us in the office) at the district newspaper in Naberezhnye Chelny, which was then a village. (Now it has become a city.) The paper was called the *Communist Banner*.

To get to Naberezhnye Chelny we had to go by steamboat, because there were as yet no railroads leading to it. Someone helped

me buy the tickets. I was still very young and inexperienced, twenty-one years old and still wet behind the ears. So I had to rely on the assistance of strangers.

We stood for two days and nights on the pier—we couldn't sleep, we couldn't sit. In fact there was nowhere to sit anyway. The suitcases were standing upright for lack of space. Finally, we made it onto a steamboat.

The journey to Naberzhnye Chelny, which normally took two days, lasted four. There was even something romantic about it. A southern night, summer, stars, you stroll up and down the deck the whole night long . . . One of the passengers was an interesting young Polish man who was fleeing Poland, and we got into a conversation. In short, I've always had an adventurous streak . . . There I was sailing into the unknown. I had no idea what a small-town paper was, what a real Russian backwater was like (and this was, moreover, Tatar territory) . . . But I still remember that night as if it were yesterday: a dark starry night, the broad Kama River—I sensed the enormity of the world, and our paltriness in the face of it. There was something absolutely enchanting about it; and something frightening, too.

We arrived at Naberzhnye Chelny. I left Mama sitting on the pier, and went alone to find the local newspaper offices.

A small village with one main street—in other words, on a single street there were several two-story houses, like they used to build them: some sort of stone structure for the first story, and the second story built out of wood. The district committee was in one such building, the executive committee in another. All the other buildings were wooden, from the ground up. A true village. Dusty, on the higher bank of the River Kama, and surrounded by forests. Beautiful.

Life smiled at me once more. The editor-in-chief, the only editor on this paper, turned out to be a wonderful human being. His name was Darichev. I remember him: a person of natural talent, a complete autodidact—he had taught himself to read and write. He was very bright, a person with deep convictions, very humane, with liberal views. In addition to all this, he was an artist, a primitivist; his work appealed to me very much.

I had to look for a place to live. No one wanted to rent anything out: they were afraid of Muscovites. I knocked on the doors of at least twenty little cottages, but they didn't let me in. It was a very unpleasant moment, but Darichev comforted me, saying, "It's all right. We'll find something for you, Lilya." Indeed, we were able to rent a room on the main street, on the second floor—but only for barter. No one wanted to take money. My terrible landlady told me, "Every month you will give me one of your belongings—shoes, a dress, a sweater. These are the terms, if you want to live in my house." I said, "What about when I run out of things?" "Then out you go," she said. "I don't need your money. What is this money worth to me?"

We had no choice. We settled into this little room. Darichev asked me, "Do you know how to harness a horse?" "Good lord!" I said. "Where could I have learned to do that?" "You can't get along here without knowing that," he said. "Every day you'll have to drive over to another village, another kolkhoz, and collect data." "Fine," I said, "show me how." He taught me how to harness and hitch up a horse in one day. It turned out to be not as difficult as I expected, and two or three days later, I set out, very nervous, because I was afraid the harness would come undone. . . I didn't understand a thing, didn't know what I was doing. Just imagine: a city girl, with Parisian beginnings, hitching up a horse and traveling through the forest to a Tatar village. In a horse and cart. And so off I went.

I found myself in a Tatar village where people could barely speak Russian. Still, the management of the kolkhoz spoke enough Russian to explain to me that the grain hadn't been harvested, that there was no way to bring in the grain because all the men had been drafted, naturally, and the women had been mobilized to cut and process peat, that only old women were left to work in the fields, and that there was not enough fodder for the cattle—in short, they painted a picture of the complete collapse of agriculture.

I took notes on everything he said. They hitched up the horse for me, and I set out again, back the way I had come. Somewhere along the road, the horse stopped and refused to budge. He just stood still. What was I supposed to do? The forest there is wild and deep, very frightening. It began growing dark. I heard strange sounds, the wind started howling. I thought I would lose my mind if I had to stay there overnight. What was I to do? I buried my head in the horse's neck and wept. Suddenly, the horse started to move again. I think it just felt sorry for me. Somehow or other we made it home. Someone helped me unharness the horse—it still wasn't easy for me. Later, by the way, I mastered it, and it wasn't at all hard. Practice makes perfect; that's a wonderful saying. Remember the passage in Bulgakov? "'How dexterously you tipple!' 'It comes with practice.'" In short, it turned out that a French-Jewish-Russian girl could harness a horse and cart like the best of them.

The next morning I went to report to Darichev. I said, "You know, things are so bad at the kolkhoz, it's time to sound the alarm." He said:

"Oh, come now! Who's interested in that? Forget everything you saw. You and I will write an article together. 'The grain has already been successfully harvested . . .'"

I said, "Are you joking?"

He said, "No, I'm absolutely serious."

I said, "Why did you bother to send me there then?"

"Just forget about all that. The paper should contain only life-affirming little pieces, full of hope and a positive outlook."

I said, "But why did I have to go there, when we could have written the article without all the fuss and bother?"

He said, "What do you mean? You have to familiarize yourself with the material."

I said, "Are you making fun of me?"

"No, you have to go there, so that when the higher-ups ask whether we are visiting the kolkhozes, I can honestly answer: yes, we are. And then we write what we are supposed to write. That's all there is to it. And that's how you and I are going to work."

I was so upset he could see the horror in my eyes. He said,

"Well, I was kind of baffled, too, at first. Before the war, we could allow ourselves to write otherwise now and then—not often, and it still had to be optimistic in tone. But now that the war is on, we can only write positive reports. At the last staff meeting, we were instructed directly: report only what is positive; but go around to the collective farms. So that's what we'll do. We'll go to farms, and write positive reports."

I must admit that my job at the local newspaper office and my life in Naberezhnye Chelny gave me real insight into the workings of the Soviet system. Until then I had imagined, like many, by the way, that arrests and terror touched only the cities—the industrial centers, where there was some degree of awareness. Here I discovered that the entire country was one single territory, rife with terror, where every second person, or at least every third, ran the risk of arbitrary arrest. There was not a single house in these Russian, half-Tatar, or primarily Tatar, villages (though villages were never viewed as ethnically mixed; a village was considered to be either Russian or Tatar) that was not a victim of this. In every family, at least one member had been arrested. They were arrested for nothing, for taking a handful of grain, for tardiness. There had been a decree that if you were ten minutes late for work . . . They imprisoned people because there was a "quota" (Darichev, who was privy to everything that was discussed in secret local authorities' meetings, told me this) specifying how many people in each district had to be sent up every month. I want to talk about this so that people who have forgotten will remember; and young people will know. They followed a plan for arrests. Broken down by district. Completely arbitrary. It didn't matter who had done what. The smallest infraction would suffice. The cobweb of bans and prohibitions was so dense that it was impossible not to transgress them at some point. Every person was breaking the law by simply breathing. They could gather the numbers they needed with impunity, and every month the KGB (NKVD) managed to fulfill its quota.

Naberezhnye Chelny is on the old "manacle and leg irons" road to Siberia. It has an ancient, pre-Revolutionary prison with very thick walls. It is not large, but very capacious. The room we rented on the second floor of a house looked out onto this prison. Just as they had been many years before, convicts were still being driven down this road. The first time I saw a convoy of prisoners, they were women. Accompanied by guards on horseback, exhausted, bedraggled figures, almost all of them barefoot. Their feet swaddled in rags, carrying satchels of some kind, and surrounded by packs of dogs. I felt I was watching some sort of horror film. It was hard to believe that I was seeing this in real life, all my misgivings about the system notwithstanding . . . I think it's important to stress that there is a vast chasm, an impenetrable wall, between speculative notions and perceptions, and what you see with your own eyes, experience with your own senses. It's one thing when I am sitting here in this room, telling you about it . . . I knew, of course, that somewhere people were being deported under convoy, that they, most likely, were barefoot, that they collapsed from weakness and hunger. I had even heard that they were guarded by men on horseback, and dogs . . . But seeing this with my own eyes . . . How can I tell you what it was like? At a certain moment, even though you are only twenty-one years old, you no longer want to live. I had the feeling that human malice had reached such a fever pitch—that certain people could look on in complete apathy at other people who were utterly broken and full of anguish—I simply didn't want to take part in life anymore. That was what I felt. I didn't want to continue living. Then I got used to it. I will say it again: you get used to everything. That first convoy, however, I'll never forget it. And then I saw convoys in winter . . . Oh, my.

26

By THE MIDDLE OF WINTER WE HAD NOTHING ELSE TO PAY WITH. Everything that the landlady would accept as rent for the room we had already given her, and we had to move. She had a girl of my age who paraded around in my clothes, and was very proud of it. She didn't display a shadow of compunction about it. This is the kind of thing she said to me, this girl Katya, "Before, you lived well in Moscow. Now it's time for us to live it up, at your expense. It's only fair."

What I earned was barely enough to maintain a half-famished existence. There were ration cards, but we could hardly pay for what the ration cards gave us a right to. You could get a bit of sugar, a bit of vodka—Mama started exchanging it for bread. Then Darichev rescued us. He requisitioned one room from the editorial office. There were three rooms, and in the smallest one he cut a door through to the outside, and settled us in it. It was an act of great mercy and kindness on his part, because otherwise we would have had nowhere to turn. We tried to rent something else, but no one wanted to rent to us; they knew we had nothing left to pay with. Not a single person was willing to rent us a room. And Darichev let us have the small room in the editorial office. This, however, brought with it another problem—heating. The editorial office was hardly heated at all. How could we live in an unheated space? Naberezhnye Chelny is hit hard by frost and cold in the winter. Nothing is more difficult to endure than an unheated space. In some sense it's even worse than hunger. In fact, we never starved; we just went around hungry much of the time.

Again, Darichev went to some other office and requisitioned two enormous logs for me. They were lying frozen in the Kama River. They needed to be dug out somehow. He went with me. But even he, a strong man, spent a whole week dislodging them from the ice. I cried the whole time. I felt terribly ashamed. During the day we worked on the newspaper, and in the evening, when it was already nearly dark, we went down to the river to chop the ice. Why he was doing this for me was a mystery, and everyone snickered about it and laughed behind our backs: "Oooh, he's in love!" I don't think he was in love. I think he felt sorry for me. And there was a lot to feel sorry for me about. Still, no one in that place felt any pity for me but him.

Day after day we went down to the river, and it seemed that even with his help we would never be able to free the log from the ice. What if we didn't manage to get them out? Would we die? I thought. Mama's teeth chattered all the time as it was, and everything was piled up on the bed to keep it warm. One had to stay in bed the whole time. Bed? What am I saying! We had two cots that he had also found somewhere for us. Without Darichev, we would have perished there.

Nevertheless, he somehow managed to cut these two huge logs out of the ice. He found someone to help him transport the logs on a cart and brought them to our editorial office. He even had time to help me chop one of them into small pieces for firewood. But he didn't manage to help me with the second. He was drafted into the army and sent off to the front.

A stableman agreed to help me with the second log in exchange for my last valuable, a penknife with ten blades that had belonged to my father. It had his initials on it. He agreed on one condition: he would keep one-third of the log, I would keep the remaining two-thirds. I had no choice but to agree. I have to say that another third of what he sawed for me (I could do the smaller chopping with an ax myself) he also stole from me. By spring, we found ourselves without firewood.

27

IN THE WINTER, THAT PLACE WAS ABSOLUTELY CUT OFF FROM THE REST of the world. The only communication we had was through phone and radio. When the river was again navigable the first steamboat came through—it was such a joyous, life-affirming occasion that everyone in Naberezhnye Chelny, young and old, rushed down to the landing docks to meet it. The steamboats that plied the Volga and the Kama were wonderful—beautiful white vessels, many of them from before the revolution, which had somehow been spared the devastation.

Besides the happiness and exultation I felt when I saw it approach, with people on board, a sign that life was continuing somewhere out there, I saw a familiar face on the upper deck. I saw a girl named Asya Goldin, who had been Mark Bershadsky's girlfriend. I started screaming at the top of my lungs, "Asya! Asya!" I waved my arms, afraid that she wouldn't see me. She did; she recognized me, and she waved back.

They wouldn't let people on the steamboat because it had a buffet in which you could buy something to eat; but I implored, and pushed my way through to Asya. She grabbed her suitcase and came down. This was a moment of pure joy—seeing a person who was dear to me in such a remote, desolate place.

Then she told me that Mark and Zhenya had both died in the first battles of the war.

The volume of Pasternak with an inscription was all I had left from Zhenya. His image has persisted through my entire life, however. I have never forgotten him. His presence has always remained.

Zhenya, my younger son, is named after him. Pavel would have been Zhenya, but Sima wanted to name his firstborn son after his grandfather. When Pavel was born, on the feast day of St. Peter and St. Paul, I decided that fate had disposed in the matter of his name, and that he would be Paul, or Pavel. My second son, naturally, was called Zhenya.

Asya had gone to the enlistment office and offered to join Mark's unit as a nurse, and now she was on her way to visit her parents to say goodbye. They lived further up the Kama, in Bondyuga. I got leave from the newspaper to visit her for a few days; then she left for the front. She did work as a nurse in the unit in which Mark and Zhenya died (they were together), and she stayed there until the end of the war.

The second event of the spring was the arrival of another person I knew: Rita Aliger. It turned out that her older daughter Tanya and her grandmother (Margarita's mother) were also living in Naberezhye Chelny. I knew them a bit. Rita was coming to see them.

I decided (my adventurous streak surfaced again) that I would leave with her when she returned to Moscow. Not permanently, of course, but for a short time. But I was so cowardly and weak-willed that I couldn't tell my mother. I said, "Mama, I'm going with Rita as far as Chistopol, where the writers' organization is. Maybe we'll be able to move somewhere to improve our lives. Let me go for a week." Mama agreed. This was, of course, a terrible thing to do. But I was compelled to behave this way. In fact, I knew very well I intended to go all the way to Moscow.

One needed a permit to travel to Moscow. There were so many decks and cabins on the steamboat that I was able to dodge the inspections. Rita somehow managed to get me a ticket at the train station in Kazan, and we boarded the train. I had a ticket, but no permit. Rita was nervous, so much so that I said, "Maybe you don't want me to travel with you? Should I go to another car?" "No, no," she said. "We're traveling together. Maybe I'll be able to help you somehow."

We didn't get a wink of sleep the whole way. There were two inspections during the journey. Both times I locked myself in the bathroom. They knocked and knocked, but finally gave up. I got off the train before we reached Moscow. I knew I would have to get off at one of the dacha districts and enter the city by commuter train. I managed to pull all this off quite well; and then I was in Moscow. From Moscow I sent Mama a telegram. I felt very ashamed that I had deceived her, but at the same time I thought maybe I could take some of our belongings back with me so we would have something to live on . . .

When I arrived at our apartment, I saw with horror that people were living in it. Each of the three rooms was occupied by different people. I made up my mind to go to the housing manager to say that I had returned for good. Yura Knabe, who was in Moscow at the same time, gave me a bottle of vodka to give to the housing manager. The manager didn't ask me for my permit, which he was obligated to do; and he freed up one room for me.

There I discovered that everything had been stolen. There wasn't a single object or piece of furniture. What grieved me most of all was that a watercolor by Voloshin, which Maria Voloshin had given Mama in Koktebel, had been filched, too. It had been hanging on the wall, which was now bare. Even though the kinds of people who were living there would have had no use or appreciation for it whatsoever.

I got the impression that Muscovites were doing quite well. Yes, there were blackouts, air raid alarms, and so forth, but compared to life in Naberezhnye Chelny . . . Here people at least got together and talked. I began seeing old friends and acquaintances. I met Leonid Pinsky every day in the home of mutual friends. I had no desire to return to Naberezhnye Chelny, however shameful it was to feel that way. I knew that in the end I would have to go back, but that made me dig my heels in all the more. Recently, it occurred to me for the first time how easy it is to become oblivious to things. How can I explain this? I seemed to forget about Naberezhbnye Chelny. Even about Mama. I didn't literally forget her—but emotionally I did. I plunged completely into the warm humanity of my Moscow life.

Soon it became clear that the war was not ending, but rather strengthening, deepening. In the spring and the first months of summer, after our forces managed to prevent the capture of Moscow at the final hour, it seemed that the worst was already behind us. But in August 1942, the German forces again began marching toward the Volga, and cut off the grain belt from the rest of the country.

On the last days of August I left Moscow. People gave me things to take with me to trade with. Everything fit into a huge zinc-plated basin—a very important household item in our lives back then. We washed clothes and took baths in it. In every communal apartment, dozens of them hung from the ceiling. It turned out that one could travel with one, too.

When I arrived in Naberezhnye Chelny, I found Mama in such a state of apathetic self-neglect and despair, believing that I would never return, that I felt a burning, bitter shame. This is one of the most painful memories in my life. When I said earlier that it is easy to become oblivious to things, this is what I was referring to. A person who escapes some terrible evil wants to reject everything associated with it. We have the faculty of protective adaptability. This was another lesson in life for me. I thought that since I myself didn't experience this separation very deeply, everything was all right. In reality, we lose sight of how much pain our actions can cause another human being.

28

THE SECOND YEAR IN NABEREZHNYE CHELNY WAS MUCH WORSE THAN the first, because, as I said, Darichev had been drafted. During the two months of my absence, a horrible woman, a Party functionary, had arrived to replace him. She simply fired me, and told us to vacate the premises.

We had no idea how we were going to make a living. What I had brought with me from Moscow was paltry—it would last a month, a month and a half, not more.

Mama tried making dolls—not toy dolls or puppets, but Father Frost figures, for decorating the Christmas tree. But the people there didn't like Mama's dolls. They didn't turn out pretty or decorative, and we had nothing to dress them in. Mama's aesthetic didn't correspond to the aesthetic of the residents of Naberezhnye Chelny. Mama had always been a very good-natured, effervescent person, but she suffered terribly in Chelny. She wrote poetry, and read. There really was no outlet for her talents there.

So we moved to a village where there was vodka distillery that made spirits out of potatoes. I was taken on as a lab assistant. The kolkhoz workers would come with their carts (or sleighs, in winter) piled high with potatoes. You would take a bucket of potatoes and run some tests. They would receive money according to the percentage of starch contained in the potatoes. Already on the first day, however, I discovered that no one bothered with the tests. I said, "Why do you take the potatoes, then?" "To eat them, of course." The potatoes were immediately boiled or baked, and the numbers were simply invented. Even though I had seen a lot by that point, I had still never encountered it in such a blatant, barefaced form. I said, "What if you're found out, what if they catch you?" They answered, "Everyone knows already."

It was a strange, double life—they sent people to prison for being late for work, but at the same time, everyone here knew that they took the potatoes, and no one did anything about it. All of this created the sense of some sort of nightmarish, unreal existence. There was a phantasmagorical dimension to it.

Mama and I lived in complete isolation. We lived happily. There is a poem in Mama's notebook about how I brought home half a liter of milk and a pine branch one New Year's Eve. Still, we sometimes began to lose hope.

It was the second winter of the war. Naturally, we had no real understanding of what was happening on the battlefront. We didn't know that a decisive battle, unprecedented in the magnitude of its cruelty, was raging near Stalingrad. Nekrasov later described it in *In the Trenches of Stalingrad*, and Grossman in *Life and Fate*. We were cut off from the world, buried under the snow that kept falling and falling ceaselessly. We were cold and hungry, there was no kerosene, and so it was impossible to read in the evening. Nothing happened where we were.

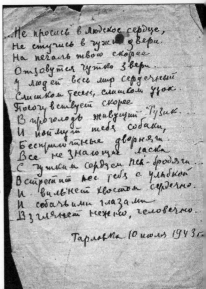

In January, Hitler's forces were routed at Stalingrad. Paulus's army capitulated, and the Nazi forces began to retreat.

After this victory, and with the onset of warm weather, I began thinking that maybe we wouldn't stay in this village forever after all.

But how could we leave? Everyone who had been evacuated from Moscow lost the right of return. One had to get a permit, and they were given out by the police on the condition that an organization could vouch that you were vitally important for the workforce, and that no one else could do your job. So for a second time I traveled to Moscow illegally and managed to get the necessary papers from the *Komsomol Pravda*. I returned to Chelny to fetch Mama, and we set out. We couldn't go by train, because Mama didn't have a permit, and she wasn't agile enough to run and hide in the bathroom, as I had done. So we took a steamboat. It was a very long journey, lasting almost a month, with numerous stops along the way. Finally, we landed at the Moscow pier. We were in Moscow again.

29

THE ROOM I HAD MANAGED TO RECOVER THE PREVIOUS SUMMER WAS still available for our use, but we lost the other two rooms in our former apartment.

The second secretary of the District Committee of our own district now lived in the larger of the rooms. She was a Party functionary with a very strict expression and demeanor. She wore blue suits, a tie, and white blouses. She was an excellent "distributor," of course. In the small room that had once been mine, and where my friends had so often gathered, lived a woman from Leningrad who had been evacuated during the Siege. She was a sweet Jewish woman. She worked as an engineer in the Leningrad lightbulb factory.

The IPhLH had been abolished. It was merged with Moscow State University. This is how I ended up as a student in the evening program of the department of philology of Moscow State University. I also began to work at the Radio Committee. There was an editorial office there which broadcast in different languages to various countries: French, Italian, and others. Once a week, Maurice Thorez came into our editorial offices to address the French people in French. It was quite a comical spectacle. No sooner did the satiated, portly, self-satisfied leader of the French proletariat arrive than he began declaiming fiery speeches about how one should throw oneself without stint into the struggle against Fascism, and suffer privations and horrors with equanimity. Being an orator of the French school, which is dripping with pathos, Thorez worked himself into a frenzy, turning completely red in the face. His son studied in a Soviet school. In the 1970s, he wrote a book rich with irony about their life in Moscow and his father's activities.

I enjoyed working in the Radio Committee, but I didn't hold out very long there. I transferred to the day program at Moscow State.

At around that time, the event that shocked us most deeply—though it might have seemed that nothing could shock us by that time—was a story I heard from a trusted source: Lev Bezymensky.

He was in Moscow on leave from the army. He reported that anti-Semitism was rearing its head in the army.

Lev, a tough person, was very obedient to the authorities at that time, since he wanted a career. Not at all inclined to slander, but rather always trying to whitewash everything that happened in the army, he suddenly told me, "You know, the promotion of other Jewish men was held back by the fact that they're Jewish."

I didn't believe it. It's strange, because, my goodness, I had found out so much, had seen so much falsehood, deception, lying—and still, this seemed completely improbable to me. There was a war on against Fascism, and the idea of "national traits," of purity of blood, was the fundamental tenet of the enemy. I simply couldn't believe that this could happen here. Deception and lies on a grand scale, yes; but not anti-Semitism.

Anti-Semitism in the Soviet Union, in my opinion, existed until that point on a very basic, instinctual level among simple folk, and even well educated people; but it was confined to daily interactions and emotions. It wasn't mandated from above. If you heard someone on the street utter an anti-Semitic remark, you could say, "I'm going to report you to the police." The police would intervene on your behalf. Anti-Semitism had no place in the dominant ideology, in the accepted doctrine. It existed, as I have said, on a mundane, instinctual level, even in the highest cultural circles—as I would find out later, it bears no relation to a person's level of education— but it was certainly not state-sponsored. It was a private, individual phenomenon. But here was Lev saying that anti-Semitism was unleashed from above, and manifested itself in the army during the distribution of medals and honors, and when it came to promotions. We found out later from *Life and Fate* that this really was the case. In 1942–1943, not only was an anti-Semitic mood discernible, but some very secret government ukases were released, as well.

It was difficult for me to comprehend why. I asked Lev, "How do you interpret this? You deal with very highly placed officers and authorities." He answered in a very paradoxical manner. He said, "It's a disease, and it's catching. It came to us by way of the Germans. There was such thorough interrogation of the generals and high officials, and they expounded their views so convincingly, that it crept into us, like an infection."

I can't say whether he was right or wrong. Moreover, I personally think that Stalin had always entertained these attitudes and feelings, to greater or lesser degrees. He did not have an untarnished past. At one time he worked as a bathhouse attendant in Baku. I met people who knew him during that period. He was small potatoes, and it is not unlikely that this anti-Semitism was always present in him, but these events seemed to provide him with a rational basis for it. Having decided to become the Father of the Russian Nation, he probably thought that such views would increase his popularity, that anti-Semitism would resonate with the masses.

In short, it seemed that by then nothing in the reigning ideology could surprise me, but this did take me by surprise. My mother had not been present during our conversation, and for a long time I pondered whether I should tell her about it or not. I was afraid that she would start remembering the pogroms, and so on. For a week I hesitated, but finally I decided to tell her, since I wasn't used to hiding anything from her. I told her, and she became panicky. For a person who had experienced pogroms at one time, who had lived in Czarist Russia, this surge in anti-Semitism gave rise to a terrible kind of fear, an irrational fear. And, in fact, very soon it became evident that finding a job with the "fifth paragraph" in one's passport was difficult. By 1945, it was no longer a secret to anyone that anti-Semitism had become state policy. It was now out in the open; so I had outstripped events only by a small margin.

30

Mama died before Victory Day, and I was grief-stricken. She died in early spring, in March of 1944. She died, of course, from oversight. She might not have had to die so soon. She died of indigestion, and from bad medicine. Perhaps if we had sought help in time . . . But they wouldn't admit her to the hospital. And I didn't want them to hospitalize her. I was afraid of hospitals, since Papa had died in one. Mama died in the space of three days, all at once, at home.

Her death was a terrible blow to me. I felt I hadn't done enough to prevent it, and that was probably the case. I didn't organize the necessary medical help, I didn't understand what was happening. I became very depressed, which was uncharacteristic of me.

I was now completely alone on this earth. I had no living relatives. My uncle, Papa's brother, had already died, as had his wife. There was simply no one left. I felt absolutely unmoored. I lived in a state of suspended existence.

A university friend of mine named Issa Chernyak invited—or, rather, almost forced—me to come live with her. In my despondency, I submitted readily. For the next year I closed up the Kalyaevka apartment again and moved in with Issa's family. They were very kind to me. Her mother, Debora Chernyak, a remarkable woman, was director of a children's hospital. She was ruined during the war, because everything she had in her home she sold to buy milk and porridge for her patients—the children in her hospital.

We graduated from university, took our final exams, and then our national exams. For some reason I began writing my honor's thesis on Scandinavian literature. I don't quite understand why myself. True, I had always loved it, but why I chose it I don't know. The topic of the paper was Russian-Scandinavian ties. Before World War I there was a time when all the Russian literary journals were keen on Scandinavia. It was understandable: northern literature was flourishing. It was actively translated and published. So I spent time in the Lenin Library and read those remarkable *Apollos* and *Northern Blooms*. I took notes, checked out books, and wrote my paper on Russian-Scandinavian ties. Samarin, my professor, said, "If you study Scandinavia, we'll accept you into graduate school." He was both head of the department at the university and head of the section of western literature at the Institute of World Literature.

I was very lucky in the people I met. Roman Samarin was a beastly person, the devil incarnate, but he showed me only his good side. He took me into a corner and whispered, "Lilya, don't think that the Russian intelligentsia is anti-Semitic; they force us to be anti-Semites, but even so, in our heart of hearts we aren't—not at all. And, you know, my stepfather, Beletsky, a famous professor in Kharkov, he was never an anti-Semite. There was never any anti-Semitism in our home!" For some reason he wanted to appear in his best light with me. Indeed, he did help me: he accepted my application to graduate school, which, for a Jewish girl in those years, was almost unheard of.

I became a graduate student at the Institute of World Literature. It pained me deeply that Mama never knew. I received a fellowship, so I would have been able to live comfortably, on my own. I gave the money, of course, to the people I was staying with.

When one is still young, it is possible to get over even enormous grief. I was in a very bad state, but it gradually lifted. I somehow managed to plunge myself into life, and it worked. Life, in some strange way, started to run its own course. I had undergone a great deal of loss. The death of my father, of Zhenya Asterman, and then of my mother. As it turned out, one can survive more misfortune than one realizes. One's supply of resilience and endurance outstrips one's expectations.

31

Victory Day was overshadowed by the fact that Mama did not live to see it. We had dreamed all those years about when the war would one day end, as everything does eventually.

No one slept for two or three days. There were fireworks, everyone celebrated in the streets, everyone ran to the stations to meet the trains with the demobilized soldiers. There is nothing to add to what Andrey Smirnov showed in *Belorussian Station*, that explosion of joy and a shared, human spirit. There is nothing I can say that has not been said better already. I would, however, like to say something about an event that occurred earlier, in the summer of 1944.

One day, a rumor started going around that German prisoners of war were being driven along the Garden Ring, from the Belorussian Station to Three Stations Square. People jammed the sidewalks. I was running some errand and happened to be not far from the Sklifosovsky Institute. Suddenly, everyone started to shout, "There they are, there they are!" In the distance I saw a dense black mass moving along the asphalt, approaching very quickly. Perhaps I had just lost my sense of time in all the excitement. First came the old generals in rumpled uniforms with epaulets torn off, in Wehrmacht service caps. They marched in Prussian step, sticking out their unshaven chins before them, and hiding first one, then the other hand in their pockets. It was bitterly cold, and their fingers were no doubt turning numb in the wind. Following them, in a disorganized crowd, came the junior officers and soldiers. Some of them were hobbling on homemade crutches, others had arms in slings, in filthy bandages. Some were barefoot. Black with dirt and sweat, emaciated, their faces skeletal, their cheeks sunken, dark circles around their eyes, with heavy, terrible stares. Rank upon endless rank, they passed . . . They turned from Mayakovsky Square onto Sadovaya-Triumfalnaya Street, and walked away down the Ring. They could barely drag themselves along. Some still struggled to hold themselves upright, others were too weak, and were bent over double from cold and hunger. It was a pathetic spectacle, but I forbade myself to pity them and kept repeating to myself that they had not taken pity on anyone.

Then I saw something that astonished me more than anything else. I saw some old women, shriveled with age, resembling black moths, approach the column of prisoners and offer them chunks of bread. Imagine how little bread we had during the war—and those old women gave away a portion of their own paltry rations. The soldiers backed away, not understanding what was expected of them. The old women, crossing themselves, insisted they take the bread. Some other women offered them mugs of water. In spite of the hatred of Germans, in spite of the horror that they had caused, and which the newspapers whipped up still more—they had, indeed, done unspeakable things, committed unspeakable acts—those women, young and old, gave the prisoners of war bread and water. They pitied them—that was what truly astonished me. That memory has stayed with me my entire life.

The Russian people surged forth into the whole of Europe. They had defeated what had seemed to be an invincible army. They saw with their own eyes how people lived elsewhere. They saw that people there lived very differently from what they had been led to believe. Soldiers from all over the Soviet Union—from Kazakhstan, from Siberia, from the Caucasus, from the Far East, having marched through half of Europe, discovered that the level of existence of ordinary people was far better than ours. In addition, the officers who were made commanders in the cities occupied by the Russian army, in the countries of "people's democracy," and in Germany, enjoyed a newfound freedom. They imbibed this new air of freedom, and became different people altogether. When Victory came, when everyone expected, and believed, that life would be different, that the air of newfound freedom the victorious army could not help but breathe would take effect, Stalin made a speech calling people cogs in a machine. Again, he had reduced them to the level of the purely mechanical, to the completely dependent status of a particle in some mechanism. It was very strange. These two moments—state-imbued anti-Semitism and "people as cogs"—set the tone for the post-war period. The illusion that the course of life might change direction for the better, even the slightest bit, evaporated very quickly.

32

THERE WAS AN ORGANIZATION IN MOSCOW KNOWN AS VOKS, THE Association for Cultural Ties with Foreign Countries. On the eve of the war, Kemenov, a person of liberal persuasion who belonged to the *Literary Critic* camp, became head of this organization. When the war began and they started looking for new people to fill the ranks when Maxim Litvinov, who was expecting to be arrested any day, was suddenly sent to the US as ambassador, Kemenov decided to do a complete overhaul of the VOKS, which had until then been a bureaucratic KGB organization. He fired almost everyone and selected young, capable IPhLH graduates, who could speak foreign languages and were freethinkers, to work there. Many of them, including Yura Knabe, were my friends. When I started graduate school, I went to them and they said, "Why don't you come here to teach French? Part-time, as a freelancer." (Being a graduate student, I wasn't allowed to be employed as a full staff member.) I began going there two or three times a week. The VOKS was located in a luxurious mansion next to Tishinskaya Square. Later, the German embassy was housed there. It was a splendid building with magnificent halls and chandeliers, and this was where the former IPhLH set up camp and tried working with new methods for an old master.

For the IPhLH folks, the "Iphlies," it turned into a kind of club. Whenever someone was demobilized and returned from the front, the first thing they did was come to the VOKS. It was a meeting place. It had beautiful draperies, parquet floors polished to a high sheen, a decent buffet—in post-war Moscow this was the lap of luxury. To use a modern expression, that was where we hung out.

There were not enough classrooms, and we often had to hold seminars at the table in the large reception hall. I remember once there was a person sitting at the neighboring table, whom I could immediately spot was a foreigner. He watched us attentively, listening, and when I had finished teaching, came up to me and introduced himself: "I am the new correspondent for *Le Monde*. You speak French so well, let's meet somewhere and spend some time together." He seemed like a charming young fellow, and I so missed speaking French. Why not? But I was afraid not only of meeting him somewhere else—that was out of the question—but even sitting there and talking to him unnerved me. I said, "Oh no, I couldn't think of it. I'm terribly busy, we're not allowed to engage in private conversations over here. You'll have to excuse me." I avoided him like the plague!

In the spring of 1946 I decided to go back to Kalyaevka to try living on my own again. I was writing my dissertation. Once I came home from the library and had not even had time to make myself a cup of tea, when the doorbell rang. A stranger, about thirty years old. I immediate guessed by his expressionless face that he was from the KGB. It was beyond the shadow of a doubt. I let him in, and he cast a cursory glance over the room, examined my books, went over to the window, and asked my permission to sit down. He was a very well behaved, very polite young man. He said, "This what I'm here for. We need your room for a month."

I couldn't believe my ears. "What do you mean? That's impossible. I can't get along without my books, I'm writing my dissertation. I have nowhere else to live."

"We'll rent a room for you in a hotel."

I balked. Why me? I can't, my books are my life . . . But he very firmly gave me to understand that it was useless to argue. Of course, if I needed my books, I could come by any time to get them; but I would have to call in advance to warn them I was coming. He gave me twenty-four hour's notice to collect my things.

I returned to Issa's house. A few days later I called under the pretext that I needed to pick up some books. A woman's voice answered—cold, flat, colorless—and told me I could come in an hour.

When I arrived at my room, two young women met me at the door. They were dressed very severely, with cropped hair and low-heeled shoes. I didn't even recognize the room. All the furniture had been moved up against one of the walls. The books were stacked up in piles in one corner. On the table was a shapeless bulky mass, covered with a sheet. It was impossible to make out what kind of object was underneath—most likely a tapping device. In those days technology did not yet allow one to eavesdrop or spy on someone from anywhere in the world. I took my books and left. Naturally, I never found out whom they were hunting down.

In the summer of 1946, Issa and I went to Gelendzhik, the vacation retreat that belonged to the university. While we were there we received a telegram. Issa's mother was gravely ill; soon afterward she died of cancer. She was apparently already ill when we were leaving for our vacation, but she concealed it from us so we would be able to vacation without undue concern. Her death was a great blow to me. I was very attached to her, and grateful for how she had taken me in and comforted me, grateful to her for simply being who she was. She was someone who carried joy around with her, whom it had been an honor to meet on the path of life. Most important, she was a person who was occupied not with herself, but with the world and people around her. Her death was as remarkable as her life. She called the hospital staff to her bedside and said in no uncertain terms, "You will do this task, so-and-so will take my place, etc." In short, she gave instructions, her last will and testament, as they did in nineteenth century novels. Then she said, "Now go, all of you. My sister and Issa and Lilya may stay." An hour later she was dead.

As often happened in our Soviet reality, the plethora of organizational and bureaucratic unpleasantness that immediately descended went some way toward helping allay the grief. Issa lived on Ermolaevsky Lane, near Gorky and Tverskaya streets. They had two large rooms in a communal apartment, where four other families were also living. The two rooms had been occupied by Issa's mother, her mother's sister, Issa, and myself. Not two days had passed when a commission arrived and said that within a week one of the rooms would be taken away. Of course, Issa would have been very uncomfortable living in one room with her elderly aunt. I felt obliged to do all I could to keep both rooms. Back in those days, there was only one way out in such a situation: marriage. We had to find Issa a husband without delay. But most of the young men had not yet been demobilized, and we only had a week. We would have to act fast. But where would we find a candidate?

Perhaps Yura Knabe would have agreed to help, but he was in a terrible situation himself. He had been kicked out of the VOKS. I will relate this whole saga in a nutshell, since it is another example of how misfortune can turn into great good luck and happiness.

Yura was expelled from the VOKS for the following reasons. During the night there was always somebody there answering the telephone. The VOKS was considered to be an important state institution, one of strategic importance, and it mandated that somebody tend the phones around the clock (though what could have posed such a threat to cultural ties in the middle of the night is anyone's guess). That night Yura shared the shift with Raya Orlova, one of our IPhLH girls. She was one of the Komsomol activists who made an appearance during the campaign of detentions and arrests. Her first husband died in the war, and her second was a highly placed Soviet official. It was late at night, one thing led to another, and at one point Yura said to Raya: "You're such a fanatical party stalwart that if the Party told you to take babies and smash their heads against a wall tomorrow, you'd do it without a second thought." Those were his words.

A week later, there was a Party meeting scheduled in which Yura was supposed to be taken on as a member. Raya stood up and said, "No, we can't accept Georgy Knabe into the Party because he is a loose cannon, as it were."

I must admit, Raya Orlova came a long way after that. She married Lev Kopelev, became a dissident, and was expelled from the country. In her autobiography, published in Germany, she tells this story about Yura somewhat differently—but that's how it really was.

The next day Yura was kicked out of the VOKS. He was crushed. His ambitions for a brilliant career were dashed. He was talented and capable, not just in languages but in various areas of scholarship. He thought his life was over. With great difficulty he was able to find a position in a trade school teaching languages. With his outstanding gifts . . .

As a result, he became a brilliant scholar. Instead of becoming a big Party functionary, he turned down the path that a person with his abilities should have been following all along. This is another example of how some piece of ill-luck can have fortunate consequences.

Three days after the housing commission had paid its visit, Noam Katzman, that little Noam who had run out to tell me I had been accepted at the IPhLH, turned up. He had served the whole war as a soldier. He had just been demobilized. So there were hugs and joy all round, and the first thing I said to him was: "Noam, have you considered getting married?" He said, "Married? I just got back yesterday!" He was from an impoverished Jewish family with many children; they lived in absolute poverty. I said, "Well, I have a favor to ask. Would you mind taking part in a fictitious marriage?" The guy had just come back from the war, he was still in his uniform greatcoat. He said, "Why not?" "Come over this evening and we'll discuss it," I said.

He came. He liked my friend Issa, and agreed. I have to say that this fictitious marriage became a true marriage within five days, and they spent many happy years together. They had two children. To end this little novella, I should also say that when Noam and Issa divorced many years later, she entered into another fictitious marriage. It seemed to be her fate. Her second fictitious marriage also became an authentic one. She married someone by the name of Panin, who is now considered to be one of Russia's great idealist philosophers. One of the characters in Solzhenitsyn's novel *The First Circle* was modeled after him. In that book, the character Rubin is Kopelev, and Panin is Panin. So he and Issa entered into a fictitious marriage. He wanted to leave the country at any cost. She managed to take him to France, and the marriage very soon became a real one. Now Issa devotes all her time to compiling and publishing his collected works. A remarkable fate.

In any case, Issa and Noam got married and fell in love, and I moved back to my room on Kalyaevka.

33

Soon afterward, I found a postcard from Lucy Tovalev, the girl from the German school with the huge dark eyes who had been arrested in the tenth grade, for which I had at once blamed Elka Nusinov. During the war, when I found out that like all students of the mathematics department, Elka had graduated from the military academy and had been sent to the front, I wrote him

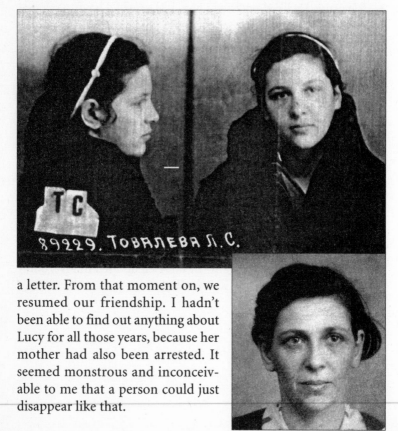

a letter. From that moment on, we resumed our friendship. I hadn't been able to find out anything about Lucy for all those years, because her mother had also been arrested. It seemed monstrous and inconceivable to me that a person could just disappear like that.

I remember being tormented by the memory of Zhenya Aster-man saying to me, "I'll find her. I'll scour every prison camp, I'll search everywhere until I find her!"

Lucy served ten years in a camp in Karaganda. First she was held for several months in the Butyrskaya Prison—forty women in a cell that measured 160 square feet, where you couldn't even roll over onto your other side at night. Then she was sent to Karaganda, where Solzhenitsyn had also been imprisoned, by the way. I won't recount everything I heard from her about her suffering, torture, and humiliation. So that the other inmates wouldn't rape her, Lucy became intimate with an inmate many years her senior, who could protect her. Soon they had a child, a daughter. By law, Lucy was not allowed to keep the child. The baby was taken to a special nursery, four miles away from the camp. Mothers had the right to nurse their children, but they couldn't stay with them between feedings, since they had to work.

Several times a day, Lucy would run back and forth along the icy road. She was completely exhausted and emaciated, and couldn't fathom where she got the strength to do it. Then her milk dried up and her daughter died of hunger and malnutrition.

Lucy fell ill. She couldn't talk, couldn't walk, didn't know where she was or what she was doing. She wouldn't have survived, but someone took pity on her and had her moved to another camp. There she took a course in agronomy and began to look after the cattle. She met a man there, a peasant, an exile from western Ukraine, and they started a relationship. They had a son, and named him Igor. Little by little, Lucy resigned herself to her life there, and stopped wanting anything else. She once told me, "It seemed as though there was nothing left of the person I once was. Someone else was living in my body. I forbade myself to remember the past. I had no desires, no hopes." When Lucy finished her term in prison, she felt no relief or joy. All the more since she had no place to go except the village in western Ukraine where the family of her son's father lived. This village had been completely destroyed several times over during the war and the occupation, and Lucy's life there was no better than it had been in the camps. To her in-laws she was a "dirty kike." Despite Lucy's many years in the camp, the very fact that she had come from Moscow, the Capital of Russian and Soviet power, made her their enemy. Completely oblivious to the reasons for her unhappiness, she wanted only one thing—to leave. But where could she go? She had no money. She didn't have permission to settle permanently in Moscow, or in any other major cities, since she was an ex-convict.

Lucy wrote me a restrained note on a postcard, saying, if you remember me, here's my address.

As soon as I received the postcard, I ran to the post office (since I didn't have a telephone) in the middle of the night to call Elka. We wired her a cable, collected some money, and Lucy came to Moscow. I let her live with me in my room. Little Igor slept in an armchair. I was afraid of what the neighbor, who was the second Party secretary of the district committee, would say. But she was very kind to the little boy, often bringing home food for him from her buffet at work—though she must have guessed who Lucy was, if only by her prison garb, a horrible black quilted jacket. Even after the war, no one wore those in Moscow. And so we lived, the three of us, on Kalyaevka.

In 1947 something happened that would completely turn my world around and change my life. I went to spend New Year's Eve with Elka Nusinov, as I was supposed to six years earlier, on the day that Lucy Tovalev was arrested. Lucy and I went to his house together. I already knew that a mutual friend would be there, someone whom my IPhLH friend Anya Grishina had told me about: a young director from the Stanislavsky Theater named Semyon "Sima" Lungin. He and I remembered that on one New Year's Eve in the past, he had gone over to fetch Anya at a place where Anya and I were both guests for the celebration, at the home of my classmate Mira (whose father was an intelligence agent). Neither Sima nor I remembered the meeting. Perhaps we hadn't even seen each other. Not only that, but Sima had been friends with Elka since before the war, and they had written plays together. But fate had decreed we would meet later.

It was a New Year's Eve like any other. The usual commotion, lots of people, lots of talk. I had no idea that this would be an epic day in my life. Afterward, Sima came to visit us on Kalyaevka once or

twice. I was absolutely certain that he had come because of Lucy. Lucy was the first person we knew who had returned from the camps. It was such a momentous occasion, so intriguing and disturbing, that my friends came over in a steady stream to see Lucy and talk with her, to listen to her stories.

Then Sima invited us to his birthday party on the 12th of January. Twelve days had passed since we had met on New Year's Eve. Lucy and I went together to the house where I was destined to live for so many years.

It was an enormous and desolate apartment, as it seemed to me then. The large room, where he received us, had massive oak furniture of the kind one might have found in a bourgeois home of the 1920s. Sima's father was an architect who also carried out finishing work, facings, and colored plastering. He had worked on this house at one time, and so was able to get a large apartment in it. There was a huge buffet, a square dining table, high-backed chairs. The furniture was covered in soot. Throughout the war, apparently, they had burned a potbelly stove there.

The walls were painted a dark blue, and on top of it there was a layer of soot. All of this was rather gloomy, imposing, and, somehow, not very welcoming. A large lamp covered with a yellow silk

lampshade hung above the table, the sort that no one had anymore, and that you only read about in novels. There was also a bell pull for calling the maid, the cook, and the servants. This all represented a completely strange and unprepossessing world to me.

There were six of us at the table. When we got up to leave, Sima approached me, completely unexpectedly, and whispered, "Stay."

I don't know what I was thinking or feeling at that moment, whether I sensed that it was fated or not—I can't say that I was in love with him. I was very strict in my habits and rules, and couldn't possibly have lost my head in that way. Nevertheless, something prompted me to stay. I stayed in that house. And I have stayed there for the rest of my life.

We lived forty-nine years together, as if in a fairytale. But in a fairytale there is a prince who has to complete heroic feats to win his beloved—catch the Bluebird of Happiness, or find a

Golden Apple. Sima, obviously, didn't have to catch any birds or pick any golden apples. It was enough for him to whisper "stay," and I stayed. The inevitable ordeals did take place, and we went through them; but we went through them together. And the ordeals were many.

34

Sima's father, Lev Lungin, had cancer. Sima cared for him tenderly and selflessly, although he was not his favorite son. His father had another son, who was serving in the army, a career military man.

We got married a year later, but we had already realized after the first day that we didn't want to live apart. I never imagined we would be together our whole lives—but we didn't want to be separated, and so things continued, day after day. For two years after the war, there was still hope of a change for the better in the country. At the same time there were rumors about continuing atrocities. People said that Stalin would not pardon the soldiers and officers who returned after being imprisoned by the Germans. He sent them to the labor camps, where some perished, and others were killed. There were discussions about anti-Semitism, and it became difficult to find a job with the "fifth paragraph"—nevertheless, there was still hope.

In the summer of 1946, Pravda published a speech by Andrey Zhdanov that he had delivered to the Central Committee the evening before. As soon as we read it, we thought: it has begun. We were already experienced. From this speech, and then from his other addresses, it became clear that another horrific offensive against anything connected with western culture was unfolding.

In this vituperative speech, the blow was aimed primarily at Akhmatova and Zoshchenko, who was one of the most beloved writers of that time. At first Zhdanov pounced on the journals that published them. Then he accused Zoshchenko of being anti-Soviet for writing base, mean-spirited descriptions of our reality. He slandered Akhmatova for vapid and disengaged poetry, alien to the Soviet people and harmful to the youth. He called her a whore and a nun (few were aware that this was a quote from Akhmatova's own poetry), in whom lechery was mingled with prayer. This lexicon had a great future, and was eventually used against Pasternak, Brodsky, Solzhenitsyn, and others.

We were very disheartened, both because we truly loved the poetry of Akhmatova and the stories of Zoshchenko, and because we understood that a new campaign against the intelligentsia had begun. The logic of these campaigns was all too familiar to us.

The Leningrad branch of the Writer's Union, headed by the poet Prokofiev, lost no time in attacking Akhmatova and Zoshchenko in their turn. They expelled them from the Writer's Union, and the press started to lambast them in one voice. They insulted them, flung mud at them, and tried to destroy them by any means possible. They were deprived of any opportunity to publish, and they fell into utter poverty. Zoshchenko was so poor that he had to rent one of the rooms in his small apartment by the night to transit passengers sent to him from one of the hotels surrounding the train station. But poverty was nothing compared with the humiliation and scorn heaped on them by publishers. At one of the writers' meetings Zoshchenko attended when he was ailing, he was greeted by shouts of "Enemy of the people!" Deathly pale, and hardly able to stand on two legs, terribly agitated, he summoned the last bit of strength he had, stood up behind the podium, and cried out, "Leave me alone, let me die in peace!" He repeated this phrase two or three times. Then he left the hall, never again to return.

Akhmatova's life was no easier. She lived in a tiny room where there was space only for a bed, a table, and one chair. A few devoted people helped her, but she had to count every penny. I met her ten years later through Vladimir Admoni, my dissertation advisor. (I wrote but never defended my dissertation.) He was the person to whom Nadezhda Mandelstam entrusted the poems of Osip Mandelstam for safekeeping.

We went to see Akhmatova when she was in the hospital. The hospital was dreadful, like all our hospitals; but this one was even worse than usual. It was an old building on the outskirts of town that had never been repaired or renovated. The reception area was a musty little room with peeling, dirty-green walls. That is where we met Akhmatova. She was very large, gray, and walked with difficulty. She wore a rough cotton nightshirt, rather dingy, that didn't even reach to her knees. On top of that was a washed-out gray robe, so narrow it wouldn't even wrap around her. At first glance, it seemed nothing remained of the slender, dark-haired beauty whose profile had been captured for all time by Modigliani. But when she entered the room, I felt I was in the presence of a queen. She was so regal that everything around her became invisible. She was offered a chair, and we remained standing.

Akhmatova apologized for receiving us down here—there were fifteen other patients in her ward, and some of them moaned without ceasing. Nevertheless, she continued to write poetry and articles, and she was finishing her work on Pushkin. I couldn't help asking her, "How do you manage to work in such circumstances?" She said, "Child,"—(I was already thirty-five)—"it is possible to work in any circumstances." I was absolutely dumbfounded by all this.

Not a single ideological campaign was ever limited to decisions taken above, in the Central Committee. It immediately had to be augmented from below. For this reason, countless letters from laborers and kolkhoz workers expressing their satisfaction with the fact that the Party, under the leadership of the wise Stalin, had picked up the broom and was cleansing and restoring order to the country, were published by all the newspapers. They praised him for sweeping away this refuse—with whom, fortunately, the authors of the letters were unacquainted—who were holding back our progress into a bright future. Meetings were held everywhere—at factories, in the Academy of Sciences, at universities, in the Unions of writers and artists. After a speech by the chairman, those in attendance voted publicly on a resolution. Unanimously. To dare vote against a resolution, or even to abstain, before a hall full of people was an act as audacious and brave as it was rare. I never once witnessed it during the Stalin era. Later, during the Thaw, people began to emerge who protested against an ideological campaign (though you could count them on the fingers of one hand). They all paid a heavy price for this. They were expelled from the Party, they were fired, forced to work as ghost writers, and condemned to a life of poverty.

It was mandatory that responsibility for these ruined reputations and lives be placed at the door of society as a whole—so that no one remained "clean." Stalin perfected this tactic, but his successors resorted to it with the same degree of enthusiasm and vigor. This tactic became one of the mainstays of the Soviet system. For this reason, later, when Perestroika began, conservatives had no trouble digging up compromising texts endorsed by the most prominent reformers.

During the campaign against Akhmatova and Zoshchenko, the Department of Philology, where I was writing my dissertation, was no exception to this rule. A meeting was organized at which all teachers and students had to be present without fail, or face expulsion. The speaker was Samarin, head of the Department of Foreign Literature. He quoted word for word everything that had appeared in the published texts. He spoke in a cold, officious tone, and, of course, in this way hoped to convey to the students that he was acting under coercion, and was not expressing his own point of view. After him, Professor Galperina, expert in French literature, took the floor. Her approach to the matter was different. She tried to persuade us of her sincerity, that she was saying what she truly believed. She stood up in front of the auditorium and looked us straight in the eye, saying she was surprised that in our day we could like such insipid poetry, smelling of mothballs. She tried to speak very frankly, very spontaneously—like an older sister. However, her words elicited more disgust than Samarin's; though in the near future, he would behave unspeakably badly as well. He stigmatized his colleagues in the department, calling them "rootless Cosmopolitans," though he told me and others in confidence that he was a true member of the Russian intelligentsia, and he wrote a report claiming that the course in seventeenth century literature taught by his colleague Professor Pinsky was saturated with an obvious anti-Soviet spirit.

This reflects one of the most catastrophic aspects of our system: it deformed the personality of every human being. Life was so difficult, so littered with pitfalls, danger was so ubiquitous, so palpable, that our worst traits became most pronounced. A person like Samarin, who in a normal society would not have caused any mischief or done any evil, became a true scoundrel in the circumstances and atmosphere that reigned at the beginning of the 1950s. Remaining a decent, upright human being required heroic courage. Yet all cowardice has its limits. Under Brezhnev, Samarin, this secret admirer of German expressionism and a lover of Rilke, became one of the most cynical conservatives.

To my shame, I must admit that I needed time to learn not to raise my hand along with others. At that same meeting of the Department of Philology, when we were supposed to vote to censure Akhmatova and Zoshchenko, I knew very well that I would not have the moral strength to abstain from voting in front of the entire auditorium, which was prepared to trample them in the dust. At the same time, I was unable to vote like the rest. It was a terrible torment for me. Finally, I decided to leave the auditorium before the vote was taken; but before that I tried to convince the people sitting around me that I had a terrible migraine. Even this faint-hearted act cost me a great deal of effort—so fearful was I to leave the auditorium.

We were not mistaken in our premonitions. The struggle against "alien influences" spread through all spheres of intellectual life: in literature, film, theater, even music. Dmitry Shostakovich, whom the Soviet authorities had lauded, they now attacked. He was suddenly discovered to write cacophony, "muddle rather than music." All the papers ground him into the dirt with great alacrity. I was later told that Shostakovich, a courageous person who had often lent a hand to others, who had written Stalin with a request or plea, was paralyzed with fear. He was afraid that any day he would be arrested; he sank into a deep depression and went silent.

In the summer of 1947 a crusade against Weisman-Morganists began, and Russian genetics was nearly obliterated.

Now, after so many years, I have no doubt whatsoever that if one were to throw out the ideological decor, what these witch-hunts always came down to was a struggle between talent and mediocrity. Throughout those years, it was the least gifted poets, the mediocre directors, and the commonplace writers who took the side of the authorities. They were desperate to hang on to their privileges and their cushy jobs, and were prepared to accuse those more talented and less cautious, who had the temerity to deviate from the reigning norms and expectations in art.

35

A NEW WAVE OF ARRESTS AND SEARCHES COMMENCED. ALMOST EVERY-one who had been arrested in 1937–1938 was condemned to a second term, and inadvertently dragged a large circle of victims down with them in their wake. People were afraid to talk on the phone; they put pillows over the receiver when they talked; apparently to no avail. Life again became hard and horrifying.

Lucy was desperate to know what had happened to her mother. The only person who might be able to give her any information was her mother's last husband, who still lived in their old apartment. Lucy went to see him. He behaved suspiciously. He assured her he didn't know anything. He had not received any word from her mother, who had disappeared without a trace. He had remarried, and didn't want to hear from her or her mother again. Still, he suggested that Lucy leave her address with him, just in case. Three days later, someone knocked on our door on Kalyaevka. Two policemen served Lucy with an order to leave Moscow within twenty-four hours. The informer turned out to be none other than her mother's former husband, the same one who had informed on her ten years before in order to confiscate her room from her—a very common practice in those days.

Lucy left Moscow, but could find work only in Siberia. A year later, her friends managed to secure her a permit as a student in a small town some 200 miles from Moscow.

Then the cosmopolitanism campaign began in earnest. It began fairly innocently, as a purely local phenomenon in theater criticism, with an exposé of pseudonyms. Several theater critics, Jewish by ex-traction, were in the habit of signing their articles with Russian names. Then several articles came out which insisted that people must sign their real names and not resort to pseudonyms. It was said that these Jewish critics who were concealing their identities under pseudonyms were spreading the wrong kind of dramaturgy, and that such remarkable playwrights as Safronov and Surov were being neglected and should be given the "green light"—an allusion to the title of one of Surov plays.

The artistic level of these plays is unimaginable today. They were such rubbish, such piffle . . . They went something like this: "You, Comrade Stakhanov, are a remarkable worker. We work even better, so let's have a competition." That was the entire content of the play. A good character argued with an even better one, and all for the good of the homeland. Several critics, including Kostya Rudnitsky, Yakov Varshavsky, Alpers, Boyadzhiev (three Jews and one Armenian) allowed themselves to ironize about such a serious theme. The reaction was instantaneous. These dramatists, pulling all the levers they had at their disposal in the Central Committee and drawing on the general mood of the times, went over into counterattack.

The word "Jew" was never written or uttered. A euphemism was invented: "Rootless Cosmopolitan." Everyone knew what it meant, though. Again, indignant readers demanded that measures be taken against these scoundrels, who had forgotten that they "eat Russian lard," as Sergey Mikhalkov wrote in his fable. At the GITIS, Boyadzhiev and Alpers, whose students adored them, were forced to repent publicly. Several of the most gifted students stood up one after another and demanded that the professors that they had admired only the day before be barred from teaching. Later, during the Thaw, many of these students became liberal critics who supported the new theater of the 1960s, Yury Lyubimov's Sovremmenik.

It was a Kafkaesque world. Unequivocally. The Kafkaesque nature of our world, it seems to me, is beautifully illustrated by two cases. The first is that of Kostya Rudnitsky, one of the most persecuted critics of that time. To make a living he agreed to write articles condemning himself and his "rootless" colleagues under a pseudonym. The second concerns the "Cosmopolitan" critic Yakov Varshavsky. During the Thaw at a session of the Writer's Union, he revealed he was the author of one of the plays of that very Surov, one of those who inspired the campaign against "Cosmopolitans." Varshavsky made public the rough drafts and letters that Surov had written him. But the governing board of the Union of Writers (and, naturally, there were many reactionaries on it) was not convinced.

Then Varshavsky asked Surov where he got the names of his characters. Surov answered, "I made them up." Varshavsky placed one more piece of paper in front of them. This was a list of residents of the house in which Varshavsky lived; all the names corresponded to the names of the characters in "Surov's" play.

Gradually, the movement against theater critics gathered steam, and spread to other spheres. It became clear that this was turning into a large-scale campaign—open anti-Semitism was gripping the country.

In 1947, Sima was fired from the high school where he taught acting. This was a Moscow high school that specialized in theater arts. Sima was staging *The Snow Maiden* there, and judging by what his students (who loved him) said, it was a very interesting production. When he was fired, the reason that was given was that he, Semyon Lungin, was incapable of teaching his students "sonorous Russian poetry."

Then he was fired from the Stanislavsky Theater, as well. They offered to let him remain as a stage hand. He accepted. He didn't tell me that he was fired; he didn't want to alarm and disappoint me. We had no money, but since at that time, just as now, salaries were delayed for months on end, this didn't raise suspicions in me. I had also decided for myself not to be dependent on Sima for money. If there wasn't enough, I should look for a source of income myself, or try to sell something or borrow money. In other words, I considered it to be my problem, and rightfully so. Sima could not have withstood this pressure; and I did not wish to burden him.

We sold all the furniture in the apartment—all that massive, imposing furniture: the dining room furniture, then the bedroom furniture, made from Karelian birch. At that time in Moscow, there were buy-ups, when they would come and take everything away in bulk. After that, we—or, rather, I—started taking things to the pawnshop. Everything that had the least bit of value . . . I had fifteen or twenty receipts from the pawnshop at one time. I was afraid I would get them mixed up. I would borrow money from one person, redeem something, then pawn it again. This was the way we lived for many years. Nevertheless, from the first day of our lives together we lived happily. All these material difficulties meant little. Maybe it was because we were young. Maybe it was Sima's wonderful gift of creating from his imagination a life that resembled theater. We were somehow always on stage, always "acting." I really don't know how to describe it—there was a festive atmosphere that kept us going, that pulled us along. We experienced many joys, simply by virtue of being together. That is what I would say—in spite of very trying material and moral circumstances, we never had the feeling that life was hard or unpleasant for us. We lived joyfully. And well. And gladly. To the fullest.

36

DURING THE WAR A SO-CALLED JEWISH ANTIFASCIST COMMITTEE WAS created per Stalin's initiative. It united well-known Jewish scholars and writers with the goal of strengthening ties with the international community, in particular with American Jews, who could offer the Soviet Union financial support for the war effort. One of the most active members of this committee was Solomon Mikhoels, artistic director of the Moscow Jewish Theater and one of our greatest actors. It was said that on more than one occasion Stalin invited him to play King Lear for him, and always praised him for his performance. Mikhoels was sent to the US to raise funds, a task he carried out very successfully.

Just before the New Year, in December of 1947, several dozen writers and other representatives of the intelligentsia, primarily members of the Jewish Antifascist Committee and people close to Mikhoels, were arrested. Three weeks later the papers announced that Mikhoels had been hit by a car in Minsk and died. No one I knew believed this. The truth came out only years later. Mikhoels was killed by the KGB on Stalin's orders. The body was discovered at dawn; his skull had been crushed by a car. Svetlana Allilueva, Stalin's daughter, relates in her memoirs that she heard her father talking over the phone about a murder, and ordering that the death be made to look like an accident.

The body was transported back to Moscow. The funeral, which was nearly a state-level ceremony, was held at Mikhoels's theater near the Nikitsky Gates.

For a long time, since the disclosure of the pseudonyms, the Jewish Theater had barely been able to function. Although the regular public was afraid to go to their performances, a handful of loyal theatergoers could be counted on to attend. The actors continued to perform for just a handful of people in the audience. Then the Jewish Theater was closed, and the building was given to the Stanislavsky

Theater, which had been housed in a basement on Kirov Street. In other words, the theater where Sima had worked as a director. He was entrusted with the task of examining the hall to determine whether the stage was appropriate for the production of a play by Sheridan, which was already in the works. Sima was happy: finally, his theater would have a real stage. He told me how he entered the darkened vestibule, and an old woman—the concierge, who was sitting in a corner—said without being prompted: "He's in there, go on up." Sima went through the dim corridor into the hall without running into anyone, and headed toward the stage. Only then, he said, did the terrible implications of his assignment become clear to him. The death of a theater is like the death of a person. With an aching heart, feeling like a traitor, he turned away and started down the aisle toward the exit. Suddenly, a voice called out to him, "Who's there? Please step in." He saw a strip of light underneath a closed door. Sima nudged it open and found himself in a spacious office. At the far end sat Mikhoels behind his desk, resting his powerful head on his palm. Sima mumbled something about the purpose of his visit as he approached, saying that it was only a matter of a few performances . . . Mikhoels pretended he believed him; but he couldn't conceal an ironic grin, and he began speaking to Sima in Yiddish. Sima grew embarrassed and confessed he didn't know the language. Mikhoels said, in Russian, "You should be ashamed, young man. It's a shame not to know your native tongue." Then he asked what play they intended to perform, waved his hand wearily in farewell, and said, "Zei gesund"—that is, "be healthy," in Yiddish.

Now, in front of that theater, a crowd of people gathered to pay their last respects to Mikhoels. There were many of us. People were terribly shaken by this mysterious and terrible death. Sima, who stood near the open casket, told me that Mikhoels's forehead was completely shattered and resembled a mosaic covered with a layer of makeup. It was snowing, and an old man was playing the violin on the roof of the building opposite. We couldn't hear him. I watched how the wind blew through his gray hair, how he wielded the bow, but the music didn't reach us down below.

As for the other members of the Antifascist Committee, none of those who were arrested survived. Among them were elderly men and women, who were executed—Peretz Markish, David Bergelson, Itzik Feffer, Leib Kvitko. The others died in prison, on a hunger strike. This is how Elka's father, Isaak Nusinov, died. During the investigation he behaved very courageously, and kept repeating to the investigator who was cross-examining him, "I was a Communist long before you were even born."

The only member of the board of the Jewish Antifascist Committee who was not arrested was Ilya Ehrenburg. And people, naturally, wondered why.

I was not personally acquainted with Ehrenburg, though I often saw him and heard him speak at writers' meetings. But his personality, and to an even greater degree, his career, was so typical for certain members of the intelligentsia that I felt I knew him well. He was a talented man, well educated, very smart; and,

nevertheless, he was unable to choose his own path. Most likely he was motivated by an instinct of self-preservation. But that wasn't all. There was also the need, without doubt sincere, to participate in what seemed to him to be, in spite of everything, a great historical moment. He preferred to accept the rules of the game completely, to play it safe. The decision he made, once and for all, to be agreeable to everything, to resign himself to everything, led him, as it did many others, from self-deception and falsehood to baseness, and did not deliver him from fear.

Sima and I, as well as the majority of our friends, judged him severely. We couldn't understand how the author of *Julio Jurenito*—a book full of irony, written in the 1920s (which has never been reissued, by the way)—a person in love with Paris, an admirer of impressionism and abstract art, a cosmopolitan in the truest sense of the word—how could he not only accommodate himself to

Stalin's regime, but also serve it? How could he write such an obse-quious novel as *Without Pausing for Breath* in the early 1930s? A book as trivial as *The Fall of Paris* after the war? Of course, we ad-mired his eyewitness reports on the Spanish Civil War in *Izvestia*; and, even more, the reports he wrote from the battlefront in the Second World War. These articles made him extremely popular. Soldiers in the trenches passed them eagerly back and forth, and even when paper was scarce would never have considered using a page of Ehrenburg to roll a cigarette. It was possible to trade Ehren-burg for bread, however. One of his most famous articles, published not long before the end of the war, was called "Kill a German"—an incitement to kill any and every German, no matter who, no matter where. Considering that we were already very close to victory, I thought it was obscene.

After the war, he enjoyed great renown. Perhaps this is what saved him during the campaign against cosmopolitanism. He wasn't some unknown critic or the author of books in Yiddish, but a folk hero. Stalin skillfully used Ehrenburg's old ties with the West. When he al-lowed him to go to Paris, he knew very well that Ehrenburg, like Gorky before him, would bear witness to the worthiness of the regime.

The same Ehrenburg, however, tried to publish *The Black Book*, which he compiled together with Vasily Grossman. This was a memoir of the sufferings of the Jewish people during the Nazi oc-cupation. This subject was absolutely forbidden. It simply didn't exist. When I saw Ehrenburg at meetings in the final years of his life, I understood that despite all the ambiguities of his life and ac-tions, he was one of the truly significant witnesses of the century, someone who embodied the continuity of Russian culture. *People, Years, Life* is proof of this. He published these memoirs in *Novy Mir* under difficult circumstances and grappling with censorship. With this work Ehrenburg went some way toward restoring our memory to us, though he didn't tell the whole truth. We must also not un-derestimate the role he played during the Thaw. In fact, the very term originated with him. Even when it seemed that he was home safe, that he was high in the saddle, he was never free of fear and anxiety. Until the moment of Stalin's death, he expected the knock on the door in the middle of the night.

37

I WAS PREGNANT WITH PAVEL, OUR OLDEST SON. MY BELLY WAS ALREADY huge. One day I came home and heard Sima's voice, and another voice that was unfamiliar to me, coming from the kitchen. I heard mention of "Soviet authorities" and "cosmopolitanism" . . . What's going on? I thought. You can hear them on the stairs, outside the apartment! And who is that person? I looked in and saw a youthful looking stranger in a checked shirt, unbuttoned down to his navel, sitting there. I called Sima into the hallway and said, "Are you mad? What do you think you're doing? How can you talk like that to a stranger? It's the first time he's ever been to our house, and it's just preposterous . . . Have you been drinking?" They were, indeed, a little bit in their cups. There was a bottle on the table; but it was obviously not the first. Sima said, "It's all right. Come into the kitchen and join us. He's one of us." I sat down with them, and only then realized with surprise what a wonderful, noble face he had. It was a face from another era. I had no idea at the time how truly he did hark back to another time . . .

This was how Vic came into our lives. Viktor Nekrasov, the writer.

He arrived suddenly, like misfortune. His play was being read in the Stanislavsky Theater. Sima, who, as a stagehand, had no real authority there, had nevertheless been invited to the reading, spoke out against the play, and used an expression for which Vic could never forgive him for the rest of his life. Sima said, "You peer at life through a keyhole." Long afterward, at the slightest provocation, Vic would say, "So, Lungin, do you still think I peer through a keyhole, eh? Do you?"

I don't know whether Sima was right or not. I know that the play had a hard time of it. It languished in the MKhAT for a year. It was reworked ten times. So maybe it really wasn't very good. I never read it.

The day after the reading, the artistic director of the theater called Sima in and said, "Mr. Flyagin (a top official, head of the district cultural board) will stage Mr. Nekrasov's play, and you can be his assistant. Of course, you won't be credited for it. It's up to you whether you want to take on the job. You'll still have to work as a stagehand. Keep working on the scenery, but, if you feel like it, you can try your hand at the play. You'll have to revise the script—here you are." Sima wanted so desperately to do some real work in the theater that he accepted. He was very embarrassed, however. He wrote a postcard to Kiev: *Dear Mr. Nekrasov, I have been given the task of working on your play. Please let me know if you can come to Moscow.* He received a reply a few days later. In large handwriting with distinctive, rounded letters, Vic wrote: *Dear Mr. Lungin, I received your postcard from such-and-such a date, I will come.*

I have to say that until that moment, neither Sima nor I had read *In the Trenches of Stalingrad*, which had been published in *Znamya*. We didn't know what kind of writer he was, what sort of person he was. Sima was dissatisfied with himself for agreeing to take on the play. It seemed unprincipled: he was against the play, and now he was going to stage it. I was afraid, and asked everyone: "Who is this Nekrasov fellow?" And Lev Bezymensky was the first to tell me: "Oh, he's a remarkable writer! He's written something akin to Remarque's *Three Comrades*." This was the first assessment of *Trenches* I would hear.

And so, Vic and Sima met at the appointed day and time. I came in at the end of this meeting—and mistook Vic for a provocateur. Free and easy behavior in a person was always considered suspect in our world. And Vic not only thought freely, he was free in his bearing and manner, in his ways of expression—in everything. He was simply who he was. He didn't try to play any role, he only said what he wanted to say, and did what he wanted to do. We couldn't allow ourselves the luxury of being ourselves. Psychologically, we were all slaves. We were resigned to our subordination, to fear, to falsehood. He did not reconcile himself to it. There was no ideology or politics behind this stance. It was simply not in his nature to be submissive. In this world where we were taught to accommodate ourselves to the system from kindergarten, Vic was a rare bird.

Our friendship lasted until the day of his death. He became like a brother to us. When he was in Moscow, he always lived with us, either alone or with his mother. Or he lived at home in Kiev, with his mother. He would spend months at a time with us. We almost always spent our summer vacations together.

The play was not a success, and Sima and Vic didn't know how to tell his mother in Kiev. They finally went to the post office and sent a cable, saying: *PLAY WAS A SUCCESS*. This became a private joke in our home: whenever something failed or fell through, but we had to pretend otherwise, we said: the play was a success.

38

By that time, we had sold everything we could sell. We lived in a completely empty apartment. We had a table and chairs, and we slept on mattresses on the floor.

I remember a certain day—it was the 4th of May. Sima and I were walking down the Arbat with Elka. The entire length of the Arbat was covered with posters announcing a production of *Green Street*.

After the arrest of his father, Elka had been kicked out of the institute where he had been working. He was unemployed, and Sima had no work, either. We had no idea what to do next. My salary could not support us both. I told them, "Why don't you try to write a play together?" Before the war Sima and Elka had written not just one, but two or three plays in collaboration. One of them—I remember the name, it was *The Mountaineer's Rope*—was even accepted for production by the university theater. So I said to them, "You could write a completely innocent, benign play, but then on a different level, so that it was written in colloquial language, with some humor, a few jokes. So it would be entertaining to watch. Think about it. Try it. There's nothing else to do, anyway."

On the 5th of May Elka woke us up at nine in the morning with a knock on the door. He had come up with an idea for a plot. The play would be called *My Patent*. It would be about two research laboratories that were working on the same thing and so began to compete with each other. The play was written in record time. The result was a lighthearted, sweet, very amusing play that Sima took to the Stanislavsky Theater. And, wonder of wonders, it was accepted. The theater, naturally, was on the lookout for just such an uncontroversial piece. Our friend Boris Levinson, a wonderful actor in the Stanislavsky Theater, who had starred in *Griboedov* and received wide acclaim, was appointed director. A gifted young actress by the name of Klavdia Shinkina, who had just joined the troupe, was given the role of the female protagonist.

My Patent ran for two weeks. Then the literary manager of the Stanislavsky visited us at home and said, "I can't help you, but I can hinder you. Give me some money. If you don't, I'll see to it that your play is banned." Sima and Elka refused, out of principle. Outraged, they sent him packing. He was later appointed head of the District Board of Theaters, a post he held for many years. One week after his visit to us a scathing article appeared, and the play was banned for slander of the Soviet intelligentsia, a subject the play had treated in too offhand and ironic a manner. Nevertheless, this was a deciding moment in terms of their professional careers.

39

Anti-Semitism had existed before the war, of course. It flared up as spats in communal kitchens; or some drunk on the street might make a slur. Anti-Semitism was alive, but it remained latent. Officially, I want to stress, it was an offense punishable by law, as a remnant of the old order incompatible with the ideas of Leninism. It grew unchecked in the back alleys and courtyards, however. When he was a boy, Sima once found himself in just such a back alley. He and his buddies usually didn't venture there, because it was the territory of a gang of older boys. The older boys didn't go to school, and they didn't work; and they all had nicknames: Hunchback, Snake, Wolf. One day, a ball rolled into their territory, and Sima had to cross the border. The kids surrounded him and yanked down his pants to see whether he was circumcised. So from the age of twelve he started to learn boxing. A few months later he went back to that alley to punch Hunchback's lights out.

It goes without saying that by the end of the 1940s, after the exultant unmasking of the Cosmopolitans, I realized that this concerned me, as well—but my realization remained on an intellectual level, rather than an emotional one. Before the repressions and persecutions, I had no sense of myself as Jewish. Sima had always said that he had a pintele Yid inside of him—a little drop of Jewishness, a "Jewish spark." Most likely he had seen something of this somewhere, in other families. His family was not religious.

In any case, I can say that when Sima sang Jewish songs—without knowing any Yiddish, but imitating the melodies and sounds—old Jewish men, among them Dezik Samoilov's father, Samuil, would sob. Samuil Abramovich always said, "It's probably an accent from some little village somewhere. I can't quite make out all the words, but I can get the gist of the song." He really believed it was a Yiddish dialect; in fact, it was pure imitation of Yiddish sounds and prosody. But Sima sang with such heartfelt sincerity that everyone cried. I think this is proof that somehow, a Jewish sensibility, Jewish poetry, was alive in him.

This was a hundred percent alien to me. It simply didn't exist. I had no idea what ethnicity I was, what "nation" of people I belonged to. I was a typical product of true cosmopolitanism. How could it have been otherwise? I had lived in Germany, had been in Palestine twice, had lived in France. My family kept no "traditions." But when the persecutions started . . . It arises unbidden when you are under attack. When I saw that being Jewish was something to be ashamed of, I began saying out loud that I was Jewish; it would have been degrading to behave otherwise.

I think these feelings of ethnicity, of "nationality" in the Russian sense of the term, were alien to the majority of young people of my generation. They had been suppressed, dampened down, during the Soviet era. Nowadays, when our families immigrate to America, for example, our children have to accept some sort of religious affiliation. Everyone claims one; you have to attach yourself to something. There was nothing like that here. It simply didn't exist. The place of religion was occupied by the great Communist Idea. Everything else was kept under wraps, muffled up, stored away, though it did live on in the depths of some people's hearts.

My Jewishness dated precisely from that moment. Based on my own experience, I would conclude that a Jew feels his Jewishness as soon as he is persecuted and violated. People say, however, that the generation of Jews that is coming of age in Israel today is very different, that they don't at all resemble the Jews of the shtetl. They are good looking, tall, strong, well built. They are a different people, with a sense of pride and self-worth. They feel Jewish under any circumstances. Here it was otherwise. There were no grounds for it, no opportunities for expressing it, perhaps. Aleksei Kapler, who was older than me by twenty years, told me that when he was in France for the first time, he was required to fill out a form in some hotels (the less expensive ones) that asked who you were, where you were from, etc. On the line about "nationality," he wrote "Jew." And the clerk asked, "Is monsieur from Israel?" There, nationality does not mean ethnicity; Jewishness is not a nationality. Nationality refers to the country you are from.

Meanwhile, children from Jewish families began to experience ever greater difficulties getting admitted to universities. It wasn't written down anywhere, it wasn't an official policy, but everyone knew about it. A friend of mine who was a young teacher in the mathematics department at Moscow State University worked on the admissions board. The dean summoned him and gave instructions (out of earshot of anyone else, naturally) to give all Jews poor marks, no matter how they performed on their exams. He refused to carry this out, but thousands of others agreed without a murmur.

At the dacha of my uncle, the academic Alexander Frumkin, we would meet Nikolai Semionov, a Nobel Prize winner in Chemistry, nearly every Sunday. One day we were all taking a walk together, and I told this story, expressing my indignation about it. To my astonishment, this person—highly educated and intelligent, a charming man whom I loved very much—said, "Lilya, it's very sad, but they're right. This hindrance is justified. The Jewish mind is too agile and capable of mastering anything it touches. A Russian can never compete with a Jew on the exams. Nevertheless, Jews lag behind Russians significantly in their creative powers. If Russians are not given preferential treatment, the Jews will become dominant in science, which in the end will only impoverish it."

On January 13, 1953, I showed up to teach my usual seminar at VOKS. Before class I had to go to the administrative office to pick up the class list so I could take roll. As soon as I entered, a secretary greeted me, saying, "I never would have expected it from your people! They have turned out to be regular killers." I was dumbfounded.

"What are you talking about?" I said.

"Here, read the paper."

Citing a report from TASS, the newspaper article said that a group of doctors—of the nine named, six were Jewish—were involved in a plot, whereby instead of treating their patients they poisoned them, on the orders of a foreign intelligence agency for which they worked. The deaths of both Zhdanov and Gorky were laid at the door of these malefactors.

The person who exposed these "killers in white coats" was a certain Lidia Timashuk. She worked as a radiologist in the Kremlin Hospital, and moonlighted as a secret agent of the KGB. They entrusted

her with the noble task of unmasking her colleagues. She wrote de-
nunciations to Stalin, and received the Order of Lenin for it. After
Stalin's death, she was deprived of it, however. One of the doctors,
Vovsi, was Mikhoels's brother. In the TASS report, he was referred to
as a "well-known bourgeois nationalist." Thus, Mikhoels brought Dr.
Vovsi orders from the Jewish-American organization JOINT.

I felt weak in the knees. Still, I appeared at my seminar and
taught as usual. Yet all through those four hours of class, it seemed
to me that my students, whom I had always gotten along with very
well, were staring at me. I immediately felt estranged.

After the "killers in white coats" incident, the campaign against
Jews was carried out on a different scale. We had not only lost the
right to work, but were exiled from the life that up until then had
been ours.

The worst thing was that people believed it, and were afraid to
go to the Jewish doctors who had not yet been fired.

There was an academician by the name of Mintz who was a
court specialist in the history of the Party. I found out from his
daughter that he was writing a letter to Stalin. In this letter, which
the most prominent Jews were supposed to endorse and sign, they
admitted to crimes perpetrated by their fellows against the Russian
people and socialism, and requested permission to expiate these
crimes. Another acquaintance of mine, the journalist Semyon
Berkin, told me he was writing an article from Stalingrad about
how the workers in a tractor factory voted unanimously on a resolution for the universal deportation of the Jews. Leon Agranovich
and Semyon Listov, friends of ours who were playwrights, came
over to our house for dinner one day and told us they had written
a play for the Soviet Army Theater, which had been received enthu-
siastically. But when the literary manager went to the artistic director of the theater to ask what kind of honorarium they should
receive (it was usually from fifteen to twenty-five thousand rubles),
the director—they called him General Pasha—replied, "Pay them
three thousand. That should suffice." The literary manager was surprised, but the "general" explained, "Fifteen hundred per month for
each of them is plenty. Then they're going to put them into cattle
cars and ship them off to Siberia anyway."

Then we got more evidence of what awaited us. Dodik Levitt was employed in Sima's theater as the head of the production unit. During the war he had worked in a song-and-dance ensemble of the Ministry of Internal Affairs. He had performed at the battlefront, and now he was continuing to organize performances of the actors' brigades of the military. He told Sima that he had recently gone on tour to Eastern Siberia, into the back of beyond—with Yury Lyubimov, by the way, who performed as an actor on these tours. At a certain moment, the pilot of the small plane they were flying in said, "Take a look over here. Can you see what that is down there?" He pointed out some large barracks, built in the shape of a letter T. Every eight or ten yards there was another row of these barracks. He said, "Those have been built for you." Dodik Levitt was Jewish, of course. "What do you mean, for 'us'?" "That's where they're going to deport you. There is already a government resolution."

Jews were expelled from the Central Committee, from the Moscow City Council, from the Municipal Committee and District Committees, from the State Security organizations, the Ministries, from the newspapers, the research institutes, and universities.

I'll never forget how the French Communist newspaper *L'humanité* published an article that was signed by André Stil, the editor-in-chief. I must admit, to my shame, that he was the first writer Noam Naumov and I managed to translate and publish in *Novy Mir*. He published a little article in the paper with the title "Bravo, Comrade!" which celebrated the vigilance of the Russian Party members who had exposed the "killer doctors."

One day Sima went to our house manager for some sort of official paper, and sitting there he found some clerk. She said, in a friendly manner, though not without spite, "Do you see these lists? They're forcing us to stay here after hours and compile them, one after another, on and on and on . . . These are your lists." Sima said, "What do you mean 'our' lists?" "They're going to deport you. These lists say who's going where, which train station they're taking you to."

People were already talking about how exactly the deportation of Jews would commence. Stalin would address the public and say, "In order to save Jews from the justified rage of the Russian people, they must be removed from the large cities and towns where they come into contact with others. They must be isolated; and this humanitarian act will be carried out to save the Jews." People said that the train stations had already been designated; the trains had been made available; when, at what time, and which buses would be used had been decided; and what, and how much, people were allowed to take with them (not more than 15 kilos per person) had been determined. Conversations kept coming back to the same subject, and living like this was very difficult. During this period, by the way, people started immigrating to Israel. These departures were extremely turbulent emotionally and gave rise to great conflict; but people chose to leave nevertheless. Everyone was asking the same question: is that the only way out, our only means of survival? Surely the authorities would try to prevent this exodus, to nip it in the bud. This matter was discussed in every Jewish home. It hung like a black cloud over the city.

I never doubted for a minute—indeed, everyone who lived through those times realized it—that if Stalin had not died, the Jews would have been deported. The prospect was just as real as the deportation of the Kabardians, and Ossetians, the Crimean Tatars, the Turks, Bulgarians, Greeks, and the Volga Germans. You know, of course, how they organized those deportations? They moved people out in the space of twenty-four hours. We are poor organizers, and yet at such moments we demonstrate true organizational genius. In the Caucasus I was told how they deported the Balkars. It was always the same scenario. When night fell, or at dawn, armed soldiers surrounded the area, gave people two hours to pack their belongings, brought the necessary number of trucks, and drove the people to the railroad sidings, where the cattle cars were already waiting. Brilliant organization. This is precisely how the deportation of Jews from Moscow and Leningrad would have occurred. I don't doubt it, even for a minute.

40

Now I will talk about the death of Stalin.

The headlines all screamed "He's Ill, He's Ill," "Comrade Stalin is unconscious," and so forth. The country stopped in its tracks. On the subway, on buses, in cafeterias, people barely spoke above a whisper, hardly looking at one another. The churches were overflowing: people prayed for his recovery.

But he did die. I have to say that the horror and grief of the common folk was immeasurable. Things were not going all that well in country. Life was difficult and frightening. All the same, not only among the common people, but among the intelligentsia, everyone was inconsolable. It had seemed (such naïve notions abounded) that Stalin was a buffer. That the others—Beria and his ilk—were far worse, and that only Stalin kept them in check.

Trains arrived, people were even riding on the roofs to get to Moscow. There was a sense of impending disaster of cosmic proportions. It seemed that history itself had stopped.

The meetings held in the Writer's Union were absolutely grotesque. People stood up to speak and broke down in tears, standing on the podium and sobbing, unable to utter a word, so immense was their grief. Some famous women critics took the floor and said, "We will survive, but what about our children? How will they live without him?" Then, in a wild, hysterical outburst of weeping, they left the podium.

I believe this was some sort of mass hypnosis. That people somehow infected each other with it. Everyone wanted to be able to see him. This mad, strange desire—to see him in his coffin—gripped the masses.

I was happy he had died. Sima shared this feeling with me. Nevertheless, we also decided to go to see him. I am ashamed to have to admit this. I truly am. Although Nanny Motya—a very important person who had appeared in our lives at around that time, a simple country woman, about whom I will say more presently—thought it was pure insanity and said with contempt, "Why are you so upset? A cur deserves a cur's death," we had the need to see this story out till the very end.

The crowd started by our gate. It wasn't too thick at that point, and it was possible to make one's way through and join it. We went as far as the Samoteka. There the road goes downhill and forms a sort of basin. It was cold. Above the Samoteka hung a cloud. It didn't seem to be raining, and it looked very strange. "What is that thing?" asked Sima. Somebody standing next to us in the crowd said, "Don't you know? The people down there are all pressing up against each other, they're sweating. It's steam." Indeed, when we looked more closely we could see that the human mass in the hollow of the Samoteka was moving forward a step, then backward a step, rhythmically, as though they were doing some mystical dance. They were shifting their feet in place, and pressing against each other. A veil of steam was rising up from them into the sky. At that point Sima said, "Nope, no way, we're not going down there." So we struggled back the way we had come and arrived home two or three hours later. Everyone knows the outcome: more than 400 people were crushed to death on that day. In addition to the millions Stalin killed during his lifetime, he had to drag so many people behind him after he died. There was, without doubt, something demonic about Stalin. That's why he always worked at night, and forced everyone around him to stay awake. No one dared leave his post—he could be called at any moment. His windows in the Kremlin were always illuminated, and the people thought, Our father never sleeps. He's working, he's always awake. Our father is taking care of us . . .

41

Isaak Pyatigorsky, Vic Nekrasov's dearest friend, was living with us. He was a simple Kievan engineer, a charming man with an exceptionally kindhearted soul. I remember once that Sima and I had gone to Leningrad on some errand, and we returned home on the 4th of April on the Red Arrow train. Isaak opened the door for us, and stood there silently in his pajamas, waving a newspaper in his hand.

The paper said that all the accusations against the "killer doctors" were unfounded. That there had been some mistake. We were overcome by a feeling of happiness I can't describe, a sense that we had been delivered from madness. It was a moment of pure joy.

One might justly consider this to be the beginning of the Thaw. It wasn't a real Thaw yet, but we were on the verge of it.

Of course, many people continued to eulogize Stalin. There were many—writers, artists—who said that his image should be exalted in film, in theater, and in visual art. Konstantin Simonov claimed that until the end of the century Stalin must remain the sole subject of inspiration. Nevertheless, within a matter of weeks and months, the first articles of a different order began to appear. But the most important thing was that people began to return. Very soon, people started to be released from the camps. Now and again you would hear that so-and-so had returned. People gathered around them to hear their stories, people talked about them, and they told each other what they had said. Somehow, a corner of the veil, which covered all the terrible dark things that had happened, was lifted. The wave of returnees grew and grew, and this, of course, created a very different climate in society. There was suddenly a great hope for something—no one knew what exactly, but in any event, something different. The fear that was linked with the death of Stalin, when we thought that things would grow even worse, dissipated very soon. Somehow, because people had started to return, there arose a certainty that it would not get worse. Whatever happened, it would not be worse. Perhaps it might even be better.

Now, instead of one, there were four masters: Malenkov, Khrushchev, Beria, and Molotov. Malenkov immediately became popular among kolkhoz workers because he relieved some of their burdens and lowered taxes. Everywhere people spoke of him as a savior: when they were waiting in line, at the market, on the commuter trains. His photograph hung in all the peasant huts next to the icons. I will never forget a story my friend Vladimir Tendryakov told me. Very few remember him nowadays, but he was a wonderful writer, one of the best prose writers of the 1960s, and one of those who wrote

most honestly and truthfully about village life and the countryside, which was very important at the time. He had gone to visit his mother in his native village. Somewhere in the north, about thirty miles from the nearest railroad. No one met him at the station, and he had to spend the night in a house nearby. There was a lad there who was about nine or ten years old. Vladimir offered him a lump of sugar. The boy didn't take it: he thought it was chalk. He had never seen a lump of sugar in his life.

Motya's sister Polka, who was unable to give the kolkhoz as much butter, milk, and eggs as they demanded from her, came twice a year to Moscow to stock up on it and then hand it over to the kolkhoz. Since she had no money, I went to the stores with her, and together we stood in several lines at a time to buy the necessary twenty kilograms of butter. (They would only allow two kilograms of butter per person.) With those buckets of butter and eggs, and with bags of millet, she would return in triumph to her kolkhoz.

The commuter trains were always packed with thousands of such women, loaded down with sacks and returning home to their villages. I remember once in the commuter train a simple fellow of about twenty-two or twenty-three years old, said to me suddenly, "Do you know what they're carrying? Bread! Look at those bags—they're bringing crackers and pretzels from the capital to the village . . . Russia is doomed!"

The first steps of the new government inspired a cautious hope, however. In the summer of 1953, Sima was with the Stanislavsky Theater in Odessa. I went to see him, taking Pavel, who was four years old, with me. One day we walked Sima to his rehearsal through the main alley of a park by the sea. Along either side stood huge portraits of the members of the Politburo. Suddenly we heard a strange sound. We walked on a ways, and saw something completely improbable: four men with axes were destroying the portrait of Beria. Sima's colleague came up to us and stood there rooted to the spot, then said quietly, "Hey, it's a Fascist coup." That's how we found out about the fall of Beria.

42

AMONG THOSE WHO RETURNED—NOT FROM THE CAMPS, BUT FROM exile—was Lucy Tovalev.

She had been rehabilitated, so she was able to return to Moscow, where she lived the rest of her life. She started teaching German at the Conservatory. The students loved her. She translated books about music, the works of composers. She translated the letters of Schumann and Beethoven into Russian—and tried never to think about the past.

Professor Leonid Pinsky was among those who returned from the camps.

He had been arrested in late autumn of 1949. The night before, he, Sima and I had been walking in some Moscow park—Izmailovo, I think. For some reason he and Sima bought a quarter liter of vodka, and while they were walking, killed the bottle. We were happy, in high spirits, and we agreed to meet again in two days. He lived in a university teachers' dormitory and didn't have a tele-

phone. One day passed after the day we had agreed he would come to see us, then a second. On the third day one of his students called and said: "I went to see Professor Pinsky to pick up my paper, and his door was sealed." That was how we knew he had been arrested.

There was little news of him while he was in prison. At a certain moment, Sima and I agreed that I should try to write him. It was a new stage in my consciousness. I wrote to the camp, and during his last year there we exchanged two or three letters. Rather, we received from him only one, because they were only allowed to write one letter every three months, or something like that. I wrote him two or three times. I was very proud of having overcome my fear, the prohibition.

When he came back, he told us what we could already have supposed. There was a literary figure in Moscow, very well known, by the name of Yakov Elsberg. He was quite brilliant, known primarily for his books about Herzen, a big talker, and a born storyteller. He was not only a scholar, but also a man of the world, so to speak. Nasty rumors circulated about him. People said that he had been complicit in the arrest of Babel. Two daughters of the writer Mikhail Levidov, arrested in 1938, implored me to warn Pinsky about the danger he was in. Suddenly, Elsberg took a fancy to Pinsky. Like Pinsky, he lectured in the university and taught literary theory. After lectures he didn't leave, but waited for hours for Leonid so he could walk him home, conversing with him on the way. It was fascinating to talk to Elsberg—he had a broad spectrum of knowledge and interests. I kept saying, "Leonid, these strolls will lead to no good." To which he said, "Nonsense, I've been talking to him for almost a year. I've already told him so much that they could have put me behind bars ten times over. That's all rubbish, just fear."

Well, as it turned out, Leonid was wrong. When he came home at the beginning of 1955, he told us that it was Elsberg who had betrayed him. That Elsberg, after every conversation, apparently, had sat down at his desk and noted down in great detail what they had discussed. The materials he had gathered were quite voluminous.

While he was in transit to the camp, Leonid made the acquaintance of Yevgeny Steinberg, an orientalist, who had been not just a friend of Elsberg, like Leonid was, but like a brother to him. Steinberg and his wife adored Elsberg. When Steinberg's wife bought a shirt or a suit for her husband, she would always buy one for Elsberg, too. They spent every birthday party together, every holiday celebration. He was their best friend. One day it came out that he had also informed on Steinberg. When Steinberg was arrested, his wife naturally ran to Elsberg that very night to tell him about it. He gave her advice about where to hide manuscripts and other things. Some of them he even took home with him. For one or two months he supported and helped them in all kinds of ways—there was a daughter, as well. Steinberg, who during the course of the interrogation realized who had betrayed him, managed to write a note during his transit to the camp and throw it out of the railroad car. Some good person found it, put it in an envelope—there was an address on the letter—and sent it to his wife. The wife received this note, in which her husband revealed that Elsberg was responsible for his arrest, but at the same time asked her under no circumstances to let Elsberg know that she knew. She must continue to behave as though nothing had happened. For five long years this woman had to maintain her friendship with Elsberg and live under his patronage. I heard this story from her own lips. When Leonid returned, he took me to her house, and she, terribly agitated, told me the whole story.

When Steinberg came home, Elsberg went to see him. He brought with him a rare edition by some Eastern author—something unspeakably valuable—and a huge bouquet of roses, and said:

Белинский в борьбе с космополитизмом

Я. ЭЛЬСБЕРГ

"I've come to repent. I'm guilty. I don't deny it. All the same, I still love you."

They kicked him down the stairs.

A great deal of effort was made to take him to court on charges of slander by Steinberg and Pinsky, among others. (They had, in the meantime, been rehabilitated.) The court dismissed the case. A meeting was held at the Writer's Union, however, and Elsberg was expelled. But he was reinstated soon after.

I would like to mention something else, and it's relevant: young people of the new generation who later became well-known literary figures, such as Vadim Kozhinov, showed a great deal of sympathy toward Elsberg during this whole affair. He taught a sort of open seminar, at which the youth could speak their minds quite freely—he was a great liberal. These young people surrounded him with love and attention, and justified it by saying, "Everyone betrayed everyone back then. There's no sense in trying to assuage one's own conscience by getting even with someone else." I think this is telling, and provides an interesting insight into motivation and motives. Of course it was all barbaric. But that's how it was. I think we need to make sure it remains in people's memories.

43

THE MAIN EVENT OF THE FOLLOWING YEARS WAS KHRUSHCHEV'S speech at the Party Congress in 1956, three years after Stalin's death. It was not published, but read out in closed sessions. It was only published at the end of the 1980s. The address was intended exclusively for Party members. Nonetheless, everyone who was even slightly literate knew about it.

It dropped like an atom bomb, though much of what Nikita said people already knew. For Sima and me there was absolutely nothing new in his speech, even the hint that Stalin had killed Sergei Kirov. And all the rest of it, too, about the "cult of the personality"—we knew all of that already, of course. Yet even for us, the fact that it had been uttered out loud, officially formulated and acknowledged, changed something. For others, for those who had tried to follow the Party line, it was earth-shattering.

Alexander Fadeyev, the author of *The Rout* and *The Young Guard*, took his own life. He shot himself through the heart. Pravda reported that this was the result of mental illness associated with alcoholism. He had, indeed, taken to drink after the war, and found his drinking buddies in the margins of society—not among writers. He would spend weeks at a time with them in the slums. Nobody, however, believed the official reports. Everyone knew that Fadeyev, as first secretary of the Writer's Union, had personally signed sanctions for the arrest of his colleagues. For the Soviet system it was a matter of utmost importance that everyone be tarnished. Every leader or official had to bear his portion of responsibility, and so give written consent for the arrest of his subordinates. The rest approved of the sentence in an open vote. Fadeyev was not a cynic, however, unlike Alexei Surkov, who was willing to resort to anything to promote himself. Nor was he a dull ignoramus like Fedor Panferov, the editor-in-chief of *October*, who wrote novels that all of Moscow laughed at. At the age of sixteen, Fadeyev took part in the Civil War and loved to repeat that he was a soldier of the revolution, and that his only goal was to serve its ends. For him, as for the majority of his generation, Stalin embodied the revolutionary project. He worshipped Stalin, and repeated on many occasions that Stalin was today's Lenin. At his fiftieth birthday, he publicly swore to devote the rest of his writing to the glorification of Stalin. All the same, Fadeyev's relations with Stalin were never simple, though Stalin did invite him to dinner a few times, in the company of close friends. Stalin loved humiliating people, and Fadeyev was no exception. Zelinsky, whom I already mentioned in connection with the fate of Marina Tsvetaeva, and who was a close friend of Fadeyev's, wrote some memoirs immediately after Fadeyev's death, which, naturally, could not be published until the end of the 1980s. In the memoirs, he recounts a story that Fadeyev had told him in confidence, about how Stalin had once called him to the Kremlin, and without offering him a seat, lectured him, saying he was a worthless secretary surrounded by inveterate spies, and that he was able see them for what they were. "Well, since you're so ineffectual, Comrade Fadeyev, I'll mention them by name. Pavlenko, your good friend, is a big spy. Ehrenburg is an international spy. Don't pretend you don't know. Aleksey Tolstoy is a British spy. Why haven't you exposed them yet, Comrade Fadeyev? Go away and think about how you've behaved."

After the official announcement that Comrade Stalin was no longer a god, Fadeyev collapsed, and after the return of several writers who had gone through the GULAG, he became unrecognizable. We heard that he was terrified of meeting people whom he had sacrificed. Zelinsky writes that Fadeyev told him a week before his death: "Now we're all in deep crap. None of us will be able to write after all that has happened, not Sholokhov, not myself . . . No one from our generation."

In our own circle, Sima and I knew people who wanted to kill themselves or fell into a deep depression after Khrushchev's speech. Even my dear old friend Noam Katzman—he was a very deep thinker, but before that moment had always tried to justify and accommodate himself to the mainstream. He was also a member of the Party. He was absolutely devastated by it.

I think there were people who believed it, but pretended that they didn't, in order to get by. There were, of course, people who did not believe, who thought that it was a ploy by Khrushchev in the struggle for power. Nonetheless, it was a decisive moment that forced every person to take a position. After this, one had to choose sides; and everyone ended up on one side or another. For many people—active and committed people who wanted to live a consistent life, rather than an inconsistent or duplicitous one—it was already impossible not to play an active role in exposing and condemning the regime in order to undermine it.

44

THE FIRST HARBINGER OF THE THAW WAS THE UNPRECEDENTED DARING of articles in *Novy Mir* that called into question the sacred doctrines of Socialist Realism and loyalty to the principles of the Party in literature. One of these was an article by Vladimir Pomerantsev, "On Sincerity in Literature." The issue containing this article disappeared from the newsstands in the blink of an eye. Sima and I had a subscription to *Novy Mir*, and fifteen or so friends gathered at our house to read it aloud. Mark Shcheglov, a talented critic who died tragically young, wrote a review of Leonid Leonov's *Russian Forest* in *Novy Mir*. Leonov was one of the dinosaurs of Stalinist literature, who were, until then, inviolate and above critique. Emil Kardin claimed that the Battleship Aurora had never given its historic salvo, which, as we all knew from our history books, served as the signal for the beginning of the October Revolution of 1917.

Then the stories of Paustovsky were published; a novella by Ehrenburg, which was called *The Thaw* and lent its name to this period; and, most significant, the groundbreaking book by Vladimir Dudintsev, *Not by Bread Alone*. It was first published in the journal, then in *Roman-Gazeta* in paperback. There was no hardcover edition. All the copies were literally read to shreds. I can say unequivocally that, throughout the entire Soviet era, there had never been a phenomenon like this. Even Solzhenitsyn's works were not devoured as voraciously as this one.

The book had something very primitive, very simplistic, about it. It touched on the lives and experiences of many people. It was, in a nutshell, the story of an engineer who had thought up a way of modernizing an enterprise, thereby saving millions of rubles, but who could not break down the wall of bureaucracy. That was the story. Evidently, every third or fourth engineer had experienced something similar. Just as Nekrasov had been the first to tell the truth about the war, Dudintsev was the first to demonstrate the absurdity of our industrial system. This was why it appealed to a mass readership. It was interesting to see how a literary phenomenon and the life of the spirit generated mass interest—not simply as entertainment, but as the true cultural property of the masses. Reactionaries, especially the writers, judged the book severely. They were afraid that once people took it into their heads to write this way, it would be the end of their own exclusive reign. They organized a discussion in the Writer's Union. There was such a press of people that the equestrian police were sent. They guarded the entrances and prevented people from entering the Writer's Union building.

A new pleiad of poets emerged in those years. First and foremost was Yevgeny Yevtushenko. There was also Bella Akhmadulina, the most talented of the group; Andrei Voznesensky; the Robert Rozhdestvensky of that era, though he later retreated. For these poets it was not a question of political positions, although Yevtushenko wrote political pieces, as well. There was something very vital, very fresh, very authentic in their work. People responded to their poems with real enthusiasm. Soon people would flock to grandiose readings in which the poets performed at sports stadiums; and even then there wasn't enough room for everyone who wanted to attend.

There has never been anything like it since. Everyone yearned for a living, breathing word. I think it was a kind of nostalgia for something alive, something warm and human. The compromised literature of those years had killed people's desire to read, but the need for poetry lived on, particularly among the youth. When a living human voice suddenly burst through this artificial dead kingdom, there was intense excitement. I should also mention that the public took part during these large-scale stadium recitals. People shouted from the spectator stands, requesting one poem after another. They were not passive listeners. It was an event, a spectacular event, in which everyone present played a role. It was a remarkable phenomenon. I don't think there has ever been anything like it anywhere else in the world—when entire stadiums filled up just to hear poetry.

One day Vic brought Yevtushenko over to our house for dinner. When he arrived, we were a bit discomfited by the impression he made. He was dressed like a bird of paradise. He wore a green jacket, a red shirt, and a lilac bow-tie. Everything clashed, you felt like you needed to don sunglasses. And his attitude . . . He was very boastful, and kept talking about himself all the time. A person who was in love with himself and admired himself above all others. It was comical. He invited us to a technological institute the following evening, where he was to read his poetry. We decided to go, although I said that maybe it wasn't worth it. But we did go: Vic and Sima and I. And it was also something I'll never forget. How many facets are present in one personality! He was a completely different man. He was dressed very severely, in a dark brown suit. He recited his poems brilliantly, and selected them just as brilliantly. To say that the place was packed would be a gross understatement. People were hanging from the chandeliers. And the response . . . He was truly a mouthpiece for the people. He dragged all the political undercurrents into the light, everything he had, and he made an indelible impression, not only on the audience, but on us.

He was Janus-faced: two diametrically opposed sides coexisted in him. I think that was the way he got by in life, and it is probably still the way he lives. He was capable of remarkable things, such as "Babi Yar." One must remember that this was the first open condemnation of anti-Semitism, and it met with a great deal of opposition. He received a great deal of criticism for it, and for many other poems. At the same time, he wrote (I can't remember which poem it was) that on his left side he carried a Party membership card instead of a heart. He wrote things like that, too. I can't just brush aside that reference to a Party card. Somehow he managed to balance both things. Nonetheless, I think his role in the evolution of ideas during this period was very significant. Later, under Brezhnev, Yevtushenko's popularity started to wane, but he continued to enjoy special privileges. He was allowed to travel regularly to America, for example. In a sense, in an era that was far less cruel, he played a role similar to that of Ehrenburg in his time. He was in touch with Andropov, the then head of the KGB, and he told me himself, when we both happened to be vacationing in the Crimea, that when Solzhenitsyn was arrested, he called Andropov and persuaded him not to exile Solzhenitsyn to Siberia. It is unfortunate that he was passed over when he wished to be elected as head of the Writer's Union. He was a person with liberal views and sympathies, when all was said and done. He simply knew how to perform a good balancing act, he knew how to stay afloat. And he kept floating.

45

IN THE 1950S THERE WERE VERY FEW RESTAURANTS, BUT THERE WERE almost always free tables in them: back then, people who could afford to go to restaurants were afraid. Some people did not want to show that they had money; others were afraid that they would be accused of imitating a western lifestyle. Low-ranking military officers were simply not allowed to go to restaurants. So the kinds of people who frequented such places were the literary public and members of the art world, and sometimes lawyers, pilots, engineers, and visiting provincial managers of industrial enterprises.

Occasionally on Sundays, if we happened to find ourselves temporarily flush, we went with our closest friends to the Nationale. This was a legendary place, where on any day of the week you would always find Yury Olesha and Mikhail Svetlov sitting at a table. They both had a wonderful wit and were famous for their aphorisms and quips. In the 1930s they were considered to be among the most promising young Soviet writers. Svetlov's poetry was part of the school curriculum, and children and adults alike all knew Olesha's *Three Fat Men*. But they were unable to accommodate themselves; they didn't know how to practice the required conformism and preferred to reject everything, having chosen what they considered to be the only consistent position: drinking to the end of their days.

Once we went out to dinner at the Aragvi, a Georgian restaurant with wonderful food and a unique atmosphere. There was no other place in Moscow quite like it. All the Moscow Georgians gathered there. They sang their polyphonic songs, made endless elaborate toasts, and drank from a horn, which they had to drink dry each time. The waiters in national dress carried platters of steaming shish kebab through the halls—the characteristic Georgian joie de vivre seemed to transport us to Tbilisi for a few hours.

One evening we were sitting at a table there with a friend, an editor at a publishing house. He left to go to the men's room and got lost in the maze of corridors, since he had already had a drop too many. He saw several doors in front of him, and tried to push one of them open—it didn't budge. He tried the second one, and it opened. He stepped inside and found himself in a spacious hall, where he saw dozens of huge tape recorders, their reels spinning. Each had a number that corresponded to a table in the restaurant. He eventually found his way back to the table where we were sitting. He returned white as a sheet, and starting urging us to leave immediately. We couldn't comprehend what the trouble was, and decided that he had just had too much to drink. Finally, unable to persuade us to go with him, he left by himself, and we stayed behind laughing at him. The next day he asked us to meet him on the street and told us about his adventure the day before. We no longer found it funny, and we never again had any desire to return to the restaurant. Now it surprises me that we were so shaken by this event. Every one of us knew it all already. We were constantly under surveillance like this until very recently.

At the beginning of the 1960s, Vasily Grossman went to take a look at his future two-room apartment in the writer's cooperative. It was still under construction, and he had to pick out the wallpaper. One of the workers came out with him when he was leaving. When they were safely outside on the street, he said, "Don't discuss anything in your new house. They've put microphones in the walls under the plaster. I don't know who you are, but I just wanted to warn you."

One day, two workers with a ladder arrived at our house, saying they had come to clean the vent grille in the kitchen. This was suspicious: whenever we need someone to repair something, it takes at least ten calls before they come, as you know. After that day we lived with Him, without really knowing whether He existed or not. We even gave him a name: Shurik. He became a silent witness to our family life, most of which was spent in the kitchen. Sometimes we had conversations with him. When we returned home from vacation we asked whether he had missed us. Sometimes Sima wished him bon appétit. Nekrasov, after he had downed a few glasses, would invite poor Shurik to share a drink with him.

Anyone could end up in a room in the Lubyanka at any time. They could stop you on the street and pull you into a car. They could phone you and demand that you show up at such-and-such a time and place. Everywhere in Moscow, in all the large hotels, in apartment buildings, even in communal apartments, the KGB had rooms for these secret meetings. Often it was not a matter of being arrested, but merely of questioning, or an offer to collaborate. Whoever agreed had to regularly inform on colleagues, acquaintances, friends. So there were always rumors about everyone. They didn't arrest me, although the fact that I had spent my childhood abroad was serious grounds for suspecting me. All the more since I had the habit of saying what I thought—within reason, of course.

There had always been an element of the mysterious, inexplicable, absurd in our life. A drama unfolds, but the mainsprings are concealed from view . . .

For a long time we were friends with Maxim Litvinov's son Misha. In the 1950s, Litvinov still lived opposite the Kremlin in a house on the embankment with his whole family: his English wife Ivy, his son Misha, his daughter-in-law Flora, and two grandsons, one of whom was called Pavlik.

Not long before the death of Stalin, there was a very disturbing incident involving Pavlik. Pavlik was no more than twelve years old. Suddenly, his personality changed. He became gloomy, silent, and he answered in monosyllables. When he came home after school, he locked himself in his room. Finally, his mother decided to talk to him about it. He refused to answer her for a long time, then burst out in tears and told her he had received an "assignment." By the entrance of the school, he admitted to her, two young men had intercepted him and said, "If you are a good pioneer, come with us. You are being given a government assignment. You will be like Pavlik Morozov. You have the same name, right? You must tell us what kinds of people visit your grandfather, and remember their conversations." They named a place where they would meet every three days. Pavlik, wanting to be a good pioneer, began to fulfill the instructions, but the thought that he would be betraying his grandfather was unbearable for him. Flora decided to take action. The next time, she showed up at the meeting with the young men instead of Pavlik, and threatened to complain to their superiors.

A nanny had lived with the Litvinovs for many years. They loved her very much. One day, she came home and rushed to embrace Flora, saying, "They've given me the rank of Major!" She was overjoyed that she had become a collaborator with the secret services.

The list of these incidents went on and on, so that we sometimes asked ourselves whether there was anyone at all who was not involved, closely or more loosely, with the KGB. As one high Party official admitted to me in a moment of vulnerability, "Lilya, the whole country is swarming with KGB agents."

I remember Leonid Pinsky telling me about his first interrogation. When he told the investigator that he had only been accused, but not yet convicted, the investigator pushed him over toward the window and said, "See all those people walking along Dzerzhinsky Square? Now *they* are the accused. You are already convicted."

46

THE UPWELLING WE HAD WITNESSED—THE YOUNG POETS, DUDINTSEV'S novel—all of this was stifled by the horrific events in Hungary. In 1956, when the tanks rolled into Hungary, there was a sense of personal tragedy in every home that had tried to embark on a new life. It was the moment of a final split among the intelligentsia. Nothing less. The first surge of freedom had resulted in a general euphoria. Everyone had participated in it. It had seemed that everything was now allowed—and, of course, that we were going down a liberal path. Now, however, it became evident that one had to take sides. One had to condone, or condemn, what had happened in Hungary. This became a kind of watershed. I still remember when Leonid Pinsky and I went to visit Mikhail Lifshitz, our pre-war idol, ideologue of a new, more profound Marxism, at the dacha he was renting in Peredelkino.

After the war I had heard Lifshitz speak once, in 1946 or 1947, at a conference on contemporary art at the Writer's Union. It was the first time he had appeared in public after the famous pre-war discussion between the "Despites" and the "Because Ofs." This time, as in 1941, many people turned up to hear him speak. By that time Zhdanov had already begun the campaign against everything that was alien to Socialist Realism. I was astonished: Lifshitz began his lecture by reading a long passage from an article in *Pravda*, in which all abstract paintings were declared to be works produced by primates. He began to elaborate on this idea, saying that impressionism was a distortion of art, evidence of decline, of decay, that there is no art outside of realism ...

At the beginning of the Thaw, however, he wrote a brilliant article in *Novy Mir* that we all read eagerly, and which seemed to suggest that he was in full sympathy with the trend of liberalization. So we went to visit him. Lifshitz loved to make pencil drawings, in a very classical style. As before, he hated modernist artists more than anything on earth (except for the vulgarization of Marxism); they were his bitterest personal enemies. So, while we were talking to him, as he was drawing in the classical manner, he revealed that he condoned the invasion in Hungary and that he shared Hegel's position that everything happens for a logical reason. Since it already happened, it had to happen. It had been an inevitable development, necessary to the Party, and we were obliged to support it so as not to weaken the foundations of the country. A rupture between Leonid Pinsky and Mikhail Lifshitz took place before my very eyes, a rupture that hit Pinsky very hard, because he had worshiped Lifshitz.

Here I would like to say, in a little digression, that courage that is, let's call it physical—for example, courage in war, when a person masters his fear of bullets or when he overcomes his fear of confronting a gang that has taken over a street—this sort of courage is quite distinct from intellectual courage. Life taught me that intellectual courage is much harder to muster than physical courage, than overcoming the instinct to save one's own skin. People find it easier to risk their lives than to admit to themselves that the path they have chosen is mistaken, to cross out that path, to refuse to go in the direction that you have been moving your entire life. I saw many examples—among French Communists, by the way, as well as among us—of noble, courageous people, who did not have the strength of spirit to make this choice. Unfortunately, Mikhail Lifshitz was one of them. He remained true to the old Marxism, albeit profound, to the necessity of Party approval, of unanimity with the Party.

The events in Hungary put an abrupt halt to liberalization. The majority of people yet again accepted the official party line: proletarian internationalism, the struggle against imperialism and fascism, and so on. The consequences very soon made themselves felt in the country—there was no more openness, and reaction ensued. Stalinists took advantage of the moment, and Khrushchev himself—drawing a lesson from the Hungarian events—demanded that writers and artists serve the interests of the Party. The novel *Not by Bread Alone*, having just been published in book form for the first time, was confiscated for "slander of the Soviet Union." Then the Pasternak affair began.

In 1957 Pasternak took a large novel to *Novy Mir*. The name of the novel was *Doctor Zhivago*. It was a novel in the classical tradition, with a protagonist who was thrust into the events of the Russian revolution, which he did not oppose, nor did he accept. This maelstrom drags him along with it, willy-nilly. Pasternak had no intention of writing a counterrevolutionary book. On the contrary, recreating the epoch through the prism of the main character's perception and his own experiences, Pasternak tried, at great cost to himself, to accept the regime, or, at least, to understand the movement that had turned his homeland upside down.

Novy Mir had begun to prepare the book for publication, but was running up against tremendous difficulties. For months on end, they failed to make any decision about the book. In the meantime, a copy of the manuscript of *Zhivago* had ended up with an Italian publisher. He was so inspired by it that he decided to publish it in Italy. The book came out soon afterward, and the great success it enjoyed in the West resulted in a huge scandal in Moscow. Seeing the turn things had taken, the editorial board of *Novy Mir*, trying to protect its rearguard, sent the Central Committee a letter pointing out the anti-Soviet character of *Doctor Zhivago*. It was one of the darkest chapters in the history of the journal. A campaign began immediately—one that would continue right up to the moment in 1958 when Pasternak was awarded the Nobel Prize for Literature.

Vladimir Semichastny, secretary of the Central Committee of the Komsomol and future head of the KGB, likened Pasternak to a pig. This was a signal for the onset of real persecution. There was a large meeting in the Writer's Union, presided over by Sergey Smirnov, the then deputy editor of *Novy Mir*. The entire literary beau monde demanded that Pasternak be expelled from the Union. Not a single person stood up for him. Worse, they took the floor to insult and abuse him, although there were plenty of people in the hall who were known to be very decent and upright—beginning with Smirnov himself, who wrote a daring book about the defenders of Brest Fortress. Boris Slutsky, a brave man and a wonderful poet, an old friend of mine, who until that time had been absolutely blameless, also took part in this affair. I must admit that he could never forgive himself for those moments of weakness, and tried for many years to explain to every person he met why he had spoken at the meeting. He assured them that he had done it with the best of intentions, trying to save what could be saved. Vera Panov, another author at *Novy Mir*, made a special trip from Leningrad and was one of Pasternak's bitterest detractors. She said that the author of *Zhivago* was simply a provocateur who had delivered a blow to the intelligentsia as a whole. I know only two people who comported themselves fairly decently, or even showed true courage. One was Vladimir Tendryakov, who called by phone to say he wouldn't be there, on the pretext that he was sick with the flu, and Vyacheslav Ivanov (today a world renowned linguist). He was only twenty-five at the time, and he was the only one who stood up for the poet's right to freedom of creative expression before a packed auditorium at the Department of Philology. The reaction was swift: he lost his job at Moscow State University and could not defend his doctoral dissertation for twenty years.

47

AFTER THE INTERVENTION IN HUNGARY AND THE STALINIST RESURGENCE, we crawled back into our shells. Still, something irreversible had happened in our minds. The wind that had fanned the first tentative sparks of freedom had not died down completely. It was merely biding its time. Meanwhile, another, parallel culture, which it became customary to call "unofficial," was gathering momentum. Semi-underground groups that met regularly to converse and socialize had formed around several unofficially recognized poets, writers, and critics. Because the books of great Russian twentieth-century poets were not being republished, and their names were being erased from our cultural history, Leonid Pinsky took the initiative to seek out old books or foreign facsimiles of publications to make copies of them. The poems of Tsvetaeva, Mandelstam, Gumilev, and Khodasevich were retyped on typewriters in copies of four (with carbon paper), sometimes even copied out by hand, then bound in small bundles and passed from one person to another. Many of our friends engaged in this practice. This was how samizdat was born. In its first incarnation it was not a political act, but rather a literary and aesthetic one, and this activity acquired ever greater significance in our lives.

One evening in 1959, Leonid Pinsky brought a young man over to our house. He looked almost like a schoolboy, with a round, childlike face, rosy cheeks, and light curly hair. He introduced him as Alik, and pulled five or six manuscript pages out of his briefcase that were sewn together and titled *Syntax*. This was a collection of new poems that could not find publication in newspapers or journals. Apart from Akhmadulina, who was published at that time in *Youth*, all the names of the contributors were unknown. Alik, who later became known as Alexander Ginsburg and played such an important role in the dissident movement, was studying at the time at the Pedagogical Institute. He had just turned twenty years old.

He adored poetry, and was an open, sincere, good-humored young man. The large room in a communal apartment that he shared with his mother and a huge German Shepherd was always full of people: young artists, actors, and, especially, poets. It occurred to him that this new wave of poetry needed to be fostered and supported. There were no political underpinnings or designs whatsoever behind his intentions. He published several issues of a journal, creating three or four print editions of each issue, then copying them. Several copies ended up in the West and were subsequently published. One day, the authorities came to search his house and arrest him.

Central to this budding parallel culture were singer-songwriters, dubbed bards (known as *chansonniers* in France). There were a number of young poets who began writing songs and performing them before large audiences. It is easy to learn a song, but much harder to prevent it from spreading. In the beginning of the 1960s, bards sprang up all over. In time, most of them were forgotten, but three remarkable names have remained. Bulat Okudzhava studied at the Institute of Literature. He was a youth from an Arbat back-yard; his father had been executed. He was exceedingly skinny, and exceedingly shy. Nevertheless, he eagerly visited the homes of strangers and sang, accompanying himself on his guitar. These songs, very melodic and musically inventive, were about daily life—about the Arbat courtyards, about friendship, about sixteen-year-old boys who went to war—but everything was deeply personal, very literally "unofficial." At that time it was impossible to imagine that these songs would become so popular.

Novella Matveeva sang in a sharp, rasping voice. She looked nothing like a singer, in the conventional sense. Overweight and suffering from chronic vertigo, no one could have called her a pretty young woman. But she had only to pick up her guitar and start to sing for her audience to fall completely under her spell. She knew how to uncover the hidden lyricism in the most mundane things. The doors of official literature were closed to her, but her noncon-formism opened the hearts of everyone who heard her.

The third name was Alexander Galich. He was the very Sasha Ginzburg who had coauthored *The City at Dawn*. When we met again, he was already known as Galich. He had become a well-known playwright and screenwriter. His comedy, *Taimyr Calling*, had enjoyed great success and earned him a great deal of money. He lived in affluence: a large apartment, antique furniture, china. He bought furs for his wife and was himself a very handsome man. This handsome fellow seemed to me to be all too elegant, and all too snobbish. I couldn't detect any trace of the Sasha from the Arbuzov studio, and had to admit to myself that I no longer had anything in common with this person who resembled someone from the Soviet bourgeoisie.

Thus, my surprise was all the greater when an excited Elka Nusinov told us about hearing Galich sing his songs at the home of I. Grekova, a former mathematics teacher, who was then publishing in *Novy Mir*. Elka said the songs were magnificent, very unusual. Then and there we decided to invite Galich to our house. And, just as it had been with Yevtushenko, we saw a completely different person.

In his first songs there was nothing overtly political. It was the genuine, crude, brilliantly captured language of ordinary people— these were the underpinnings of his ballads. For example, a ticket collector's lover jilts her, marries the daughter of an apparatchik, and now moves in the highest circles. And the whole song is a dialog between Tonechka, the ticket collector, and the fellow who describes his beautiful life to her. "I now live in a house that is like an overflowing chalice / I even have trousers that close with a zipper." He tells about how his Pops comes home in the evenings and always offers him "a glass or two" and "tells him a few Jewish jokes." But his heart is longing for Tonechka, who is standing in front of a cinema "all a-shiver, teeth chattering, not betraying him, nor forgiving."

Then his songs started to express more overt political protest. There was a song in which Khrushchev invites a highly placed foreign official to go hunting. They set loose the dogs to flush out wildfowl in the woods and the fields where the soldiers killed in the war are lying buried in the ground.

Galich had found his calling. He wrote and wrote without stopping, and his songs added up to a true encyclopedia of Soviet life. His popularity was astounding, comparable only to that of Vladimir Vysotsky for the following generation. Thanks to homemade recordings on domestic tape recorders, he was known even in the farthest reaches of the USSR. This could not be met with anything other than an answering blow. He was invited to perform in a club in Akademgorodok, a branch of the Moscow Academy of Sciences near Novosibirsk. He received thunderous applause, and the enormous hall sang along with him. Three days later, an article came out in *Pravda* accusing Galich of anti-Soviet propaganda. From that moment, already under Brezhnev, the authorities made life more and more difficult for him.

48

AT A CERTAIN POINT, I REALIZED THAT I COULD NO LONGER DO WITH-out a second child. Although I was already forty years old, I decided that I would have another one, come what may. I wanted a girl. I had always dreamed of having a girl. That's why I have always so dearly loved the wives, and before that the girlfriends (my boys were real heartbreakers), of my sons. It is as though I'm always looking for my own daughter among them. I gave birth to another son. We called him Zhenya, after Zhenya Asterman, my old IPhLH love.

Our first attempt to struggle out of poverty was the play *My Patent*. Although the play closed after only two weeks and the opportunity to work in the theater was severed, Sima and Elka immediately started working on a film script, *Midshipman Panin*. This was based on the memoirs of an old Bolshevik, Vasily Panyushkin, that had been published in *Novy Mir*. They wrote it very quickly and easily, and Misha Schweitzer, one of the new generation of post-war directors, who had already made a name for himself after directing a successful film with Tendryakov, decided to take it on.

Typical of the new cinematic wave was the return to the time-worn theme of revolutionary history in our film tradition, but now with a different approach—turning it into an adventure story by means of humor and a quick pace. So they had fun with it as they wrote.

There was a funny episode in which Midshipman Panin carouses in Paris, and when the Arts Council reviewed the film script, they strongly objected to this breezy lack of restraint that later proved to be the source of the film's main appeal. There was one more review session scheduled, and Misha Schweitzer called us the night before and said, "Listen, I can't defend your project. I refuse. I'm afraid to do it." This dashed all our hopes. Sima and Elka were sure they had written a very good script.

Apropos of how much one can do for someone else—that evening, Vladimir Tendryakov came by. Sima said, "You know, Misha refuses to plead for our script at the Arts Council tomorrow. He won't defend *Midshipman Panin*." Vladimir grew irate. "What? He refuses? Well, we'll see about that. I'm going to call him." He did, and said, "Misha, if you don't defend the script tomorrow, if you don't say 'it's this, or nothing,' if you don't stand up for *Midshipman Panin*, I'll never speak to you again. Forget you ever knew me." And Tendryakov was, at the time, a very attractive, influential figure, the embodiment of conscience and honesty. And Misha didn't want to lose him . . . In short, Misha Schweitzer vouched for *Midshipman Panin* at the review, and it was eventually filmed.

That brought in some much-needed money right away, and some acclaim and notoriety, because it was considered to be a film of a new type, one that "opened new horizons."

As for myself, however, I couldn't find any work. I continued teaching at the VOKS, but I was paid by the hour, a mere pittance, and, naturally, I wanted a real job. My colleague Boris Gribanov headed a program in literary translation at Detgiz, the Children's State Publishing House. He said, "Lilya, I'd love to help you out, but right now we have a quota for Jews, so I can't give you a French translation. We have many French translators already. Now, how about the Scandinavians? I know you study Scandinavian literature. Go ahead and find something to translate. We don't have any Scandinavian translators at the moment, so I can be straight with the bosses."

I dragged home huge bags full of books from Scandinavia, unbelievably beautiful books that had been sent to the publisher through the mail. We didn't publish books as beautiful as these back then. They all had glossy covers and wonderful illustrations—and they were absolutely vapid. I hauled home these bags of books, and fumed, thinking, It's so awful that I can't translate something from French, so-and-so gets a French book, and so does so-and-so, but they won't give me anything . . .

49

W<small>HEN ONE DAY, ABOUT FIVE MONTHS LATER</small>, I <small>GOT ANOTHER BATCH</small> of these remarkably beautiful books, and one cover in particular caught my eye. On it was a drawing of a little man, flying with a propeller on his back. It said: *Karlsson på taket*, which means Karlsson on the Roof. I started reading, and from the very first page, I realized that this was no ordinary book, that it was something miraculous, the kind of book one could only dream of translating. I realized it was remarkable in its intonation, its humor, and its simplicity. It was unique in the inventiveness and fantasy of its imagery. I called Boris very late at night and said, "I've found a brilliant little book." "Are you sure?" "Yes!" I said. "And you don't need to look it over. You'll see, it will be a colossal success!"

The spirit of the times was already less bureaucratic than it would be later, so Boris was able to say to me, "Sure, go ahead. Translate it. No one can object to a decision I make."

This incident had nearly the same significance in my later life as my decision to "stay," when Sima asked me to on the 12th of January. In terms of work, I had drawn a very lucky ticket indeed. To think that I had moaned about not being able to translate French! Had I translated a French book, no one would have paid the least bit of attention to it; and I wouldn't have noticed. Now, though, I had landed in the remarkable world of Astrid Lindgren, the brilliant children's writer.

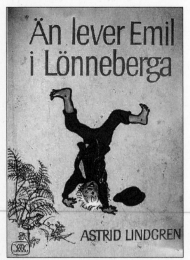

When I had already begun translating, I dutifully wrote a review of the book for the publisher, as one is expected to do. I wrote that Astrid

Lindgren would one day be a famous writer, because unlike any other writer, and so on, and so forth. Only a year or two later did I find out that she had long before received the Hans Christian Andersen Award, the highest children's literature award in the world, that she had already been translated into more than thirty languages, and that she was the world's premier writer for children. So much for walls and barriers ... By the way, the same thing happened to me with regard to Saint-Exupéry. The same Boris Gribanov gave me Saint-Exupéry's book *Wind, Sand, and Stars* to review—a marvelous, unexpectedly profound work. I was so carried away by enthusiasm I wrote a twelve-page review of the book, which no one really does. I also wrote that one day, Saint-Exupéry would be a world-renowned writer. Several months later a French exhibit opened, and in the books section I saw several bookshelves full of works about Saint-Exupéry. I was not given *Wind, Sand and Stars* to translate, unfortunately. My humble enterprise did not bear fruit. Still, I am proud of the fact that twice, when I anticipated future fame, I was actually sensing fame that was already fully-fledged.

Astrid Lindgren was like a character from her books. She was wonderful—slender, tall, very cheerful and lively, and very spontaneous in all her reactions. Zhenya was three years old the first time she came to our house for a visit. He was already asleep. She woke him up immediately, sat him down on the rug, and started playing with him. That was Astrid Lindgren. We took her back to the Rossiya hotel that same evening. The #2 bus makes a turnaround there, and she got out of the bus and started dancing. At one in the morning, when she was saying goodbye to us! The mood was so infectious

that Sima and I had to respond with our own fancy footwork in the empty bus on the way home.

It was her vital spirit that was so infectious. Once I asked her, "What makes you tick?" I knew her biography. She was married to a small businessman and worked as a secretary in his office. She had children; no higher education. A farmer's daughter. ("Emil of Lönneberga" is a story about her father, embodied by the boy Emil.) I asked her, "Where does your imagination come from?" She said, "Oh, that's easy to explain. I grew up in the shadow of a great love. When my father was seventeen, he went to a fair and saw a girl there. She was fourteen years old and wore a blue dress and a blue ribbon. He fell in love. He waited until she turned eighteen, then asked her to marry him. He adored her. We were a fairly poor farming family. We had just one farmhand and one farm girl (that's what they call poor farmers). My mother milked the cows and did all the work. But every morning began with a prayer by father—he thanked God for sending him this miracle of a wife, this miracle of love, this miracle of emotion. We grew up in the shadow of this great love and adoration. And this is what made my brother and me who we are." I said, "What about your mother?" "Mom died ten years ago." I said, "What about your father?" "He's still living." "How could he have survived the death of your mother? It must have been terrible." She said, "No, not at all. Every day he thanks God that he was the one to have to bear the pain of parting, and not her." I was amazed. That was Astrid Lindgren.

Being able to translate four of her books (each of them consists of three separate parts, so there were actually twelve in all) was not only a great joy, affording me great professional satisfaction, it also made me well-known in my world. Translating these books helped me get by in life. It helped me deal with fierce house managers, get airline tickets that were not supposed to be on sale, pass through customs posts, and, in general, make the heavier and darker moments of our lives lighter, and easier to survive. Then came *Pippi Longstocking*, Astrid Lindgren's first book.

From a letter from Astrid Lindgren to Lilianna Lungina:

Dear, sweet Lili,
I am so ashamed, so terribly ashamed—it's unbelievable how time

flies! I received your letter in July and was horrified when I heard about Sima's illness. I didn't get both letters, only one, dated 30 September. The other one must have gone astray. I have just had no opportunities to answer any letters this summer, I've been so sad—I haven't been able to think about anything but my brother, and I haven't done any work at all. I have thought about you very often, though. What good news that you're translating *Emil* and *Bullerby* [. . .] 300,000 copies of Karlsson—it's magnificent, isn't it? Are your children eating the books, by any chance? The Theater of Satire keeps staging my plays again and again. I wonder what the playwrights who also write drama think about it?

Armenia—that must be wonderful; I'm so glad that you and Sima were able to vacation there. I went away for a bit, too. I was in Switzerland, in a small Alpine valley. Unbelievably beautiful.

Please give Margarita a big hello from me, and decide on a time when it is convenient for both of you to come to visit me. My little apartment is still occupied, but soon it will be free again; I'm just not exactly sure when. Be sure to give my greetings to Sima and Zhenya.

My dear Lili, please don't forget about me. I always think about you. Next week I am going to Holland on a short trip.

All the very, very best!
Your Astrid

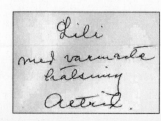

So, I had made a name for myself. When you have a name, even the fact that you are Jewish is viewed indulgently. I remember when Boris said, "If you knew German, I would give this book to you." I said, "You know, maybe I do know German, let me give it a try." He gave me a book in German (titled *Trevan*, written by an anonymous author). I discovered, of course, that I could still read German fluently. Thus I entered the world of translators.

Translating is a great joy. For me, the art of translation is akin to playing a piece of music. It is an interpretation. I would never venture to say that one translation is better, one worse, than any other. They are all different; every person has an individual preference. For example, I translated stories by Heinrich Böll, and there were other translations. The other translations and mine result in completely different Bölls. I think that the fate of Remarque, who was not considered here to be a writer of the first rank (which is absolutely untrue—he was a superb writer), was determined by the quality of the translations. Alas, they were inadequate. Vulgar translators. The love scenes, which are wonderful, conveying feelings at the highest pitch of ardor, came across as banal and trite. As I am personally acquainted with these translators, I saw their self-portraits in the translations. When one translates, one captures oneself in the text, like leaving a signature.

I still didn't understand the mechanisms of official Soviet life. I was very happy that I finally had work. (Before that, Noam Naumov and I had translated several books from French, but no one was interested in them. So Noam started translating from Spanish, since there was less competition, and more opportunity there.) I never thought about the need to make my position more official. Vladimir Admoni said, "Lilya, you have to join the Union of Writers." I said, like a little nitwit, "Why should I do that? What need do I have for all those official Soviet offices and organizations?" But he was adamant: "Lilya, you must join the Writer's Union." In short, he forced me to do so. He began pressuring Sima; and I did finally join. I'm proud of the fact that it was Emmanuil Kazakevich who recommended me, for *Karlsson on the Roof*. He loved the book. It turned out that the very fact of being a member of the Writer's Union gave one the right to work. Many talented people who were not in the Union, and whom I tried to help, were always refused, on the grounds that they were "not members of the Writer's Union." I said, "But how can they be members of the Union if they haven't translated anything yet?" "They have to be in the Union."

Starting in 1964 or 1965 my professional life, as well as Sima's, was on a roll. There was work. More or less all the time. Regular employment.

Sima and Elka worked with amazing film directors. The screenplay *Welcome! or No Trespassing* was filmed by Elem Klimov. It became a classic of children's cinema. It really was a brilliant film, and Klimov became very well known. A few years later they made *The Agony*, a film about Rasputin, with Klimov. The film had to wait ten years for permission to be screened. There were two films with Roland Bykov, *Attention! Tortoise*, and *The Telegram*, which also became children's classics, and *There Once Was a Singing Blackbird*, with Otar Ioseliani.

50

I<small>T WAS</small> 1961. E<small>LKA</small> N<small>USINOV CALLED US AT ONE O'CLOCK IN THE MORN</small>-ing and said:

"Get dressed!"

I said, "We're already asleep!"

"No, you have to get dressed right away, I'm coming over to get you."

"Why? What happened?"

"You'll see."

In those days, there were things one didn't talk about on the phone. We got up obediently and got dressed. He arrived, and said, "They say that today they're removing him from the mausoleum." He, meaning Stalin. "Let's go to Red Square." And we went.

We were astonished. Already some distance from Red Square there were crowds of people, and the square itself was packed. People stood in groups talking to each other. But what I want to recall for you is this: young boys turned to us, almost cursing, and said: "How could you have allowed the idolatry of Stalin to continue, this cult of Stalin? You are guilty, all of you, your generation is guilty." Elka got embroiled in an argument with them, trying to explain that people had been afraid, that they were governed by fear.

"Why were you afraid? Why aren't we afraid, then?"

Explaining to them that the times were different now, that the fear had dissipated; that, before, the fear had been a phantom, but nonetheless palpable, tangible—that the sense of fear is connected with the mood of society as a whole, that it . . . I would describe it thus: it is not an individual phenomenon, but something general, something shared; a commonality. But it was impossible to explain it to these young people. We stood there as though they had a right to sling mud at us, as though we were to blame before these youths, who were saying, "We're not afraid of anything. Everything is different for us than it was for you." Incidentally, in the Brezhnev era they came to understand perfectly, I think, what it meant to be afraid; but this was another time, another atmosphere. For the time being, it seemed that freedom had arrived. That night, Stalin was not removed after all. We stood on the square until four in the morning. Everyone older than twenty-five felt answerable to these young people. And something wouldn't let us leave.

51

Vɪc Nᴇᴋʀᴀsᴏᴠ ʜᴀᴅ ᴀ ᴠᴇʀʏ ᴄʟᴏsᴇ ғʀɪᴇɴᴅ, ʜɪs ᴇᴅɪᴛᴏʀ ᴀᴛ *Nᴏᴠʏ Mɪʀ*. His name was Igor Satz. He was a scion of the Satzes, a well-known Moscow family. Igor's sister was Anatoly Lunacharsky's wife; his cousin was an artist at MKhAT. Igor Satz lived in a room above the Smolensk grocery store. In this building the apartments were arranged along corridors, like a hotel: in each room lived a family. The rooms were long and narrow, as I said, like tunnels or pencil boxes. In Igor's room, both walls were lined with bookcases. He lived in that room with his wife Raya. Tvardovsky, editor-in-chief of *Novy Mir*, and a great poet, often came by to have a drink with them. Igor liked to drink, too, and lived conveniently just above the store. Satz had a great deal of influence over Tvardovsky. During this period, when we had just met, we liked Igor very much. He was reputed to be a very astute and unusually talented critic. Later I read only his article about Zoshchenko, nothing else—I think there were more discussions around this. But he was someone from the *Literary Critic*—that is, a thinker, a progressive from even before the war.

In the narrow space between the bookcases stood a small newspaper table, and people would sit around it drinking. The evening I saw Tvardovsky for the first time, Sima and Vic and I were the first ones to arrive. We sat at the table with Igor and his wife. Nekrasov dominated the conversation. He talked, he held forth, he was like the host at a banquet. Then Mikhail Lifshitz, who was also good friends with Satz and visited often, arrived. And dominion passed over to him. He was now the center of attention; he was the head of the table.

Suddenly, Tvardovsky appeared. I was excited to be seeing him in this setting, so close up. We were vaguely acquainted, because I had done translations for *Novy Mir*, and I wrote short reviews of translated books. He was a large man, very tall, broad-shouldered, with a round face and small, piercing eyes—bright blue eyes, and an exceptionally penetrating gaze. Later I had the chance to observe that he was, as they say, all eyes. He saw everything; nothing escaped his gaze. As soon as he arrived, both Vic and Lifshitz faded into the woodwork. Tvardovksy reigned at the table now, and everyone listened to him alone. I was able to witness myself, for the first time, the significance of his personality, his I, which held absolute dominion over others.

He had a very original way of speaking—with a specific accent, characteristic of his place of birth, and he never raised his voice, since he was certain that everyone was listening only to him. He went silent not to let other people have a turn speaking, which would never have entered his head, but to search for a more exact expression.

The power of his personality, which surprised me that evening, came to the fore in the journal, in his relations with his editors. He tried to speak to the authors he published in the same manner, as well. Tvardovsky's relations with them were always strained and complicated, whether it was Nekrasov, Voinovich, or, later, Solzhenitsyn.

In contrast to Vic Nekrasov, Tvardovsky was in no sense a free and easy human being. On the contrary, he was bound not only by his membership in the Party and the board of directors of the Writer's Union, but also by his role as editor-in-chief of the most controversial journal of the time. Tvardovsky came from a peasant family. During the era of collectivization, his father had been dispossessed as a kulak and sent into exile. On the one hand, a sort of idiosyncratic peasant psychology forced Tvardovsky to revere those in power. On the other hand, it tormented him to have to bear this reverence inside himself, as he was an exceptionally honest person. It sickened him to have to act against his conscience. He was like a chained-up giant. He was trapped between his feelings and the demands of the Central Committee, which called the shots in the life of literature. He envied those who didn't have to compromise or make concessions. When he received permission from the Central Committee or the censor to publish something after many long days of wrangling, but on condition that he excise one or another passage, the resistance of the author drove him into a fury. Vic told us that Tvardovsky shouted at him: "You criticize everything, you're dissatisfied with everything, you blame the Soviet authorities; but at the same time, the lard you eat is Russian! The bread you eat is Russian! Yet you are enamored with anything from abroad!" And when Grossman, a friend of Tvardovsky's, but at the same time someone who hated the regime, wrote travel notes about Armenia, Alexander Tvardovsky did what was nigh impossible and secured permission to publish them. He wanted very much to publish them, and considered that he had won an important battle, all the more since this would be the first publication of a work by Grossman since *Life and Fate* had been withdrawn from circulation. Censorship, however, demanded that one episode be jettisoned—that in which an Armenian raised a toast to two peoples, Armenians and Jews, because they had both been victims of genocide. Grossman could not even think of making concessions. Tvardovsky was beside himself with fury. He pounced on Grossman, accusing him of not being willing to understand anything, not wanting to make the smallest effort to help him.

After our meeting at Satz's, Alexander Tvardovsky and I met more frequently, and even struck up a friendship. One morning he called very early, at about nine. He was calling Vic, but he included us at the same time. "I must come by to see you this very minute," he said.

By ten he was already at our house. He had brought a manuscript with him. They were pages torn out of a school notebook, lined paper for mathematics problems. The pages were filled with dense type, and the manuscript was titled *Shch-854*.

"Last night," he said, "I read this manuscript twice through, and I must read at least part of it to you. I can't not read it; it's an astonishing manuscript." We immediately called Elka Nusinova, who answered right away. Oh, and Tvardovsky demanded vodka, so Elka got hold of some and brought it over. The five of us sat in our living room, and while we drank our vodka, we listened to the story that everyone knows now, the story that became a world classic: *One Day in the Life of Ivan Denisovich.*

Even before Tvardovsky's call we knew about the existence of this manuscript. Lev Kopelev had taken it to *Novy Mir*. Lev Kopelev was a literary critic and translator, and later a famous writer, who was exiled, and then settled in Germany. Lev had been imprisoned in his time in a so-called sharaga. The sharaga was a prison that functioned, at the same time, as a scientific research institute. Because there were so many talented and brilliant people in prison, the Soviet authorities decided to make use of them and organize prisons where they could work in their areas of specialization. In one of these special prisons, Kopelev had been incarcerated with a colleague, a high-school mathematics teacher by the name of Solzhenitsyn. He had ended up in prison because of his correspondence with a friend: the censor intercepted the mail from the field post office. In the letter, Solzhenitsyn expressed doubts of a political nature, and he was sent to prison. When he was released, Solzhenitsyn wrote the story. Lev didn't understand the entire significance of the story, but he took it to his friend Anna Berzer, the wonderful literary critic and head of the prose section at *Novy Mir*. Anna (Asya) Berzer later became Vic Nekrasov's editor, and my very dear friend. At that time, Asya was renowned in literary circles for her brilliant, witty articles that took aim at Stalinist writers and hacks. But her special gift was for discovering new talent. She knew, like no other, how to bring the best out of writers, to get them to give all they were worth. She was the one to whom Yury Dombrovsky dedicated his novel *The Faculty of Useless Knowledge*, saying that were it not for her, the book would never have been written. Solzhenitsyn, too, pays tribute to her in his memoirs.

So Lev Kopelev brought the manuscript to Asya and said, "Read it. I think it's good." I should say that at this point in the Thaw, other manuscripts written by people who had been in the camps and in prison had already started to appear. None of those manuscripts had made the sort of impression on anyone that this one did, however.

The publishing process at *Novy Mir* was complicated. They could delay publication out of considerations of precedence and other matters that had nothing to do with the content of the manuscript. Members of the editorial board, citing the "interests of the journal" as a pretext, were sometimes guilty of cowardice. After she read the manuscript, Asya turned immediately to Tvardovsky. This was a breach of protocol. Their "Mount Olympus" was on the second floor. That was where the journal management conferred and held sessions. The rank-and-file employees were on the first floor, and did not have direct access to Tvardovsky unless there was a very good reason for it. Still, she went to see him, put the school notebook on his desk, and said, "I beg you to read this." She told us over the phone about the remarkable manuscript.

Alexander Tvardovsky had a unique trait—I observed this more than once, but in particular in the case of *Ivan Denisovich*—he knew how to delight in something. This is not a gift that all talented people, or people in general, are endowed with. He was in raptures about Solzhenitsyn's story. Many things contributed to this. Tvardovsky held truly grassroots views: he believed that truth and depth of understanding of life reside only in the people. He was very wary of the intelligentsia. The fact that Solzhenitsyn had chosen an ordinary man for his protagonist, that he was not a member of the intelligentsia, but "Ivan Denisovich," a regular guy, won Tvardovsky over completely.

We sat at the table, munching on sausage and cheese, and drinking our vodka, getting slowly drunk, while he read. He couldn't stop; but some scenes, the scene about the dye, for example—that was one of the episodes in the book—he reread three times. He was so taken with it, he told us, "Let them fire me, let them ride roughshod over me, let them do whatever they want— I'll go straight to Nikita (Khrushchev) and read it to him myself. If this doesn't help it to get published, I no longer want to work. It's a matter of life and death for me. It's my duty to see it through to the end."

Since we parted at around midnight, having been drinking since nine in the morning, naturally, we thought it was the vodka talking in him. Him? Going to Khrushchev?

After such a long bout of drinking, he was unable to make it home on his own and someone had to accompany him. Since Elka Nusinov drank less than the rest of us, the task fell to him. He led Tvardovsky up to his apartment in a high-rise house on the embankment, propped him up in front of the door, and rang the bell. Tvardovsky's wife saw Elka in this role all the time. She concluded that he was an inveterate drunkard, that he was the instigator of all this, and that he kept plying poor Tvardovsky with drink. Elka had to live with this inglorious reputation. That evening, too, Elka told us, Tvardovsky was very drunk when he took him home, and he kept repeating: "I'll go straight to Nikita, I'll go straight to Nikita." His wife said, "Why are you leading this poor man astray? You should be ashamed of yourself, he's already talking about Nikita."

Nevertheless, it did happen. Tvardovsky managed to get permission to see Khrushchev when he was vacationing in the South. He read the book aloud to him with the same intense rapture that he had read it to us, even permitting himself to read several key passages twice. Khrushchev was captivated—because he, too, was just such a simple man. He could relate to everything, grasp every detail, on its own terms. He gave the go-ahead, saying, "Let's publish it. But you have to change the title."

Well, everyone knows, everyone remembers, except perhaps the youngsters, what an event it was when *One Day in the Life of Ivan Denisovich* appeared in print. An event of universal significance in the country. Think about it—it's remarkable how important the publication of books and poems have been in the liberation of this unfortunate country from its enslavement.

I believe Solzhenitsyn's first books are true works of art. I don't think he ever achieved anything higher than the standard set by his first books—which were peerless. In my opinion, *One Day in the Life of Ivan Denisovich* is a sublime aesthetic achievement. And *Ma-*

СОДЕРЖАНИЕ

tryona's House is also exceptional in its artistry and depth. At that same time, it is politically resonant. The life of our countryside in its entirety was illumined through this one story.

Politics cannot be the defining feature in the art of the written word. If a political position is apparent on the first level of the work, some affirmation of a political stance that is only embellished with artistic devices, it can't be considered a work of art. *Not by Bread Alone*, for example, is a political work plus some literary aesthetics thrown in. Dudintsev simply added this artistic dimension to enliven the work. The aesthetic dimension is not intrinsic to it.

The desire to read *Ivan Denisovich* was driven by an interest in politics—or, rather, not in politics per se—but by an interest in life. The mass readership it enjoyed, the fact that every literate person read it, and was expected to read it—that was politics. In this country politics has never been purely politics. We have never had real politics. It seems to me that politics has always assumed the form of some sort of terrifying mass event—that is, it has merged with the terrifying "lived life" of ordinary people. Our politics doesn't unfold in the sphere of political debate or competing doctrines. Our politics is a dimension of some sort of mass action or event that always tells on the lives of people in the gravest, most difficult way. The urge to read *Ivan Denisovich* was an effort to discover a form of life that was also a mass phenomenon or experience, but until that time had been concealed from us, hidden out of sight. People wanted to find out from a person who had been there, and was a reliable and truthful witness, what life was like in the camps. This was what led to its popularity, and captured the interest of readers. Once you started reading, you came under the sway of a true work of art. Unequivocally. For me, there can be no doubt about this.

I think that that what guaranteed the artistry of *Ivan Denisovich* was Solzhenitsyn's decision to write about a happy day. He didn't describe a difficult day in Ivan's life, but showed instead what a good day in prison looked like, when everything fell into place. This created the possibility of perception. A person cannot take in an overload of gore and misfortune. But Solzhenitsyn's approach, I would say, is like a bitter pill with a sweet coating, making it easier to swallow.

Subsequently, the stories of Varlam Shalamov appeared. Shalamov returned home in the wake of Solzhenitsyn. I met him through Leonid Pinsky, because many returnees from the camps frequented his place. He was very different from Solzhenitsyn. When I met him, I saw a man who was not yet old, but who had aged prematurely. He looked like a Rembrandt portrait of an old man. Life had left a terrible mark on him, distorting his expression. He was covered in wrinkles, and had a terrifying, heavy gaze. He was a person who had been completely crushed by the system.

His stories, which are wonderful, are no less trenchant and revealing than *One Day in the Life of Ivan Denisovich*. Shalamov's stories were not published here, but we were able (through my active
efforts, I might add) to send them abroad for publication. Some
French doctors I was acquainted with smuggled the stories out on
their persons, taping the pages under their clothing. They were published in France. They made no impression, however—no one read
them. It's only now that Shalamov has become so well known. Now
he is being republished. But at that time, the truth that he revealed
about the camps, the lives of the hardened criminals, or urkas—he
wrote a great deal not only about the political prisoners, but also
about the hardened criminals, about that side of life in the camps—
was a pill so bitter, without any coating to make it palatable, that
the print run was not sold out. And the reviews were so-so . . .

He took all of this very hard. When the persecution of Solzhenitsyn began, he even allowed himself to speak out. In the same issue
of the paper that announced that Solzhenitsyn would be exiled, a
letter from Shalamov protesting the fact that his stories had been
published abroad without his consent appeared. This was not true.
He had given his permission. He was demonstrating his bitterness
that the stories had not met with any response. It was as if they had
fallen into an abyss. He couldn't understand why.

He died a terrible death. I saw him once when he was visiting
Leonid. Then he fell ill, and could no longer live alone in his apartment. He died in complete obscurity, in the district home for the
elderly, in terrible circumstances—the conditions were comparable
to those in the labor camps. Now he has become a great writer in
the West. Here, too, in fact. His works are published, and republished, in volumes this thick.

I say all this to convey just how important it was to describe a
happy day of Ivan Denisovich.

Solzhenitsyn visited our home twice. The first time, he came
to see Nekrasov. He talked to him like a schoolteacher giving a good
scolding to a pupil. He tried to impress upon Vic that he needed to
change his way of life completely: to get up early in the morning,
work ten times harder, and write at least four or five hours a day.
He drew up a daily schedule for him, using red and blue pencils.

Vic, a living embodiment of freedom, was squirming with laughter, but Solzhenitsyn, paying no attention to this, went on, "First and foremost is that you stop drinking. You will drink nothing but mineral water." Solzhenitsyn didn't see the people he talked to. He didn't speak—he preached.

The second time he visited, he came to listen to a recording of Galich. Still standing in the doorway, he told us he only had twenty-two minutes to spare. He listened to the beginning of a song and said, "This one's boring. Play the next one." He listened to two or three to the end, the ones expressing the greatest realism. The whole time, he kept glancing at his watch, and exactly twenty-two minutes after he had arrived, he stood up as though he were adjuring a meeting. Then he left, without saying a word. Already completely captivated by the music, we felt bewildered by his departure.

The last time I saw him was in 1971 at Tvardovsky's funeral in Novodevichy Cemetery. For Tvardovsky, who had been removed from his post at *Novy Mir* a year before, life had lost all meaning. We were transported by a bus hired by the Writer's Union. The police were blocking the entrance, trying to disperse the crowd that formed in front of the gates. Ordinary people were prevented from paying their last respects. Everything went very smoothly and quickly, as if they were afraid for the funeral of Tvardovsky, who had fallen into disfavor, to last too long. Not a single sincere word was spoken—only official speeches. Then, when they began lowering the coffin into the grave, Solzhenitsyn, who had been expelled from the Writer's Union two years prior and was leading a semi-underground existence, with a decisive gesture, the gesture of a man who had every right to do so, shoved aside everyone standing in his way and strode forward. He wanted to be the first to throw a handful of earth in the grave. Then, solemnly and boldly, he made a sign of the cross.

52

KHRUSHCHEV ALWAYS ACTED IMPULSIVELY. HE WAS TWO-FACED. IN THE matter of *Ivan Denisovich*, he had behaved like a good czar: wise, understanding, sensitive. Several weeks later at the exhibition in the Manège, however, he revealed his other face, that of an evil czar: irascible, intellectually limited, imperious.

A small group of art critics decided to seize the opportunity (as they thought) and to organize a large exhibition of modern art. This was the first time in thirty years that such an exhibition had been held. It would be all the art of the 1920s and 30s—Aristarkh Lentulov, Robert Falk, David Sterenberg, Pavel Filonov, and so on— who had been banned and disgraced for decades.

You can't imagine the joy we felt viewing these remarkable canvases, which had been waiting for their hour in the dark underground storage rooms and cellars of museums. Lines formed at the ticket windows long before the actual opening of the exhibit. Thousands of people visited it—to the bitter disappointment of the academic artists, headed by Aleksandr Gerasimov, who imposed a veritable dictatorship on the Union of Artists. The old guard sensed a threat on their iron grip, and decided to take action. On their invitation, Khrushchev visited the exhibit four or five days after the opening. He understood what was expressed in words, but he couldn't make head or tail of what was conveyed in the language of visual art. His escorts, however—those who had invited him and accompanied him through the exhibit—prompted him in his conclusions. Khrushchev, shocked and dismayed by the spectacle of all these nudes, geometric figures, and deformed heads, walked from painting to painting mumbling a single word: "Pederasts," which he pronounced "pederasses." Only Ernst Neizvestny, a wonderful sculptor, was able to offer a rebuff; but it was fruitless.

This provocation by the old guard, this setup, did bear fruit. The next day, all of Moscow was in stitches, and everyone kept repeating "pederasses," like a mantra. The exhibit in the Manège, however, which had almost been the harbinger of a new era, was closed down. Later, after his fall from power, Khrushchev expressed regret about this, and complained to Yevtushenko, who was paying a solitary visit to him: "They didn't fill me in properly. Why didn't you explain it to me?"

The Manège was the first warning. Very soon afterward, the writers were also called to heel. First, Khrushchev invited about thirty of them to dinner at his Moscow dacha. A meeting like this was unusual in the relations between the intelligentsia and the leadership, and the guests arrived full of optimism, believing in the possibility of open, sincere discussion. Their optimism was in vain. Khrushchev quickly grew irate, turned red, and began shouting, "You must work for the Party, you have to stand up for the Party position," and added threateningly that he would not tolerate any deviation. Margarita Aliger tried to say something about freedom of self-expression, but Khrushchev gruffly pounced on her, and she ran from the table in tears. She told me afterward, with a bitter smile, that not a single person had tried to defend her.

At just this time, an incident occurred in our family that I think characterizes that period, at least in part. Our son Pavel was fourteen years old. He was in the seventh grade. He was enrolled in a school that taught intensive French as a foreign language. The director was a retired colonel who ran the school with an iron fist. Pavel was a live wire, given to mockery, always ready to fight if someone tried to pick on him, or to make his classmates laugh during lessons. He was not what you would call well-behaved. Rather, he was an inveterate disturber of the peace, and the teachers were not averse to the idea of getting rid of him. Since he was at the same time one of the brightest students in the class, they just had to put up with him. Finally, though, they saw their chance.

One day Pavel brought some large reproductions of the impressionists to school and tacked them to the wall. There are books with perforated pages that can be removed to function as posters, and our French acquaintances gave him such a book as a gift. He had wanted to share his delight in the discovery with his classmates; but a scandal erupted. The director turned it into an ideological struggle: this demonstration of "decadent bourgeois art" was not a run-of-the-mill prank, but an act of political provocation with the goal of destabilizing the class. Pavel was summoned to a meeting of the Pedagogical Council, along with his father.

The night before, the director had warned us that if we didn't want Pavel to be expelled from school, we should not try to defend him in any way. He would reward us for our good behavior by allowing Pavel to remain enrolled. Sima and I submitted, since we believed it was important for Pavel to graduate from this school, which had a good reputation and facilitated one's chances at getting admitted to the university. It was also because of our faintheartedness and our lack of independence. For two hours the teachers cursed Pavel, calling him every name in the book. They said he was a bad influence on his classmates, that he was full of vices and bad habits, and, as a teacher assured us, dangling a Manet Nude in front of our faces, that his lack of patriotism posed a danger to the whole class. Sima sat there silently, as he had been instructed to do. He didn't speak a word in defense of his son, who was astonished at this betrayal. Sima never forgave himself for it.

None of this, by the way, prevented them from kicking Pavel out of school.

53

MEANWHILE, THE AUTHORITIES BEGAN ALLOWING WRITERS TO TRAVEL abroad in small groups. Konstantin Paustovsky, who at that time was in semi-disgrace because of his anthology *Tarusa Pages*, was nonetheless scheduled to travel to Paris, and Vic Nekrasov joined him. Needless to say, Vic had long dreamed of going to Paris. He had lived there until he was four, and as a little boy in long ringlets had played in Parc Monceau. He was in love with Paris, as we all were, and dreamed of visiting it again. The possibility of the journey was up in the air. Would they allow them to go? Would the trip come through? The authorities had promised.

In our house, a fiery debate broke out. Paris. That was where my friends, the friends of my childhood, of whom I had spoken so much, were living. I had found out that Lida had married Jean-Pierre Vernant, and that he had become a well-known academic. Of course, I very much wanted (while there was the slightest opportunity—we didn't know whether it would last) to make contact with them again. And so, in our house, especially within our circle of friends, crazy debates raged about whether I should do this or not. My friends, in particular Noam Naumov, said, "You've lost your mind. Why would you want to do such a thing? Who are these French people to you? They're complete strangers. They lived completely different lives. If you strike up a correspondence, you'll destroy Sima's career, they won't let him work anymore." They were the same old arguments. I said, "Who are you to be telling me these things? You yourself made samizdat." "Well, that's a different matter. Sima has made such a brilliant start in his career, what he and Elka are doing is so important. Their films push back the limits of what is possible—it's far more important than your letters to your French friends. Don't stand in his way." That was the way many reasoned. Sima told me, "You must do what you yourself want to do; I'm all for it." He pressed

Vic very hard: "You must find them." I vacillated and fretted. I didn't know what to do.

Sima was a morning person—he got up early and often went to bed before I did—and I was a night person. I didn't like getting up in the morning, and I was used to working at night. It was the same that evening. Sima had already gone to sleep, and Vic and I stayed up talking. Vic said, "Come on, aren't you going to write? Now's your chance, it might be the last one." Something broke in me, and I said, "All right. I'm going to write a letter." So, sitting in the kitchen at one in the morning, I wrote a long, long letter, six pages, then grabbed a painted khokhloma bowl as a souvenir, and said, "Here, Vic. Try to find them."

The next morning they didn't bring Vic's travel passport. Noam said, "You see? It's fate. You wrote a letter, and he couldn't even go on the trip." Paustovsky and his daughter Galya went alone. They did bring Vic his passport the next day, however, and he set off for Paris.

Ehrenburg's daughter Irina had a friend whose name was Natasha Stolyarov. She and her father lived abroad for a while, and returned to the Soviet Union at around the time that Marina Tsvetaeva did. She was an eighteen-year-old girl who had come back to help build socialism, and within two weeks of her return was arrested. In her book *Journey into the Whirlwind*, Yevgenia Ginzburg recalls how they led a slight young girl with enormous, clear eyes into the cell. This was Natasha Stolyarov. After that they wouldn't allow her to live in Moscow. Ilya Ehrenburg took her on as his secretary, and for this reason she was able to return. She was the first in my circle to start a correspondence with her friends in Paris. It was she who (not without my prompting) organized the safe delivery into the West of Shalamov's manuscripts, with the help of her French friends. Natasha had given me the Vernants address, which I entrusted to Vic.

The address was incorrect. It turned out to be the address not of Lida, but of another friend of mine—Zina Minor. Yet by an incredible coincidence, Jean-Pierre Vernant's brother lived in that same house. When Vic called the concierge and asked for Vernant, he was directed to the apartment of Jean-Pierre's brother. When the brother opened the door and saw a person who didn't know French and who spoke Russian, he assumed that he was looking for his brother, Jean-Pierre, who was married to a Russian. Lida and Jean-Pierre lived in a suburb near Paris, and this was how Vic found them. Chance. Happenstance.

Vic immediately became a friend of the Vernants and spent the remaining days of his trip in Paris with them. He brought me back a pile of gifts and a long, long letter from them. It was even longer than mine to them had been. I began my letter saying: "Perhaps you don't remember that girl who long ago left Paris to return to Moscow. So much time has gone by, thirty years." In her response to my letter, Lida wrote: "How can you possibly think that I don't remember you? We talked about you so often, reminisced. You were part of our lives." When we finally reunited, it was as if we had never parted. That was just before the New Year, 1964. And at Easter time, they came to visit me in Moscow.

54

THEY STAYED IN THE METROPOL. IN THOSE DAYS, WE WERE NOT ALLOWED to enter hotels where foreign tourists were staying. We agreed to meet by the exit of the Smolenskaya subway station.

I think I was afraid of the first moments of our reunion. I took my four-year-old Zhenya with me for moral support. Like a lightning rod, so to speak. Here is my boy. Ah, your son!—to deflect attention from myself at first. I was so apprehensive about that first moment. Although we were still fairly young, I was afraid—would we even recognize each other? So that they could recognize me, I said I would be holding a child in my arms. I saw them coming up the stairs at the station, and I realized that they were my own people, they were family. Lida was very pretty, as she had always been—perhaps even more so than she had been in her youth. We came here, to our house, where Sima was waiting for us.

Before they came, I had done a bit of fixing up around the apartment. I was ashamed that my house wasn't up to the standards of Europeans. I remember how, the night before, we had reupholstered two armchairs whose springs and cotton stuffing were falling out. It was ridiculous, of course. The sense that we had found each other without ever having lost each other took over immediately. The paint on the lightbulbs had still not been wiped off after our modest renovations, and J.P. grabbed a ladder and a rag and went to work. It was like our brother and sister had arrived. That's how it felt. Sima didn't speak French, but he and J.P. made themselves understood to each other by relying on their hands. Lida spoke Russian well. She became a Russian teacher in a lyceum, and spoke very fluently, though like a foreigner, trying to use more idioms. It was funny. When it was time to eat, she said to me, "We're going to stuff ourselves like hell," thinking that this was colloquial Russian.

J.P. had already been in the Soviet Union. Soon after Mama and I had returned to Moscow in 1934, a group of young French Communists traveled to the Caucasus. J.P. was a Communist. He found me here—I haven't mentioned this yet—and I took them to the Park of Culture. In spite of the burning of the effigy of Chamberlain and other disturbing impressions, I wore my Young Pioneer tie, and I wanted very much to show them—I remember feeling this—how wonderful it was here, perhaps even better than it was in France. I wanted to show it in a better light than it really was. For two days we walked around Moscow, and I engaged in agitprop for Soviet power. Then J.P. and I lost track of each other for some thirty years.

Now we sat and told each other about our lives for several days in a row. I found out that Vernant had been one of the main figures in the French Resistance. During the day he taught in a lyceum, and at night he was the leader of the Resistance for the entire southwestern district. He had taken part in some terrifying assignments—he blew up railroads and whatnot, wore a stocking over his face instead of a mask. He was always expecting to be arrested. He had been awarded a medal by de Gaulle that only six-hundred-some people in France received: the Compagnons de la Libération. Every year de Gaulle invited them for breakfast at his residence, and shook hands with each of them as they entered.

Lida was also a Communist. At first, of course, we tried to avoid discussing the subject, but on about the third day I said to J.P., "How

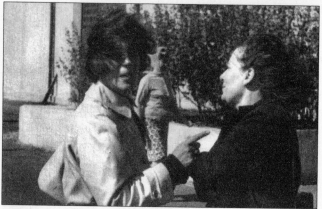

can you possibly be a member of the Party? It has been so hard for us to find out the truth: we had to keep guessing, we had to struggle to get to the bottom of things—but everything is made public over there! You have so much material about it at your disposal! How can you remain in the Party?" He said, "In the first place, we hadn't read the anti-Soviet material. It was absolute rubbish, like something concocted by the devil; it was taboo. Now," he said, "I do read, but in my youth, we refused to read that stuff. Besides that, you know, as long as I am in the Party, I enjoy a broad audience. I can try to lead the Party onto another path. If I am outside the Party, I'm no one. Just a solitary individual. And I don't want to be just a solitary individual."

He said all of this only toward the end of his stay in Moscow. It had an unexpected finale. It coincided with the trial of Brodsky in Leningrad.

I had seen Brodsky before. He had addressed the translator's section at the Writer's Union. He looked very funny, a boy with a bright red shock of hair, and a face covered with freckles. He sat on the edge of his chair, and when he was asked to read his translations he said, "Why should I read you translations? You can translate yourselves. I'd rather read you my own poems." And he began reciting his stunning poetry. He read his poems like all Russian poets do—without any expression, not thinking about the meaning, just falling into the rhythm. Everyone present was captivated. It was immediately clear that this was a true poet, very complex, a completely new kind of poet, different from any we were familiar with. Now he was being tried for "parasitism."

On the last evening before the Vernants' departure, someone brought over a transcript of Brodsky's trial, which Frida Vigdorova had written down. I gave it to Lida to read, and then said, "J.P., I want to translate it for you. I don't want you to leave without having read it. Not only that, you must take it with you." When Lida was reading it, she started to cry; it deeply offended her Communist ideals. And J.P. said, "All right, I'll take it to France and give it to my comrades to read." This was the note we parted on. I later found out that Lida had fallen ill, so shaken was she by the collapse of her ideals and illusions.

They had had an argument. Lida said that they shouldn't show it to anyone on the age-old pretext that one mustn't "play into the hands of the enemy." We'd heard that one before. J.P. insisted on doing so. He is one of those people who have the intellectual courage about which I was speaking, an intellectual courage that is so difficult to come by. He said, "The truth is above anything; things are what they are. This document exists, so people should know about it and read it."

When they returned a year later—they visited every year—I was proud to find out that he had left the Party. I think J.P. benefited greatly from this, because it gave him much more time. He had been a propagandist and had had to address worker's rallies and meetings all over France. Now he began to study in earnest, and soon became a scholar with a worldwide reputation. He founded a new branch of scholarship called Historical Psychology. This was an attempt to analyze historical phenomena from the point of view of the psychology of those years, and not from the point of view of contemporary consciousness. His primary work, which immediately made him a name throughout the scholarly world, was about the origin of rational thought, starting from classical antiquity. He was in fact a Classics scholar.

55

ONE DAY IN THE FALL OF 1964, SIMA OPENED PRAVDA AND SAID, "Lilya, Khrushchev has been removed." I nearly fainted. He was removed as a result of a coup organized by Mikhail Suslov, and the country responded to this, for the most part, positively. Khrushchev had never been a popular leader. The peasants were particularly unhappy with him because of his crazy ideas—to overtake America in the production of milk and meat, or to plant corn everywhere, completely disregarding the specificities of climate. Life became simply unbearable for the peasants. Malenkov had allowed them to raise livestock for themselves on their own land, but under Khrushchev this was again taken away from them. I saw with my own eyes in the village of Lukyanovo near Ryazan how the peasants killed their own animals when the district commission was dragging off a pig from the neighboring farm. These draconian measures still didn't provide Moscow with the amount of meat that it required, and a mass slaughter of horses was carried out in the kolkhozes. This is the real reason that horses became such a rarity, and why they are pointed out to children as if they're seeing a dodo bird.

Khrushchev's image was not in keeping with that of an all-powerful leader to whom Stalin had entrusted the people; and he was not particularly respected in the cities, either. People said he was a "peasant's peasant," and laughed at him. He did not inspire esteem or admiration. I had a reliable barometer: taxi drivers. And the Moscow cabbies called Nikita a clown. When Khrushchev banged on the podium with his shoe at the UN, he made himself look ridiculous. As the years went by, those who felt nostalgia for the old order remained dissatisfied, and the liberal intelligentsia was disappointed with his caprices and his dictates. Finally it became unbearable.

Still, I think Khrushchev is undervalued. Nowadays we would do well to remember the role he played in de-Stalinization. He destroyed the myth, ended the terror, and opened the gates of the GULAG. Of course he never intended to revise the system; just to make it slightly more humane. In spite of his doctrinaire tendencies, there was something touching, almost childlike, about him. He wasn't indifferent to the misfortunes and difficulties of people, to the hell of communal life, and he was the first to defend the right of every family to have a separate apartment. The construction of inexpensive housing on a massive scale was begun under Khrushchev, followed by a new plan to build more comfortable cooperative housing. Moscow turned into a gigantic construction site. Of course it changed the appearance of the city. The lanes, little parks and squares, and old wooden houses surrounded by gardens, alas, almost disappeared; but thousands of families acquired hope. It is hard to imagine the joy people felt at the thought that they would get their own two- or three-room apartment. It didn't matter that these apartments in five-story buildings had no elevator, that they all looked alike: a forty-square-foot kitchen, no hallway, adjoining rooms. For months these construction sites were a destination for Sunday family outings. Of course, twenty-five years later these "Khrushchev slums" were already shabby, their facings warped and peeling; but it is impossible to overestimate the importance of Khrushchev's decision to give millions of people the chance to live decently.

No repressions followed Khrushchev's removal. They didn't imprison him, didn't send him to Siberia; even the press didn't humiliate him. He simply retired and lived either in his Moscow apartment or at his dacha, which they didn't confiscate from him. There was none of the usual violent and bloody settling of accounts. This, naturally, surprised the liberal intelligentsia. For the broad public, Brezhnev, with his imposing appearance and bearing, his unhurried speech, and his weighty, calm demeanor, corresponded to their notion of a leader, and they said about him: He'll take charge. Very soon it became clear that he loved automobiles, and drove them himself, at maddening speeds. This only added to his prestige. At that time, owning a car was the epitome of happiness and well-being. This passion meant that he was a human being, just like the rest of us.

We thought that now we might stand a chance to become a more or less normal country, and perhaps live with a modicum of comfort and tranquility. Among my close friends and family, only Sima remained skeptical. He stared at Brezhnev on the TV for a long time, then said, "The manner of a provincial actor who is trying to give himself airs. The face of a bulldog, an empty gaze, completely mechanical speech. Listen to how difficult it is for him to say the simplest words. No, no good will come of him."

Yet life did become easier. In the stores there was meat, salmon, and caviar at reasonable prices. In the winter we could even buy oranges and bananas. It was easier to find clothing. Synthetics were very much in fashion back then: Nylon, Dacron, and so on. Imported furniture was available—from Hungary; rugs from Czechoslovakia and Finland. People developed a taste for comfort, and trips abroad began to be organized—primarily to the people's democracies, but also to Scandinavia, to Italy, France, and England. This opened up a little window into another world. Everyone flocked around those who returned from these trips. People would even pass up an evening at the theater to catch a person newly arrived from a trip abroad, their impressions still fresh in their minds. They were expected to describe things in the minutest detail. It was precisely these concrete details that were so interesting: what the hotel was like, what kinds of papers they had had to fill out, what kind of furniture the room had, what was in the stores, what the people on the streets were wearing.

There was also an undeniable cultural boom, which had already begun under Khrushchev. The young poets passed over the baton to the theater. Oleg Efremov, whom people already knew from his successful acting debut in *The Little Humpbacked Horse*—which appealed to adults as well as children—decided to take advantage of the Thaw and create his own theater. To the surprise of nearly everyone, the Sovremennik Theater ("Contemporary Theater") was born. It was aimed, above all, at those who wanted to speak and hear the truth. It had a young troupe that was united both by friendship and by a common goal: to revive a theater that was faithful to the Stanislavsky system of acting. They didn't question Soviet values, but simply wished to move theater arts closer to reality, similar to the writers who were publishing in *Novy Mir* and to the new wave of poets. The theater enjoyed unbelievable success. Every premiere was an event and signified a victory over censorship. Sometimes the censor won out, however. Galich's play *Sailor's Silence* was banned after the dress rehearsal because it recounted the history of a Jewish family. Nonetheless, the Sovremennik overcame this trial, and throughout the sixties it remained one of the few places that everyone always wanted to go.

During that period, Yury Lyubimov, who was then an actor in the Vakhtangovsky Theater and taught in the Shchukin Acting School, staged Brecht's play *The Good Woman of Setzuan* with his students. It was performed without sets—only tables and chairs, in a rehearsal hall. The entire arts community of Moscow rushed to see it, curious about how it was possible to create such magic with such minimal means. Then Lyubimov managed to get hold of a venue in a former movie theater on Taganskaya Square, and opened the famous Theater on Taganka, which soon became the most popular theater in Moscow.

Unlike Efremov, Lyubimov was very much interested in innovating theatrical forms. He rejected the Stanislavsky method and naïve realism. He produced plays based on the poetry of Pushkin, Mayakovsky, Voznesensky, and young poets who perished during the war. There was a play called *The Fallen and the Living*, which adapted stories and novels for stage, and sought a new metaphor each time. I would call it a theater with a burning conscience, which expressed all the ills of society. Lyubimov always pushed the boundaries of possibility, and he had to contend with censorship even more often than the Sovremmenik did. When he produced a classic, he made extensive reference to the context in which we were living. This was especially apparent when he staged *Hamlet* with Vysotsky. The audience was completely one with the Danish Prince in his struggle against the rotten royal court. Lyubimov was a man of passionate emotion, and theater was his life. He was present at every performance. He had his own seat in the audience, where he sat and signaled to the actors with a flashlight, controlling the pace of the play. In his work he was absolutely unbending. He refused to make the slightest concession to the authorities and the cultural officials. People left his plays feeling purged. This was probably why the tickets cost so much on the black market.

Anatoly Efros didn't even have his own dedicated space. He worked in the theater on Malaya Bronnaya Street, but the head of the theater finally began to allow him to do whatever he wanted. All of his plays, especially his productions of the classics—Shakespeare, Gogol, Turgenev, Dostoevsky—were beautifully staged. Naturally, the theater nomenklatura resented this and took it as a personal insult.

The unofficial, alternative culture grew steadily in significance. On Mayakovsky Square a base had been laid, and then waited for years to receive its statue. At around six in the evening, around this base for the future statue of Mayakovsky, groups of youths would gather to listen to the poems of Tsvetaeva and Pasternak, whom the young people recited alternately, and, most important, to recite and listen to their own poems. Soon these young poets—Vadim Delone, Leonid Gubanov, and many others who never published a line—formed an original association that they named SMOG (an acronym for the "Youngest Society of Geniuses"). In their manifesto, which they read fearlessly on the square, they expressed a certain political position; they were against the Soviet way of life, for example. They decried the formalism and limitation of the Komsomol, and demanded complete freedom of expression in word and deed. The crowd on Mayakovsky Square swelled from one day to the next, and unleashed public debates. Every third person there was a KGB agent, but the event was allowed to continue for some time. Then they began dispersing the gatherings under the pretext that they were blocking traffic. Some of them were driven away in cars, interrogated, then set free; sometimes they were tried for parasitism and banished from Moscow. They were able to rid themselves of SMOG fairly easily, but the seed had already been planted.

After that, the practice of visiting nonconformist artists' studios took hold. In fact, calling them "studios" was an overstatement. These artists worked in the same cramped spaces where they lived with their families and children. Natasha Stolyarov introduced us to this circle. Despite having lived in the camps for more than twenty years, she preserved a surprising independence of thought. She ventured to do things that it would never enter our heads to attempt. In addition to the Shalamov stories, she managed to smuggle out many other manuscripts to the West. She seemed to want to make up for lost time, and her boundless curiosity pushed her to meet as many new people as she could. For example, she traveled to Ryazan and knocked on Solzhenitsyn's door, without any prompting or letter of introduction.

Natasha took her friends to see the artists she discovered now and then. They were very disparate, and had no desire to unite into any sort of grouping or school. What drew them together was solely a strong resistance to any of the demands or tenets of Socialist Realism.

Oscar Rabin, for example, depicted the world as he saw it: half-decayed barracks, like those in which he lived with his wife and their two children in Lizanovo, near Moscow, with the corpses of dolls lying in dingy snow, heaps of trash in a dump, columns of gray smoke, and, very often in the foreground, an enormous bottle of vodka. The subjects of his paintings alone, not to mention his painterly execution, challenged the conventions of Soviet art. Exhibiting his canvases somewhere was out of the question.

Ephemeral exhibits lasting a day or two were organized at these apartments. Leonid Pinsky, for example, once displayed watercolors and oils by Anatoly Zverev. They are now worth a fortune, but Zverev himself died in wretched poverty.

Then several research institutes mustered the courage—for which there was sometimes a high price to pay—and organized exhibits of these "cursed artists," abstract painters, surrealists, hyperrealists, and others, in their own conference halls.

They received the right to show their work publicly only a decade later, after they had first tried to organize their own show in a vacant lot in Moscow. That exhibit was destroyed with bulldozers and street sprinklers. This event went down in history as the Bulldozer Exhibit. This barbarism, the destruction of these pieces of art, resonated widely, and the artists were then permitted to exhibit their work for one day in Izmailovsky Park. Thousands of visitors showed up. We were there, too, and we rejoiced, though we realized it was only a partial, imperfect victory, and a paltry concession on the part of the authorities.

The beginning of the Brezhnev years was marked for us by our reading of the first political novels, published abroad. Twenty-five miles from Moscow, in Sheremetevo, was the dacha community of the *Literary Gazette*. In the summer, the employees of the publication vacationed there, and in the winter one could rent these cabins fairly cheaply. An entire little phalanstery took shape there. Every Friday we went there to ski, but our rucksacks were stuffed with manuscripts and copies of banned books—*The New Class*, by Milovan Đilas, and *The Technology of Power*, by Abdurakhman Avtorkhanov, for example. The distribution of these could land you ten years in prison. The copies were often so faded it was nearly impossible to make out the text. The dachas of the *Literary Gazette*, the premier organ of propaganda for the Communist Party, thus served to undermine it. The dwellers were not dissidents; but we supported the struggle of the dissidents for civil and human rights, which would emerge at the end of the 1960s, beginning with the trial of Andrey Sinyavsky and Yuli Daniel.

56

In the summer of 1965, Sima and I were vacationing with the children in Koktebel, in the Writer's Home. Vic was there with us—we always tried to spend the summers together. On the third or fourth day of our stay, Asya Berzer arrived.

We were just leaving the Poet's House, that is, Maria Voloshina's, whom we had been visiting, and I said, "Look, there's Asya. She looks so gloomy . . ." We rushed down the steps and gave her a hug in greeting. She responded listlessly to us and said, "Something terrible has happened. They've arrested Sinyavsky and Daniel."

I knew about Daniel, because he translated poetry, and I had met him in the Translator's Department. We knew that Sinyavsky was a brilliant critic. He had written an article on Boris Pasternak in *Novy Mir*, in which, for the first time since he won the Nobel Prize, someone dared admit the true significance of Pasternak as one of the greatest poets of the twentieth century. Sinyavsky taught a course on Russian Literature in the MKhAT studio school.

Somehow, in recent years, we had grown unused to the authorities seizing people from this milieu. Asya walked with us along the tree-lined lanes, speaking in a whisper, saying that everyone in Moscow was afraid, and no one understood why this was happening. This threw a dark shadow over Koktebel, of course.

Gradually, news filtered through about the reasons behind the arrest. It transpired that both of them had written prose under pseudonyms—Sinyavsky under the name Abram Tertz, and Daniel under the name Nikolay Arzhak—which they sent abroad and had published there. Someone ratted on them, as they say. Someone denounced them, and they were arrested.

So we returned to Moscow. We were already different from the way we had been at the beginning of the Thaw. We felt we had to act. We simply couldn't look on passively. We had to come to their defense. All the more since Andrey Sinyavsky's wife had just given birth to a child. We had to make ourselves heard, to speak our piece; but we had no idea how we would do this.

On Constitution Day, the 5th of December, on Pushkin Square, for the first time, probably since the end of the 1920s, there was a protest demonstration. Friends called to tell us where and when it would take place, we called other people, and so on . . . Before, it would have been unthinkable to talk about such things on the phone—and a few years later it became just as unthinkable.

About ten of us met at the Mayakovskaya subway station and marched along Gorky Street to Pushkin Square. It was about six in the evening, and, in spite of the frost, the square was packed with people. There was no way to tell who came especially for the demonstration and who just happened to be walking by and joined in. Still, it was clear that something was being planned. There were more police than usual, black Volgas lined up in rows along the sidewalks, and in the nearby lanes; and, of course, dozens of KGB agents. We had come more as spectators than as organizers of the event, and we stood there not knowing what would happen next. Suddenly, in the center of the square, the crowd seemed to thicken, and I saw banners being unfurled above people's heads. It all happened in a matter of seconds. There was hardly even time to read the slogans, which said: RESPECT THE CONSTITUTION! and FREE SINYAVSKY AND DANIEL! before they disappeared. A commotion began. Voices were heard shouting and protesting, there were police whistles, and loudspeakers were turned on—or maybe it was just megaphones: "Clear the area! Clear the area!" People didn't lose any time, and a minute later the square was almost empty. We also cleared out, but I managed to notice some plainclothes policemen pushing two young men into one of the cars that had earlier drawn our attention. These two were not the only ones. The majority of the future leaders of the dissident movement were arrested on that day.

The trial of Andrey Sinyavsky and Yuli Daniel began two months later, in February. The intelligentsia immediately divided into those who were ready to defend them, and those who, on the contrary, considered them guilty. We experienced this very palpably, especially since this political trial—the first since the war—did not go on behind closed doors. Access was not open to the public at large, but tickets were distributed to members of the Writer's Union and the cinematographers. One could go and listen to how it all unfolded. A new era. I wasn't able to attend, but Sima was present in the court session at which two writers, Zoya Kedrin and Arkady Vasiliev, who assumed the role of volunteer district attorneys, testified for the prosecution. They testified in particularly insulting terms.

But Sima's impressions of the court proceedings were not entirely negative. He was surprised and heartened by the testimonies of several people who witnessed on behalf of the defendants and testified to their innocence. There was a young man by the name of Popov who worked as an apprentice to Sinyavsky's wife, Maria Rozanov, a jewelry maker. They worked in a very small room, and met every day. The apprentice, a seventeen-year-old boy, looking boldly at this body of important and powerful people sitting before him, defended Andrey Sinyavsky, telling them what an honest and wonderful person he was.

Despite the best efforts of the Writer's Union, they could find hardly a soul to endorse the sentence, apart from six unknown Uzbek writers and Mikhail Sholokhov, who announced at a writer's congress that he was ashamed of those who tried to defend Sinyavsky and Daniel.

On the other hand, a letter was written that later came to be known as the "Letter of the Sixty-Three."

Sixty-three people, including Sima and myself, signed a letter of protest against the suppression of the written word through the arrest of writers. Immediately following this, there was a wave of repressions. Each of the signatories was called to account by a corresponding professional organization—some by a writer's organization, some by the cinematographer's—and each one was called upon to make a written renouncement of what he or she had done. I must say, to the credit of the signatories, not one of them, apart from the sixty-fourth, who withdrew his name immediately, renounced the letter. People were punished, banned from being published. Their contracts were annulled, they were denied the right to make films based on their screenplays, and so on. However terrible it was, however harsh the sentence, there was still a sense that things were proceeding against the grain, that they weren't going completely smoothly, that there was resistance, albeit weak resistance. So the country was moving forward, it seemed. At the same time, something was happening in Sima and me, in our psychological development, in our respective psyches. By this time, we were already allowing ourselves to think and do more than we had before; we struggled with the feeling of fear, and tried to stamp it out, to eradicate it.

I do want to add something, however, to be completely honest (because I want to be as honest as I possibly can in this account). When Alik Ginsburg was released from prison, he gathered material on the Sinyavsky-Daniel case and published the so-called *White Book*. He gave one copy to Nikolai Podgorny, the chairman of the Supreme Soviet, and the other copies he distributed among friends, with the request that they pass them on to others when they had finished reading them. He was arrested again. Sima and I were asked to sign a petition about him, but we refused; because at just that moment, at the end of the 1960s, I had received permission to go to France—I'll say more about this later. I desperately wanted to go, if only to connect my adult life with my childhood. I was afraid that they wouldn't let me out, I told myself that one more signature wouldn't matter . . . I was terribly ashamed of myself. It tormented me, but I still didn't sign. I am saying this by way of confession. That is the way it happened. It seemed easier to sacrifice a general cause, I won't deny it. We were running a risk, each time—risking our livelihoods, our careers. But the risk was somehow generalized, and this three-week trip, a very concrete matter, I didn't want to sacrifice.

To some degree, my disappointment that the "Letter of the Sixty-Three" had been ineffectual played a role, as well. That letter had carried no weight whatsoever. It was completely discounted in the balance of fates. Sinyavsky and Daniel received long prison terms for publishing their works. We received proof that our opinions, our voices, had no influence on the outcome in the least. And, of course, this also undermined our enthusiasm, put a damper on the desire to sign letters and petitions, all the more since the cost was so high to us personally. That's just how it was. It was what it was.

57

The Sinyavsky and Daniel affair backfired on the KGB, however, because at just that moment, what eventually became known as the dissident movement began. This was a movement of those who opposed the authorities, not only in conversation around the kitchen table, where most liberal discussion in Moscow took place, but also in the realm of action.

Everyone did what she or he could within the limits of what was legal, and Sima and Ilya, in particular. Everything that they wrote pushed the boundaries of what was permissible. They didn't have a single play, a single film script, that might not have been banned at some stage. Literally, not one. Nonetheless, they felt, as did many other people, that it was important to work within the framework of what was legally sanctioned, for it gave one access to an enormous audience. The honest, truthful word can give rise to other associations that can inspire people to think and to evaluate, and has a large sphere of resonance. They thought in particular about the provincial young people who were deprived of everything. Here in the city, at least, there was samizdat—but in the provinces, there was nothing at all.

Thus, some people thought that it was very important to work absolutely honestly, and on the boundaries of what was permitted, while not transgressing those boundaries flagrantly. In the field of translation, that meant translating books that stood only a slight chance of squeezing through the censor, but still sometimes managed. In the theater, Zorin tried to write plays of this kind. Khmelik's play *My Friend Kolka*, which criticized dead forms of Pioneer organization, was also a borderline piece of art. A whole group of young artists tried to make people think, look, and imagine, without transgressing the legal norms too flagrantly.

There was another group who did not believe that legal methods could accomplish anything. Yet others believed one should combine both forms: that it was necessary to work both legally, and in non-sanctioned ways.

Alik Ginsburg was the first one to act openly to protect freedom of thought guaranteed by the Constitution. During the trial, he and the others accused with him not only refused to admit their mistakes, as had always been the case in the past, but stood up for the legitimacy of their actions firmly and convincingly, and defended their innocence. They appointed as their defenders people who, for the first time, defended them not according to the rules of Soviet justice, but according to their conscience. As a result, they themselves became victims of repression.

Two of them were especially close to me. Boris Zolotukhin, Ginsburg's counsel for the defense, had just begun a brilliant career as a prosecutor, but he made a moral choice and became a defense lawyer instead. He soon became very well known, and was tipped to be the most likely candidate for the post of chairman of the Collegium of Advocates, at which point he agreed to help Ginsburg. He paid for this with expulsion from the Party, then from the Collegium of Advocates, and was banned from practicing for twenty years.

Dusya Kaminskaya was a very beautiful, elegant woman who adored dressing well and ordered her clothing from famous Moscow tailors and dressmakers, the last ones remaining from the past era. She held receptions in her very tastefully appointed apartment. She also inculcated in us a taste for antique furniture, which everyone used to throw away, preferring imported wall units. Dusya was the first in our circle to dare to entertain foreign journalists. I met the correspondent of *Le Monde*, Jacques Amalric, and his wife Nicole Sand, at her home. Although I wanted very much to invite them to my house, I never mustered the courage.

Risking the loss of this luxurious life, and, of course, fully aware of what was in store for her, Dusya began to defend the dissidents. Vladimir Bukovsky had made a great impression on her. She admired his toughness, his precision of judgment, and his strict code of conduct. He defended the Crimean Tatars and Pavel Litvinov, whom, as a boy, KGB agents had prompted to inform on his grandfather—a former People's Commissar of International Affairs. Ultimately,

Dusya and her husband, Konstantin Simis, also a wonderful lawyer, were forced, under threat, to emigrate. They were offered a choice: emigration or the camps.

There were only a handful of dissidents, but they could not have undertaken anything were it not for the fact that they were surrounded by countless sympathizers. The trials that went on now behind closed doors, in contrast to the Sinyavsky-Daniel trial, attracted great crowds. They stood outside during the court session, in this way expressing their support for the accused. I will never forget the feeling that I had during Ginsburg's trial: a feeling of fear—what if they nail me?—mixed with joy that I had overcome this fear.

Perhaps the most important thing was reading, though. Beginning in 1968, issues of the *Chronicle of Current Events* began to appear regularly. The *Chronicle* was a true means of communication. This bulletin, on twelve to sixteen sheets of flimsy paper, spread all the information regarding the opposition throughout the country. If the police found this little brochure on someone, that person would be sent straight to prison. With unprecedented persistence, the KGB tried to arrest the authors of the *Chronicle* and thus to put an end to all opposition activity. They didn't succeed, and the *Chronicle* continued to appear. This was proof that the struggle continued, and we began to hope again.

The *Chronicle* and other samizdat materials were often lent for one night, for one day, or even for just a few hours. Whoever could, and wasn't afraid, copied them. This created a form of social interaction in Moscow in which people began to drop in on each other in the middle of the night. If someone's lights were on, you could call on them, knock on their door. If you brought something with you to read, you were a welcome guest. This facilitated friendships, communication. It was a new kind of friendship, friendship on a new basis. I have always noticed that people form friendships more easily when they have a common cause. This is why J.P. Vernant, my French friend, told me: "There is something in the friendship you have here that reminds me of the Resistance." Of course. It was the same phenomenon. When you have a common cause, when you are being persecuted, when you are threatened with danger, it is completely natural that people unite, that they express solidarity with one another, and begin to understand each other better on the level of emotion, of spirit. They confide things to each other that aren't connected with this activity, relate to each other with greater openness, with greater trust. It seems to me that the significance of the dissident period in the intellectual life of Moscow—and Leningrad, Kiev, Kharkov, I think—was also important in that it was a time when people who didn't know each well before, who were holed up in their little burrows, suddenly came together and recognized each other.

A sense of fraternity took hold, a readiness to reach out, an interest in one another, and plain sympathy. In this oppressed country, under the fixed gaze of the KGB, a gaze that had grown more intense, a new spirit of kinship took hold in people. This, I think, was very important, and people haven't talked about it much. Nevertheless, when foreigners came here to visit, they all noticed it. "The way you experience and maintain friendship," they used to say, "is different from how we do it. At home, when we socialize or communicate with one another, we don't really have much to talk about. We talk about where to find a place to park the car, or where you can buy the best cheese, or, in the best case, about the latest film or exhibit. Here in Russia you have exceptionally substantive conversations, and this creates a greater cohesiveness among people."

And it really was like that. Conversations were substantive because each person had to make a decision about how to live. For that reason it was interesting to hear someone's opinion, and to find out about someone's own experience. This kind of intimacy, this solidarity between intellectually honest people, was a byproduct of samizdat and dissidence, something ancillary to the primary and immediate concern. What was the *Chronicle of Current Events*, in fact? Before, when they arrested a person, especially in the provinces, he would disappear without a trace. It was like she or he had been wiped off the face of the earth. Now, the *Chronicle* would document it, reporting that in, say, Nizhny Tagil, so-and-so was arrested because he was found carrying a book of, oh, I don't know, Sinyavsky. Now, at opposite ends of Russia, people read about this, people knew it was going on. The importance of this was inestimable.

Another significant moment in those years was that people began collecting money and goods and sending them to the camps. Many political prisoners had no help or support. Their relatives and close friends were afraid to support them, and renounced them. Wives, and even parents, but especially wives and husbands, renounced one another. In the camps, it was very difficult to survive without help from outside.

An entire system of collecting goods and money was organized, and all the honest people in our circle participated in this, as did we. There were specific days, and people, who were in charge of gathering the things and sending them to their destinations. This also fostered mutual trust. I collected some money in academic circles, for instance. My uncle, Alexander Frumkin, and his wife, my aunt Amalia—now I can talk about this, since they both died a long time ago—contributed money very willingly, but they repeated a hundred times over: "Don't let anyone know where it came from. It's an anonymous donation, don't let on who gave it." Many others said the same thing. When it became possible to donate things through other people, rather than directly, many people were willing to help, all the while carefully concealing their involvement.

I think that it must always have been thus. Although the fear that was present under the Soviet system had never existed in more civilized times. Perhaps only during the Inquisition. Well, under Hitler, too, of course. There, too, as we are finding out, there were people who tried to help the Jews, tried to resist. There were far fewer of them there than there were here, however. It was easier to do here, of course. Our chaos, our disorganization, the disjointedness of different aspects of authority, assured that much of what could not have gone unnoticed in a civilized country, say, a country like Germany, remained undetected here. I want to stress, however, and to remind those who yearn for the past: people immediately alerted the authorities of the arrival of any stranger in any village. In every village there was an informer. This system of informing gave better results in the authorities' oppression of dissidence than any other. I know many stories: even in the most remote area, the back of beyond, you could never go unnoticed. You could never escape attention, someone was always on the lookout. The only way to save yourself—and some managed to avoid being arrested—was to disguise yourself as a forest ranger and leave for the backwoods. There is a Leningrad actress, Alexandra Zavyalova, whose father had been a big boss on the municipal level. When he realized that he was going to be arrested, he took his daughter and went deep into Siberia as a forest ranger, thus escaping danger.

Regarding help. In an honest person, I know this from my own experience, there is a great need to suppress fear and to help someone else. This is a need of the soul. One simply feels humiliated if one doesn't dare do this. What it is, is . . . now I've found the right word: it is a humiliation not to dare to extend your hand. It is as though a person is drowning, and you walk right past, whistling a tune.

For a person who is not entirely corrupted, who is not completely rotten or decadent, who has remnants of understanding left, it is natural to extend a hand. Although those sixty—or fifty, at the time—years of Soviet power, of course, destroyed, spoiled, many of the people who at one time in the past would naturally have done so. Still, it's impossible to completely corrupt and destroy a people at all levels. I want to recall here again how those old women offered bread to the German prisoners of war. It's a phenomenon of that nature. There is still a sense of pity, of compassion. Compassion for the suffering—this has always been a trait of the Russian character. The urge to help, to give a piece of bread, to offer a piece of warmth. I think it was something of that order.

58

A REMARKABLE EVENT OCCURRED AT THE END OF THE 1960S: THE Prague Spring. Alexander Dubček, the new secretary of the Communist Party of Czechoslovakia, became a hero for the Soviet intelligentsia. We believed that he was the embodiment of our dreams. Since we knew that it was unthinkable for us to call socialism into question, and we knew that the system was unshakeable, "socialism with a human face," the formula offered by Dubček, completely won us over. We saw in it a way out, a path that we could follow, too. All the more since our leaders did not seem to want to force the course of events. There was nothing in the papers about it; we listened to the BBC, Deutsche Welle, and Voice of America. Sometimes we sat by the radio for nights on end, following the news. Tuning into those broadcasts was not easy. We had to lie on the floor or cram ourselves into a corner of the kitchen or the bathroom. Out of safety concerns, people exchanged news on the street. I met Asya Berzer every day by Mayakovskaya subway station after she got off work. She told me what people were saying at *Novy Mir*, and we compared notes.

The situation seemed to be developing favorably, and at the beginning of August, Sima and I, Pavel, Zhenya, and some friends traveled to Lithuania, to the Ignalina District, on vacation. There we went canoeing down the small rivers from one lake to another, and in the evening we would find a pretty spot to set up camp. In these forests, you could walk for hours without seeing a soul. We picked boletus mushrooms and berries, and the events in Czechoslovakia seemed very distant. Nonetheless, in the evenings we listened without fail to our trusty transistor radio, which informed us about the progress of the negotiations between Dubček and the Soviet government. Then the batteries ran out, the radio fell silent, and we had no news for several days. We returned to Vilnius, where we were to board the train back to Moscow, feeling no alarm or concern, and very happy and carefree.

We bought newspapers; nothing interesting there. We still had a few hours before our train, and we went for a walk in a nearby park. Suddenly, coming toward us, we saw a man behaving rather strangely. He was listening to his transistor radio, pressing it to his ear. As soon as he noticed us, he quickened his pace, as though frightened of something. This brought me up short; I had no idea why he was behaving in such a way.

We arrived again at the station, and as we hadn't been able to book berths in the night train to Moscow beforehand, we were all scattered throughout different compartments. I tried to fall asleep, despite the mumbling of the radio, which was piped through the train and never turned off. Suddenly, in a fog of sleep, I thought I caught the name "Dubček." I listened more closely, and in a few minutes understood that he was in Moscow. "Dubček is in Moscow," the radio said, and it announced that in Czechoslovakia a full-scale counterrevolution was underway. The radio kept repeating this phrase over and over, without any commentary.

No one around me even budged. Apparently, no one paid any attention to this news. Shaken, I went to look for Sima. He was already fast asleep and hadn't heard anything. I even started thinking, Maybe I only dreamed it? But a few minutes later the latest news bulletin announced that the entire Czechoslovakian leadership was in the Soviet capital. From this moment, we weren't able to sleep again the whole night, certain that something terrible was happening.

In the morning at the Belorussian station, several friends met us, including Elka. With a gloomy expression on his face, not even bothering to greet us, he said, "Pavel Litvinov was arrested." Then he told us everything we were so afraid to hear: the leaders of the Czech Communist Party, headed by Dubček, had been brought to heel and sent by force to Moscow. Czechoslovakia was occupied by forces of the Warsaw Pact countries, tanks had rolled into Prague, hundreds had been killed, freedom was extinguished . . .

Our papers, of course, published only the official information: the USSR had offered armed assistance to the brother nation of Czechoslovakia as per their request. This was spiced up by falsified reports describing the joy of the Czechoslovakian people, saved from counterrevolution by its big brother.

No one protested, no one spoke about the shame that we ex-
perienced. No one, with the exception of four courageous women
and four men, who went out onto Red Square, and, by St. Basil's
Church, had just managed to unfurl banners reading FOR YOUR FREE-
DOM AND OURS, and CZECHOSLOVAKIA, WE'RE WITH YOU! when they
were arrested. I knew four of them personally: Pavel Litvinov and
Larisa Bogoraz-Daniel, the mathematicians; and the poets Natalia
Gorbanevskaya (who had come with her child in her arms), and
Vadim Delone. Almost all of them were involved in publishing the
Chronicle of Current Events.

They were tried and convicted. None of them pled guilty. Gorbanevskaya was forcibly removed to a psychiatric hospital. The others received sentences of several years of exile in Siberia and in
outlying regions of Kazakhstan. I think the end of 1968 was one of
the saddest periods of our lives.

59

Right up until 1973, the dissident movement grew, as did the government's attempts to suppress it. The trials followed in quick succession, one after another.

One day I went into Asya Berzer's office at *Novy Mir* and saw a person who looked nothing like the sort of people who frequented the offices of literary journals. Tall, bony, with a face covered in deep wrinkles, as though it had been carved out of stone, he had hands with huge palms, broken nails, toughened by frost and hard work. I couldn't help noticing them, because they stuck out of the short sleeves of his jacket, that was apparently too small for him. He spoke in a hoarse voice, with a slight rural accent, not articulating his words completely, and he had a bit of a stammer. When he said goodbye, he was the first to hold out his hand awkwardly to Asya, which is considered a sign of poor breeding; but he was beaming, his face lit up with a charming, childlike smile. This was Anatoly Marchenko. He had just returned from the camps and had brought Asya the manuscript of his book *My Testimony*. This was the first text about the camps not of the Stalin era, but of the Brezhnev era. From this book it became clear that the system had remained unchanged. How could such a text be published?

But Marchenko was not a man who would take this into account. He was the son of a collective farm worker. His universities were the camps, and he never ceased struggling. He dedicated his freedom to helping political prisoners in all possible ways. His freedom, however, was short-lived. He was arrested repeatedly, and he spent most of his whole life incarcerated, declaring a hunger strike in protest against the illegal imprisonment of others, and their poor treatment in prison. He died in 1986, two days before the announcement of his release. Several times the KGB offered him the possibility to emigrate, but he refused.

At the home of my friend Flora Litvinova, I met General Grigorenko for the first time. I remember how surprised I was to see such a guest at her house. He had the look and bearing of a typical Soviet apparatchik. Thick, solid, square, almost bald, with powerful gestures; his manner of speaking betrayed his peasant origins. It wasn't by chance that he looked like one of the nomenklatura. Only recently Grigorenko had occupied one of the most prestigious posts in the Frunze Military Academy: he headed the Department of Cybernetics. He took Khrushchev's address very literally, and began to think; and, gradually, step by step, he discovered all the layers of corruption in the system. This involved long and arduous inner psychological work, but when he had arrived at his new convictions, he could no longer remain silent. He started to fight within the Party itself, unmasking those who opposed the process of liberalization.

His fiery speeches were not appreciated; he was urged to repent. But no threats could deter him. This son of a peasant, elevated from his origins by the regime, sacrificed everything—his position, Party, professional scholarly activity—and became one of the staunchest and most courageous fighters for human rights in our country.

He defended the Crimean Tatars. The authorities, of course, could not reconcile themselves to the fact that one of theirs, moreover, a general, was capable of sacrificing his career in the name of the purity of the ideas of Leninism. In their view he was more dangerous than any dissident. Therefore, arresting him was not enough.

He had to be declared insane. When I next saw Peter Grigorenko, several years later, years he had spent in a psychiatric hospital, he had changed drastically. He was returning from hell, and had turned into a tiny, skinny old man. He had lost his brave demeanor, but the expression in his eyes expressed his former unbending will, which they had tried to break with the use of drugs. His wife said that she had seen him crying like a baby on a cot in this hospital-prison. Then, one brave doctor had started giving him shots of vitamins instead of neuroleptic drugs, and little by little he revived and gained strength, only to begin his struggle all over again, the moment he was released from the hospital. He was a person with the same kind of courage that Andrei Sakharov had. They both made the choice to risk everything—fame, honors, money—and never stinted or spared themselves to speak the truth, only the truth, at all costs.

After the Soviet tanks crushed the Prague Spring, we weren't able to recover from the blow. Members of the liberal intelligentsia fell en masse into a deep depression, convinced that Soviet power was all but invincible.

In contrast to the 1960s, so vital and full of hope, the 1970s began very somberly. The Stalinists had gained strength, Solzhenitsyn was expelled from the Writer's Union, which reviled him in every way possible, beginning with a terrible campaign headed by Sholokhov that resorted to all the old tricks—letters sent by workers and kolkhoz members expressing outrage that such a person "walked this planet." Tvardovsky was finally removed from his position as editor-in-chief of *Novy Mir* after a long battle, the final episode in which was a letter signed by thirteen writers demanding his resignation.

After that, the trial of Yakir and Krasin began, which, for all practical purposes, put an end to dissidence. Peter Yakir was the son of a famous general in the Red Army, executed by Stalin in 1937. He himself had been arrested at the age of fourteen. After spending seventeen years in the camps, he returned to Moscow in 1956. He became one of the most vibrant and vocal people to expose Stalin's crimes. Viktor Krasin, whose father died at Kolyma, was arrested several times, the first time when he was nineteen years old, at the end of the 1940s, for criticizing Marxism-Leninism. He was a math-

ematician, and one of the founding organizers of the struggle for
civil and human rights. He was considered one of the staunchest
members of this movement.

Now they were both arrested, and soon rumors started making
the rounds in Moscow that both of them had "broken" during the
interrogation. They had confessed everything about the system of
publication of the *Chronicle of Current Events*—microfiche, corre-
spondents, diplomatic mail, and the names of the underground
couriers. We found out that one person after another was being interrogated at the Lubyanka, and the list of those summoned grew
longer from day to day. One day, a friend of ours invited us to walk
in the woods near Moscow. In fact, he wanted to tell us that he had
been interrogated by the KGB several days prior, and warned us
that our turn was just around the corner. He had been surprised
when he received a letter from prison, signed by Yakir, with the request that he hand over the books and papers that he had hidden
in his apartment for him. He was even more surprised when he realized the amount of information the authorities already had at
their disposal.

I knew Yakir well, and was not terribly surprised at his behavior. In spite of all his energy and ardor, I had always had the feeling
that he was a broken person, and I didn't like his manner of luring
people into dissidence without asking their opinions. I found this
kind of offhandedness and carelessness dangerous. But why Krasin
had surrendered, no one could understand. Whatever the case may
have been, the authorities appreciated their willingness to cooperate and rewarded them with relatively light sentences. It was
broadcast on television: they admitted their guilt and repented
during the trial, which was staged like a grandiose show. While this
trial was being fabricated—and it dragged on for months—fear
returned with new force. Like everyone who was more or less
closely connected with dissidence, we got rid of everything that
might compromise us—books, samizdat texts, letters from abroad,
and every day we waited for a search to begin. The atmosphere felt
poisoned: it wasn't so much a matter of lack of trust, but of disappointment and despondency. We even lost the desire to see our
friends and spend time together.

60

In the 1970s, we experienced a great misfortune in our lives.

The Northern Fleet invited Lungin and Nusinov to travel along the coast of Europe to Odessa on a large military ship. *Midshipman Panin* had enjoyed great success in the Navy, and Elka and Sima began to be treated by the sailors as "one of their own." They went to Severomorsk and boarded the ship; three days later an unthinkable tragedy occurred. On the nineteenth of May, Elka died on board the ship of a coronary artery spasm. It wasn't even a heart attack. There was a large medical ward on the ship, and they tried to revive him, but to no avail. This happened in Norwegian waters. The ship then sailed back into Russian waters. A small steamship was sent to meet it, and in front of the crew, lined up in formation (around two thousand people serve on such aircraft carriers), and with military honors, Elka Nusinov's coffin was lowered by a hawser into the boat. Sima returned to Moscow with a zinc coffin on a military transport plane.

This was a defining moment in our lives. We were overcome by sadness and a sense of loss. Until that moment, everything that Sima and Elka wrote they had written together, even the shortest article. They had always collaborated. Sima didn't think he could work alone. He had never even learned to type. He lolled on the divan, while Elka sat at the desk and typed. Now Sima would have to learn how to write all over again.

61

FOUR YEARS LATER, WE WERE BESET BY MISFORTUNE OF ANOTHER KIND.

Vic Nekrasov, at one time one of our most beloved writers, even a laureate of the Stalin Prize, later simply a famous writer, fell into greater and greater disfavor.

I think Vic was perhaps the freest person I've ever known.

All in all, the damage that these seventy years inflicted upon the human being was much more terrible than the disasters in the economy, the ecology, and national relations. The deformation of the psyche, the destruction of the personality, are irreparable. The Civil War, collectivization, mass killing, then another horrific war, altered the genetic legacy of the nation. Those who perished were the cream of the crop, the most honest, the bravest, the proudest. To survive, one had to adapt, to lie, and to submit.

Of course, I saw people who resisted, and not only dissidents. Each of us tried to do what we could. For someone in the arts, honest work, expressing one's opinion, not making concessions and backing down, was a form of resistance. Not raising one's hand at a meeting when everyone else did, signing a letter of protest—that, of course, is already another form of protest. Nevertheless, all of this was an uprising of unarmed slaves. We understood perfectly well that we were engaging in madness, that this effort was doomed to fail, because the government, the Party, the KGB, were omnipotent. The only person I knew whose personality remained untouched by this, who was free of these deformations, was Vic Nekrasov. He was not an active fighter, he didn't seek direct confrontation with authority like others, nor did he challenge the system head-on, like, say, Solzhenitsyn. But everyone I knew, including Solzhenitsyn, was, unlike Nekrasov, a child of the system; despite their dissent, despite everything, they bore its stamp.

Vic behaved absolutely naturally in any situation. He wasn't afraid of anything, and he didn't bow to any authority. One day, just by chance, I overheard him talking on the phone to Surkov, the chairman of the Writer's Union. He was a spiteful, shrewd, and dangerous man, a typical apparatchik. To my great surprise, Vic expressed his indignation and anger about the persecution of Boris Yampolsky, a very good writer from Kiev. In a peremptory tone Nekrasov demanded that this campaign against him be stopped. I was sure that no one would allow himself to speak to Surkov like that; but on the other end of the line, I heard him mumble something in response, an excuse or a promise.

I often wondered where Vic had acquired this independence of spirit, freedom of manner and behavior, this sense of his own self-worth. Perhaps it was his blue blood, his aristocratic origins? But I saw other representatives of the Russian nobility who were servile time-servers. Alexey Tolstoy, for example, though not just him. Perhaps it was because Vic had spent his childhood in Switzerland and France? In the atmosphere that three wonderful women—his grandmother, his mother, and his aunt—who absolutely adored him, created for him?

His elder brother Nikolay was killed in the Civil War at the age of seventeen. He was murdered on the street by Red Army soldiers for holding a French book in his hands. As a class enemy.

There was no one else like Vic. With his artistic temperament and his spontaneity, he lived in a totalitarian world as he would have lived in any other world.

Before the war he had been a brilliant student of architecture, but he hadn't received a diploma. The academic committee wouldn't accept his project, which was imbued with the spirit of Le Corbusier, the architect Vic most revered. In that year the campaign against constructivism was unleashed. It was deemed to be a bourgeois tendency, hostile to the Socialist aesthetic. For many years after, Stalinist Neoclassicism was championed. Nekrasov was urged to take on another project if he wanted to receive his diploma, but he preferred to abandon architecture, rather than to abandon Le Corbusier. He decided to become an actor, hoping that this occupation would provide him with more independence. As a result he ended up in the municipal theater in Krivoy Rog in two capacities—as the *jeune premier* and the set designer. Then the war started.

Vic loved to repeat that he became a writer by chance. After the second time he was wounded, at Stalingrad, the doctor advised him to draw or write every day, in order to return mobility to his fingers: "to exercise the small motor skills." Vic chose writing, since, as he was lazy, he loved lying down, and he could write without standing up or sitting at a desk. Thus, lying on his stomach on his sagging divan, and scrawling with a pencil stub, he wrote *In the Trenches of Stalingrad*.

When he finished it, he gave the manuscript to a typist without any intention of publishing it. It wasn't in his nature to go running from one journal or publisher to another. He simply wanted to let his friends read it. One of them, unbeknownst to Vic, sent the manuscript to Vladimir Alexandrov, a critic who was part of the Lukács and Lifshitz group before the war. Alexandrov read it, was in raptures over it, and submitted it to the journal *Znamya*. Very soon after that, the book was published.

For the first time, those who had been in the war were able to recognize themselves in a novel. For the first time, people discovered descriptions of what they had experienced firsthand on the printed page. At the same time, the book challenged the whole tradition of glorification and exaltation of WWII. Immediately, voices were raised in protest. They accused Nekrasov of "deheroicization," of imitating Remarque—and this was a crime. The book was nearly destroyed. Suddenly, by some miracle, the book received the Stalin Prize. Books that were awarded this prize became sacred and inviolable, all the more since, according to rumor, Stalin had added *In the Trenches of Stalingrad* to the list himself. There were several editions of *Trenches*, many reprints, and it was one of those rare instances when official recognition and popular fame coincided. It is difficult to imagine how popular Nekrasov was throughout the country: he received thousands of letters, people recognized him in the street, on the train, people came up to him and expressed their gratitude and delight.

But fame didn't change him. He remained the same old Vic who had lived in a communal apartment with his mother, a doctor, who ran up and down the stairs of Kiev houses day after day tending to sick people. Although he had suddenly become a national treasure, a famous and wealthy man, he still managed to preserve his integrity, his clarity of vision, and his notions of good and evil.

He didn't change his way of life. The doors to his beautiful apartment on Kreshchatik, which the Writer's Union had given him, were open to everyone who needed his help. In contrast to most of the intelligentsia, who tried to go with the flow, Vic was a natural-born individualist. Therefore, he occupied a completely unique place in the literary milieu. At the height of his fame, he was chosen as a member of the board of the Writer's Union. They tried to push him down the career path, and tempted him with privileges connected to the position; but for him, observing these rules of the game was out of the question.

At meetings of the board of the Writer's Union, where everyone spoke and acted according to established rules, he was the only one to say what he really thought. Thus, he became an inconvenient witness to the machinations that were started there. He never resorted to the bureaucratic jargon that was de rigueur in official circles, and he shocked people with his relaxed attitudes and manner. A T-shirt in the summer, a checkered shirt unbuttoned to the navel, and pullover sweater and jacket in the winter. Others wore suits and ties in every season. Perhaps they wanted to reprove him, but they didn't dare. There was something in him that inspired respect.

The first signs of trouble began in the Kiev branch of the Writer's Union, because Vic wrote in Russian, and not in Ukrainian. At that time, the Ukrainian nomenklatura was distinguished by its dogmatism and nationalism. For these mediocrities, the presence of a celebrated Russian writer was unbearable. Suffice it to say that *Trenches* was not published in Ukraine—unprecedented for a book that won the Stalin Prize.

To convey some notion of the atmosphere in this milieu, Vic loved telling this story. Once he was walking with one of the local poets past the Kiev House of Writers, and Vic couldn't keep from mumbling: "Robbers' Den." His companion did not hesitate to inform on him at the next meeting, and added, "Do you know what I told him? I said, 'No, Viktor, it's not a robbers' den, it's the headquarters of progressive humanity.'"

In short, little by little an atmosphere of hatred and spite grew up around him. Vic traveled more and more often to Moscow, and spent the night on the divan in our living room. Several years later, when Vic's mother, whom he adored, retired, he began bringing her with him. They lived with us for months at a time. The shelves in our room were loaded down with journals and books with Vic's stories. We would sit in the kitchen talking and eating for hours on end—for some reason I remember the smell of herbs, dill, parsley, and tarragon, that wafted through the air as we sat around that table. Vic had his own spot by the window, and he wouldn't let anyone else sit there. Those were years of disappointment, fruitless struggle, bitterness—but, at the same time, in a strange way, years of great joy. When I recall how we sat around the table talking, the first thing I hear in my mind is our bursts of laughter. Vic's stories, Sima's stories about the discussion of the screenplay for *Welcome! or No Trespassing*, vacationing near Riga, in Apšuciems . . .

One of our greatest shared joys was the filming of *Ilich Outpost*, although it didn't have a happy ending. Nekrasov had a rare gift: he took delight in the work of other people. In 1960 our mutual friend Marlen Khutsiev, who was just over thirty at the time, invited the beginning screenwriter and poet Gennady Shpalikov to make a film about the younger generation. It was truthful cinema, cinéma vérité, in which the characters were taken directly from life and depicted in all the complexity of their feelings. Shpalikov was the first director in Soviet cinema to capture in dialogue the living speech of young people. The principle photography took many months. Aiming for perfection, or, perhaps, apprehensive about showing it to Goskino, Khutsiev kept reshooting some of the scenes. Vic passionately loved the way Marlen worked on film, this new manner of describing life in cinema. He spent all his time at the Gorky Studios, and once a week invited us to view the dailies.

We shared his enthusiasm; we also felt that it was unprecedented in Soviet cinema. Nekrasov wanted to talk about the birth of this masterpiece in *Novy Mir*. He wrote a little piece in which he stressed the natural acting of Nikolay Gubenko (the future Minister of Culture), who played a young worker and didn't look at all, Nekrasov said, like a mustachioed record-breaker who could only speak in slogans. This remark cost Vic dearly. There was some meeting or other in the Hall of Columns, or in the Kremlin, and Khrushchev reviled Vic. He said dismissively, "Who is this Nekrasov? I don't know him! For me, Nekrasov was a great 19th century poet. But this one? What right does he have to criticize our workers?" From that moment on, things started going downhill. The film was banned, and when it came out two years later, it had been reedited by the censors beyond recognition. Seeing what happened with *Outpost*, the young actors and the screenwriter took to drink. Nekrasov was no exception. Before that he had liked to drink like everyone else, but without getting drunk. But Vic had an obsessive desire to avoid growing old. And so, urged on by the desire not to be outdone by the younger people, at a certain moment he became a real drunkard.

Some time after this scandal, he nevertheless got permission to travel abroad. At first his impressions were published in *Novy Mir*, and then published in a beautiful volume with Vic's own pen and ink drawings. The book was very successful. It offered an authentic picture of life beyond the Iron Curtain. I believe it was a dispassionate, truthful account, rapturous and at the same time ironic.

For his objectivity, Vic paid a high price. The journalist Melor Sturua, London correspondent for *Izvestia*, printed a pamphlet with the title *Tourist with a Walking Stick*, in which he accused Nekrasov of painting a false picture of life in capitalist countries, serving the interests of imperialism, and slandering the Soviet system. The campaign against Vic intensified, and the doors of journals and publishers were shut to him for all time. He became more estranged from official life, although he never became part of the opposition. He was never a dissident in the literal sense of the word. His conflict with the authorities was moral in character; it grew out of an aversion to falsehood and demagoguery. At the same time, he supported young people fighting for human and civil rights and tried to protect them; interceded for detainees and for the disgraced; and signed petitions and letters. Every year Vic traveled to Babiy Yar, to the ravine near Kiev where the Fascists executed thousands of Jews. The Central Committee could not forgive him for a speech he made, dedicated to the memory of the victims. Amid the anti-Semitism that reigned then, his speech was an act of defiance.

He began to notice that someone was always following him on the street, watching his comings and goings, and gradually he got the sense that they were trying to push him out of the country, to get rid of him. It had already become customary to banish people. They had kicked out Solzhenitsyn, forced Rostropovich to leave, along with Galina Vishnevskaya, who was guilty for having offered

him shelter. They kicked out the biologist Zhores Medvedev, Sinyavsky and Vladimir Maksimov, Vladimir Voinovich, Lev Kopelev, Raya Orlova, Alexander Zinoviev, and so forth. Not to mention all the scholars, scientists, artists . . .

For Vic, the last straw was a search in his house that lasted for almost three days. They took away two sacks of manuscripts, a typewriter, books . . . And he wrote a naïve letter to the Central Committee of the Ukrainian Communist Party. He felt so much a part of this world, this country, so deeply bound to its life through his *Trenches* and so forth, so organically implicated in it, that he couldn't imagine that they might really want to get rid of him. He thought he needed to address the issues point blank, and they would immediately give him the "green light." He wrote a letter, which he showed to us, protesting that they weren't publishing him, that they were dogging his footsteps, following him around, that people wrote articles against him. He demanded that the confiscated manuscripts and books be returned to him—they were books by Aleksandr Kuprin and Ivan Bunin published abroad. Why, he wrote, couldn't he keep them in his home? He demanded that the persecution cease, that they publish him in an edition of so many copies . . . That kind of letter; full of indignation and demands.

He called us, very satisfied with himself. "Look how quickly it's all happening," he said. "They have called me in, two days from now, for an interview." At the interview they told him to leave. Good riddance. No one's stopping you. He was stunned. Psychologically, he was not prepared for this kind of response, or for departure. He had been absolutely certain that when he explained his position so clearly and succinctly they would have no recourse but to apologize to him. Although they had railed at him, he remained a child of fortune. He was lucky in life. People loved him very much, they took care of him, women adored him. In fact, he didn't really take all these trials and tribulations very seriously; he didn't think they could change the very course of his life. Now, suddenly, they were telling him: Get lost! No one's keeping you here.

He had an uncle in Switzerland, a professor at Lausanne University. In 1974, Vic left, on the pretext that he was going to visit his uncle. It was already clear, however, that he was leaving for good. For Sima and me it was a terrible blow. We couldn't imagine our lives without Vic. Since we couldn't get permission to go abroad, it was clear that we would never see each other again.

Sima and I decided to see Vic off in Kiev. We went to the Kiev Station, and just before it was time to leave we bought tickets for the train. In Vic's compartment there was a single traveler, a man of about sixty, who pulled out a bottle of cognac as soon as the train started moving and said, "You're going to see Nekrasov off? Let's have a talk." I nearly fainted. We had just bought the tickets. How was this possible?

We talked all night. He conversed in a strange, sly manner. He knew everything. Knew whom Vic met with, where he had been, where we had been; he knew everything. Only when we were arriving in Kiev did it come out that he was the secretary of propaganda for the Kiev City Council of the Communist Party. He was one of the people who had facilitated Vic's departure. The night we spent talking to this person was one of the most unpleasant I have ever experienced. It was almost metaphysically unpleasant. I started feeling that although we were living in different times, life was transparent, someone was always watching, nothing remained secret. When we parted ways, he asked with a smile, "So, I look like a demon, don't I?" I said, "Yes, you do."

In Kiev, two young men with briefcases trailed us wherever we went, with microphones sticking out from their briefcases, like swan's necks. This was obviously intentional. It was so blatant that it could only have been meant for us to see. When we boarded the plane to fly back to Moscow, we noticed that these two young men were sitting right behind us.

In the same year, 1974, Alexander Galich was also forced to leave the country. On the eve of his departure with his wife to France, we visited him to say goodbye. The apartment was empty. There were no pictures on the walls, no rugs, no dishes or lamps, no curtains on the windows—nothing. Everything but a few stray pieces of furniture had been given away to friends and relatives. Only Sima and I, the composer Nikolay Karetnikov, and Alexander's brother were there. We felt like crying, and the conversation was starting to fall apart when, suddenly, Alexander grabbed the guitar and sang us a song he had just made up: "When I return . . ." The last line went: "But when will I return?"

We were all sure the answer was never.

The authorities got rid of everyone who could have served as an example to others. Exile, banishment from the country, prison, hospitalization in psychiatric wards—anything to force people to stay silent. When these people had been expelled, when they disappeared from our common existence, the country became mired in a swamp of mediocrity, the whole culture was impoverished. The small traces of individuality, morality, intellectual integrity, were destroyed and scattered.

62

SAKHAROV REMAINED. HE WAS DETERMINED TO RESIST AND TO TAKE action, no matter what, no matter whether they followed him and his family around the clock for days on end and tapped his telephone line, and despite the threats from the KGB that became ever more serious. He seemed not to know fear. He was afraid of only one thing: that he wouldn't know how to express what he wanted to say precisely enough. His only concern was to stand up for his convictions to the very end. They tried every trick in the book to compromise him, to turn public opinion against him, to hold him up to ridicule: through slander, and every kind of base accusation against his family and his person that they could muster. Needless to say, there was an avalanche of letters from workers, peasants, and academics . . . Alas, it would be wrong to claim that the scholarly and scientific community did not subject him to shabby treatment. No one rose to his defense, no one spoke out publicly against the harassment he had to undergo. The Soviet government knew how to control minds. Twelve musicians announced that they were "outraged by the actions of Sakharov," among them Shostakovich and Khachaturian, two world-renowned composers—people who, one would have thought, had the luxury of being independent.

Unanimity of opinion was explained not by faith, as in the Stalin era, but by submission and obedience; and the authorities paid their lackeys well, with a complex system of privileges. I experienced this personally, during a trip to Moldavia.

Sima was chairman of the jury of a film festival or some sort of competition in Kishinev. This transformed him to an honorary member of the nomenklatura, and we were housed not in an ordinary hotel, but in the hotel of the Central Committee of the Communist Party. It was a luxurious building with expensive carpeting, and nearly empty—so much so that the silence was unsettling. At the same time, there were a great many service personnel everywhere. They were very obliging. We intended to go to the restaurant, and we asked the maid—in a black dress with a white apron and lace cap—where it was located. She answered in an apologetic tone that they only had a dining room. We went there, and what a dining room it was! It had been a long time since we had seen such white tablecloths, laundered and starched, in the best traditions of pre-Revolutionary Russia. We were equally surprised by the smoked salmon, various types of caviar and cuts of meat, and so forth. But what surprised us most of all were the prices. Everything cost mere pennies. True, as in all dining halls, wine and beer were not on offer. The only one who had the right to a bottle of vodka, covered by a white napkin, was the first secretary, who was sitting a little to the side on a raised area.

There was a broad network of "closed" grocery stores where everything was sold at greatly reduced prices. The father of our friend, the lawyer Boris Zolotukhin—former head of the Government Committee, at the ministerial level, and now retired—received monthly rebates to the sum of one hundred rubles, which he was able to spend there. He shared these rebates among his family members and two sons, and this was enough to guarantee the family a steady supply of the best meat and fish. There were also clothing distributors: the wives and daughters of managers and officials shopped on the sixth floor of GUM department store in Moscow. In every region, city, and even in villages, everywhere there were local Party committees, there were also "closed" buffets, as well as warehouses, where one could acquire imported furniture—Finnish, Yugoslavian, and even Turkish.

When a gigantic hotel was built by the Central Committee in the center of Moscow, almost directly opposite the French embassy, one of our Pavel's girlfriends, who was a fashion designer, was commissioned to design pajamas and bathrobes especially for the guests of the hotel. There were specific requirements: there had to be four pockets on the pajamas for guests who stayed in the Deluxe rooms. The guests in the other rooms had to be content with pajamas of another color and a single pocket.

There had to be a whole army of service personnel to satisfy the demands for luxury and comfort of this privileged class. All these employees of "closed" stores—housemaids, waiters, and cooks, who had such riches at their disposal—began to trade the goods they now had access to. They not only became rich, but played an important role in society. Let's not forget the Beryozka stores, where one could buy only with hard currency or a chit, if the money had been earned abroad. For ordinary people, these stores held an irresistible attraction, and soon the chits were being traded on the black market, too.

Butchers and managers of grocery stores quickly realized that it was in their interests to have private clientele, for whom they would put aside the choice pieces in exchange for money that went straight into their pockets. Drugstores traded in imported medicines on the black market, not to mention the doctors and hairdressers, who, not in the least afraid of the law, served private customers and earned big money doing so. Or the teachers who helped prepare students for the entrance exams at the universities. It was not easy to keep things competitive. Everyone knew that admission to the university was expensive. First, a certain number of spots were reserved for children of the nomenklatura (this was called the "rector's list"); and, as for the others, the examiners often bargained directly with them. Almost all the high-school students, even those from working class families, paid fifteen or twenty rubles for private lessons in order to get admitted to the university. Groups of teachers conspired with the examiners, whom they paid to ensure certain results; and they themselves got money from the families for their services.

This was how the parallel economy was organized. It developed very rapidly and spread throughout every sector of society. Only members of the intelligentsia—important scholars and scientists, writers, cinematographers—did not need to seek extra income. The government paid them well, already—bought them off, in other words. They received trips abroad (as the highest reward), not to mention vacations and plane tickets, over and above their salaries.

In this way, almost imperceptibly, a strange society characterized by consumerism without consumer goods took shape.

The entire country, from top to bottom, regardless of social background or category, drank. People drank everywhere—in organizations and schools and institutions, in offices, on shop floors in factories, on the stairs of residential buildings, on the street, in train and bus stations, on the trains, at any time of day or night, before, after, and during work. On the factory floor, workers couldn't turn on their machinery without taking a nip of vodka or home-brew, because after their drinking binge the night before, their hands would be shaking. To stop the tremors in their hands, they needed the hair of the dog to "recover." The day began with col-lecting change to make a "booze run." Vodka didn't go on sale until eleven, so you can imagine what time they actually started work-ing.

The Party bosses were lenient toward tipplers (in spite of the fact that according to statistics published under Gorbachev more than half of all crimes committed were carried out in a state of in-toxication), since most of them drank themselves. Moreover, vodka possessed an exchange value: every worker or government official could be paid with a certain number of bottles.

Vodka became a religion. With no hope for change of any kind, people found an outlet in trying to make their lives more bearable and comfortable, in entertainment, in oblivion. Some wanted to save up money, to receive privileges. Others wanted to hold themselves aloof, insofar as it was possible, from official life. At a certain moment we stopped going to meetings of writers and cinematographers, we avoided the Writer's Home and the House of Cinema, and even refused to eat in the restaurants where there was a preponderance of black market traders. The atmosphere was strange: a mixture of weariness, indifference, and cynicism, like a feast during the plague—only this feast, people assumed, would go on for centuries.

63

ALL MY COLLEAGUES IN TRANSLATION TRAVELED ABROAD, BUT THEY wouldn't let me go anywhere. I submitted my papers time and time and again, and I was always refused.

They wouldn't let Sima go, either. Elka had once gotten permission to travel to Yugoslavia, but not Sima—despite the fact that they were inseparable. Once, the man who was the director of the House of Cinema, who had previously spied on us, most likely—judging from the fact that he had been kicked out of England with a group of spies—told Sima, with whom he had a good relationship, "Take a good look at the people you socialize with. There's your problem." I think that was simply an excuse, because Elka and Sima shared the same friends and acquaintances.

Another time, Nikolai Sizov, who was a big film producer, tried to send Sima abroad to work on a film script, but they again refused to give him a travel passport. Sizov tried to arrange the matter through his own connections, and finally said to Sima irritably, "They just don't want to let you! They don't want you to go abroad!" So the reason remained a secret. I would give a great deal to be able to peek at our KGB files. When Leonid Pinsky returned from the camps, he told me that at one of the interrogations—and they interrogated him often, and very painfully; his legs were like two logs, because during the questioning you spend the entire night with your legs down, either standing or sitting, and in the day, in your cell, you can't lie down either—he told me that one or two of the interrogations were specifically about me, and there was a special record of it. Naturally, he held firm: he would never under any circumstances have said anything about me, nor about anyone else.

Suddenly, the secretary of the Union of Cinematographers summoned Sima and said, "Hand over your documents, you can go abroad. It seems I came to an agreement about you." Sima also asked him, "Do you know what they were holding against me, what the problem was?" "We're not going to talk about that," he said gruffly.

Sima went to Italy with a group of filmmakers. I lay on the couch, looked at the map, picturing him going from city to city. I accompanied him in my imagination.

Four times I got a refusal formulated in the same way: *Your trip is not considered viable at this time.* Then I wrote to the Ministry of Internal Affairs, since the OVIR was under its auspices, and I got the standard form letter in response, saying there were no grounds for reviewing the decision that had already been taken. After the fourth refusal, someone told me, "You aren't writing to the right place. Don't write the Ministry of Internal Affairs, write directly to Andropov." I wrote Andropov, although people, close friends, criticized me for it: "How can you write to such a vile person? It's inappropriate to correspond with him for any reason." But I thought, I don't care. I want to go to Paris. So I wrote to Andropov, saying that I'd received four refusals to my request to go visit my friends. People like me, members of the translator's section of the Writer's Union, that is, all went abroad. If I couldn't go, I would like to know the reasons why I was an exception to this rule. I was certain that I would receive another standard letter stating the same thing the others had.

I was visiting the famous philologist Koma Ivanov in Peredelkino with one of Lida's colleagues, a teacher, when little Zhenya, who had somehow gotten hold of the number, called me, shouting, "Mama! Mama! A postcard came, and they want you to pay a fee of 200 rubles! That means you're going!" That was how I found out that I could finally visit France.

I traveled by train, primarily because I couldn't imagine that in only three days I would actually be there. The impression would have been too jarring, too intense. I needed to arrive there gradually.

With every hour I passed some sort of stage on the way. Here was Brest, where we transferred to another gauge of track—it's narrower in Europe—and now we were on the other side of the station, and it was already "abroad," which for me was like a breath of something mysterious and alluring in those years. I couldn't tear myself away from the windows. Poland was gray and dismal, but I stared transfixed out the window. Then Berlin. East Berlin, that is. Those terrible, terrifying German policemen with dogs came in. We had to exit the compartment. They searched under the seats, they groped in the luggage racks above; they knocked on the walls, as if they expected to find a whole army of dissidents hidden between them. Belgium, France; and in three hours twenty minutes the train would stop at the Gare du Nord, the Northern Station, in Paris.

64

SIMA, VIC, AND I USED TO LOVE TO PRETEND WE WERE IN ALL KINDS OF imaginary situations. The last summer before Vic's departure, when we still had no thought of parting, we rented a little house in Saulkrasti, near Riga, and spent the whole summer there—Sima and myself, Vic, and our little grandson Sasha. And we pretended: imagine that I (Lilya) get permission to go to Paris, and you (Vic) meet me at the station. You have a little Peugeot, and we drive here, and we drive there . . . In short, we played out an imaginary life in Paris, which, of course, seemed absolutely unattainable and improbable.

When I got off the train in Paris, Vic Nekrasov was there waiting for me, on the platform.

With him were Lida, J.P., and other very close friends of mine: Dusya Kaminskaya and Konstantin Simis. We, too, had thought we were parting forever when they left.

This is apropos of the idea I expressed earlier: you shouldn't assume that a loss (if it's not a death, naturally) is necessarily a disaster. It can turn out to be the other way around. Bad solutions to problems can turn into something good. In short, when I arrived in France, there on the platform stood not only Vic Nekrasov, but Dusya and Kostya. Our mutual friends had collected money for them so they could be there to meet me, too. It was wondrous, seeing those from whom I had parted forever.

Again, I felt that life had come full circle. That I had never left there. I experienced Paris as my own city, my hometown. I belonged here.

When we arrived at Vic's house, I saw that his French room had been arranged in just the same way as his room in Kiev. It was an exact copy. He loved what he was used to, and it was such a strange feeling when I entered . . . He had hung his beloved paintings and photographs in the same way, flowers were arranged in the same places—everything mirrored his room in Kiev.

Our dream of Paris had come true. Three years later, I received permission to go there with Sima, and the second part of our dream came true: to be there all together.

After that we went to Paris a number of times. We traveled the length and breadth of the country with Vic. We swam in the Mediterranean. We went to Switzerland, high up into the mountains. We have amazing photographs against a background of everlasting snow. Vic loved taking pictures. He was a brilliant photographer. At some point, I hope that either I or one of my children will be able to publish an album of photographs: *The Paris of Viktor Nekrasov*. It needs to be published. Each time we went to Paris, we received a photo album as a gift. We have five of them.

In spite of the rumors that circulated around Moscow, Vic was not unhappy living in emigration. He had always dreamed of traveling, and was now finally able to travel almost the whole globe. He was invited by universities all over the world to speak and teach, and he continued to write. After each of our trips to France, we managed to smuggle copies of his books back to Moscow, where people waited impatiently for them. He was not wealthy, but his needs were few. Vic didn't like cars, or expensive restaurants. He preferred small Paris bistros, where he would drink his coffee over a newspaper in the mornings. His expenditures consisted of books and albums of art. In Paris, when invited to eat with friends, he would request tea, sandwiches with sausage and cheese, and vodka. Still, he remained a stranger there, cut off from his language, from his country. I remember how he pasted some beautiful black and white photographs of Paris in one of the albums he presented to us, and said, "I haven't become French, but I am a Parisian."

Once we visited Toulon together. Toulon is the military port of France. As one walks from the train station, at every step one comes across a slogan that reads: "If you've never seen a warship, you've never been in Toulon." We arrived in the evening, and stayed in a third-rate hotel, because we had to count every penny—we never had any money there. In the morning, when we had just set out to look at the warships, a downpour began. We ducked into the first café we came to, and stayed there the whole day, because that's what the weather is like in the south of France: it clears up for a bit, and down comes the rain again. In the evening we had to go back to Paris, so we never did get to see the warships.

On the day of our departure from France, Vic brought us a little box that he had covered with dark red velvety paper. On the top of the box was an inscription in French: "If you've never seen a warship, you've never been in Toulon." Inside the box were three tiny toy battleships, glued to the bottom, and the words: REMEMBER TOULON. This gesture was very much in the spirit of Vic. I would say it expressed his very essence. It was one of Sima's and my prize possessions, and now that I am alone, I still cherish it.

65

Toward the end of the 1970s, life changed. Even the appearance of Moscow was altered. Social inequities came out onto the street. People stopped trying to hide their wealth; it became conspicuous. Foreign-made cars with Russian license plates appeared, and girls paraded their silver fox coats—whether they were daughters of the nomenklatura, or foreign-currency prostitutes providing their services to foreign tourists. More people began flocking to the restaurants, sometimes waiting hours for the privilege to enter and spend all their money on carousing. The wealthiest people didn't have to wait in line—a few banknotes in the pocket of the bouncer, and the doors opened for them like magic.

At the other end of the spectrum, a new category of the population appeared: limitchiks. These were young people, most often from rural areas, who were hired to do the hardest work in the jobs and industries where there was a labor shortage. Every factory, every construction enterprise, received permission to hire a limited— hence the name limitchiks—number of collective farm workers or people from small towns and settlements. At first they were housed in dormitories on the outskirts of the city. Then they gradually moved downtown. They were easy to spot—by their rudeness in lines or on the buses, by their tacky clothes, and by their swagger. In contrast to Muscovites, they evidently had abundant patience and energy, and to acquire residence permits and a separate room for themselves they were prepared to wait many years.

For example, our nanny, Motya, had a cousin, Tanya, who came to Moscow when she was eighteen as a limitchik, after she was hired at the ZIL automotive plant. A tiny, frail girl who had never been anywhere but her native village, she dreamed, of course, of moving to the capital. All over the Soviet Union, hundreds of thousands of young girls echoed the refrain of Chekhov's *Three Sisters*: "To Moscow, to Moscow." So Tanya realized her dream and ended up in an enormous factory, where she was supposed to operate a tipping bucket with melted metal, which rolled along a rail suspended from the ceiling. The pay depended on the amount of metal moved through the system, so neither she, nor any of her friends on the shop floor, paid attention to the safety regulations. Accidents were the rule, rather than the exception.

When she was hired, they promised her her own room in three years. Then the three turned into five. In the end, she received what they had promised her only after ten years; and at what a price! Sima and I went to her housewarming in this room, where she had moved with her husband, also a limitchik, and their small child. It was an enormous sixteen-story building with twenty entrances, which looked out onto an empty lot. On each landing there were four three-room communal apartments. Families with children lived in the two larger rooms, sometimes with a grandmother who had moved from the countryside, and the small room—a hundred square feet—was occupied by a single mother with a child. All the furnishings were exactly the same in all the rooms: a folding-bed, a child's bed or crib, a wardrobe with a mirror. In the center of the room was a table with four chairs under a plastic lampshade. There was a refrigerator, a TV, and on the wall, there was always a rug, a symbol of abundance. In the tiny, forty-square-foot kitchen were three identical tables—one for each of the women. On the day we visited, all three women were smiling and friendly, of course, but there was palpable tension in the air. Not two months had passed before Tanya and her neighbors had come to blows.

Meanwhile, these paltry little rooms that the limitchiks received from their factories, which built the houses for their employees, gave rise to the resentment and envy of native Muscovites. Many of them had to wait longer than the newcomers, and to live in worse conditions. The hatred that the native residents felt for these strangers was comparable to the hatred of Jews.

One shouldn't think that anti-Semitism disappeared during the Brezhnev era. On the contrary, it was more tenacious than ever; it simply assumed other forms. It had become more mundane, less threatening to life and limb—but it was every bit as virulent. This was especially palpable after the victory of Israel in the Six-Day War, which filled Soviet Jews with pride—even those who were completely assimilated. At the same time, it called forth hostility in the authorities and a significant portion of the population. Later, when Jews were offered the possibility of "leaving the country," the anti-Semitism grew more acute. Countless times I heard people discussing the fact that Jews could no longer be trusted, that they dreamed only of emigrating, that this was not their homeland, that it was foolish to allow them to get an education, it was a waste of government money, that they didn't have the moral right to occupy a post or job here. Even respected figures reasoned in this way. These views were always fortified with envy: "Why them, and not us? They are always getting preferential treatment!" The envy was that much stronger because they didn't dare allow themselves to formulate it.

Other than everyday anti-Semitism, there was also "intellectual" anti-Semitism, so to speak. There was a right-wing branch of the dissident movement, active already since the 1960s. It united such disparate figures as the mathematician Igor Shafarevich; a corresponding member of the Academy of Sciences by the name of Emelyanov—a kind of ideologue, an ignorant fanatic whose writings were distributed in samizdat; or the well-known literary critics who were associated with the journals *The Contemporary* and *Young Guard*: Kozhinov, Palievsky, and Mikhailov. Oleg Mikhailov formulated the essence of the fateful role of Jews in the history of Russia most categorically. He claimed, for example, that Russians had developed a taste for hard drinking because of the Jews, that Jews had carried out the October Revolution, that they were responsible for collectivization, that they worked for the GPU (KGB) . . . All this with the secret goal of causing harm to the Russian people. As for Russian culture of the 20th century, the legacies of Babel, Ilf, Mandelstam, and Pasternak had distorted and damaged it. It had lost its originality, its national character. Then, in the eighties, the same accusations were leveled by the Pamyat ("Memory") organization, and spread by the publicists Begun and Evseev in brochures published, primarily, in Belorussia.

In short, the desire to emigrate grew stronger and stronger among scientists, scholars, doctors, and even musicians, among those who wanted permanent jobs, and especially among young people, whose prospects were limited. Our younger son Zhenya, who was a very successful student and had become a theater critic, spent an entire year looking for a job. Everywhere, he was greeted with open arms—in the theater, television, at journals—and they assured him that he was the very one they had been waiting for. But as soon as he filled in the infamous "fifth paragraph," his ethnicity, on the application, he was informed that there were no vacancies. In the places where he knew people, they whispered, "The Personnel Department wouldn't hear of it." After many attempts to get a job, and many rejections, he decided to leave the Soviet Union.

It was harder and harder for a Jew to get a higher education. Several departments—mathematics and physics, in particular—turned into unassailable fortresses.

If you already had a job, the only way to keep it was to go unnoticed. Keep a low profile. If you wanted to work, you had to reconcile yourself to mediocrity. A Jew would never be appointed to a position with a high degree of responsibility, even if he were a genius. If he had long occupied a certain place in the scientific or academic hierarchy, it was impossible for him to transfer to another place, because no director or manager wanted to take that risk. He feared that it would compromise his institute.

Many people in the scientific community submitted their documents for emigration. But submitting them did not necessarily mean you would be able to leave. No, they could refuse you. After a time, you would be allowed to submit them again. And again they would refuse you. You became a refusenik. I didn't know many personally, but I knew a few. Of course, like all normal people, I was indignant at the fate to which they were condemned: to be forcibly retained for years on end, to be fired from their job, to be treated like an enemy of the people, their departure considered to be treason. They were ejected from society, they were confined to their own little circle and communicated only with one another. So as not to starve to death, they sometimes managed to find work, if only as guards or night watchmen. They no longer cared what was happening in the USSR. Mentally, it was as though they were no longer here.

We lived in a completely different milieu, however. The situation was truly different in the theater, the movie industry, journalism—the sphere of free professions, where one didn't have a permanent post, and there was no need to deal with a personnel department. In these fields, in which professional qualities played, if not a major role, then at least a significant one, it was still possible to work, although it wasn't easy. The managing board of the main publishing houses, for example, not only Detgiz, as I have already mentioned, but also Khudozhestvennaya Literatura, received a directive saying that the number of Jewish translators should not exceed a certain percentage.

Among our friends, almost no one wanted to leave, and we never even considered it ourselves. We felt deeply rooted in Russian culture; all our work was connected with the Russian language. Although this land spurned us, we felt it was our own. This was where the graves of our relatives and friends were. The landscapes of central Russia—mixed forests, meadows, onion domes of white churches overlooking meandering rivers—all of this made up our life, with both the bad and the good, and we had neither the desire, nor the courage, to start all over again from scratch.

The years passed, and nothing changed. People like us withdrew further and further into the shells of our personal lives. It was like we weren't there, though we were physically present. Our only refuge was our work. We tried to do the best possible job, maintaining a certain intellectual level, and struggling for maximum leeway from the censor.

Everything that Sima and Elka had done, I want to stress again, was always banned at first. But at the cost of struggle, they managed to push through *Welcome! or No Trespassing*, and the play *The Goosefeather*, which was produced by the wonderful Nikolay Akimov in Leningrad. They even wanted to ban the film *Attention! Tortoise* for ideological reasons. They seriously thought that the image of a turtle in the pathway of a tank was an allusion to the Prague Spring, to Czechoslovakia. (Also diminutive and ancient, like the turtle!) Nevertheless, they let the film pass. But *Agonia* was shelved and collected dust for many years. My translation work, however humble, helped make a small aperture in the Iron Curtain separating us from the rest of the world. Indeed, after reading Boris Vian or Colette, a person can't help but look at things differently.

The more decrepit the system grew, and Brezhnev along with it, the more meaningless everything became. The same empty slogans were repeated over and over—like a mantra, like an incantation. They seemed to cast a spell on us. Stalin had crippled us with fear, and under Brezhnev we were paralyzed by senility.

He gradually became a comical figure. They said that he couldn't walk anymore by himself, that someone had to move his limbs like a puppet, that he fell asleep during negotiations. Both the intelligentsia and the people laughed at him. He would often award himself new medals, he became a member of the Writer's Union as the author of three books, which were in fact written for him by journalists. Watching him on television, the way he cleared his throat and mumbled the text of his speech, seeming not to understand a thing he was reading, everyone started impersonating him. There was never a party or gathering at which someone didn't impersonate a speech in the manner of "dear Leonid Brezhnev." He became the butt of countless jokes: There's a knock on Brezhnev's door. He goes to the door, slowly reaches for his glasses, pulls a piece of paper out of his pocket, unfolds it, clears his throat, and reads out: "Who's there?"

We didn't know who was actually running the country, who was making decisions. More often than not, people pointed to Suslov. He was a sort of secret counselor who was in charge of ideology and had served under Stalin. But there was no certainty about anything; everything happened in secret, anonymously. The only important event of those years, one which shocked us out of our stupor, was the war in Afghanistan. Children were sent to war and perished for an unjust cause. I must say that at first people experienced a sort of curious pride in the thought that the empire was expanding and our army was once again fulfilling its "international duty." Only a few voices were raised in protest: Sakharov, Larisa Bogoraz, Sergey Kovalev . . . But when the recruits began to die, and mothers began to receive telegrams and lead coffins, many acknowledged the tragedy. It is impossible to overestimate the contribution of Gorbachev in ending it.

Every week new rumors came out that Brezhnev was dead. People even said that it was a fact, and that his body was being stored in a refrigerator so the country wouldn't panic. Motya brought this bit of news. A woman who had worked for Brezhnev and whom Motya used to meet in church at vespers on Saturdays told her. We already tried to guess about who his successor would be. We were rather ambivalent about it, however: we were certain that nothing would change no matter who it would be. Finally, Brezhnev really did die. His successor was Andropov, but he also died very soon after taking the lead. Andropov was succeeded by Chernenko. He, too, didn't live very long. People called the road from the Hall of Columns, where they bid farewell to their leaders, to the Kremlin Wall, where they buried them, the "corpse-bearing trail."

Gorbachev's appointment came as a complete surprise to us, but I have no memories whatsoever of his accession to power. He was just one of them. We didn't expect anything from him, and we entertained no illusions. If he had managed to rise so high, to go up all the steps in the ladder of hierarchy, it meant that he was docile and conformist enough to forego his conscience—in a word, he was indistinguishable from any of the others. It was hard to imagine that a person who had overcome all the obstacles on his path toward the position of General Secretary of the Communist Party of the Soviet Union could cherish the desire to change something, and had the necessary moral courage and imagination for this. Nevertheless, something akin to an earthquake occurred very soon . . .

Sima and I would never in our wildest dreams have been able to imagine that we would witness such a turn of events. We didn't even expect anything of the sort for our children. Yet, suddenly, in our lifetimes, the Communist empire was crumbling, and in the first free elections the people rolled back the nomenklatura candidates. We still didn't dare believe it, though. We didn't yet have the feeling that victory had arrived and that everything else was behind us.

I spent the final months of 1989 in Paris. I watched on television the crowds of people on the streets of Warsaw, Budapest, Sofia, East Berlin, and it shook me to the bottom of my soul. The people who embraced by the Wall, which had taken the lives of so many and had become a symbol of non-freedom and coercion—this is an image I will never forget. I will never forget the determination with which masses of people demanded the regime be abolished, and achieved victory through unity of will. As I watched this, I thought: They liberated themselves through a broad popular movement. What about us? What did we do? Perestroika was brought upon us from above, without struggle. This is the biggest difference between them and us. This explains why the people of Eastern Europe are moving toward democracy much faster. Of course, they could never have begun the movement toward freedom without the blessings of the Kremlin, without the choice made by Gorbachev; that much is clear.

Then I returned to Moscow and watched on television how the final bastion of totalitarianism in Eastern Europe fell. In Romania, blood was spilled, a great deal of blood; but that was the price of freedom for them. People went out onto the streets not because they wanted to kill each other, not because they were moved by hatred, but by the will to topple the dictatorship. Whereas in our country, there was a sense that the air was brimming with hatred. Throughout the past years, Sima and I kept remembering, alas, Pushkin's famous words about Russian mutiny. We were haunted by the memory of the Civil War. Perhaps we were mistaken, though; perhaps we were misled by the fear that is in our blood. Perhaps we will avoid a new tragedy.

66

MOTYA WAS BORN IN THE VILLAGE OF NIZHNEE MALTSEVO, NEAR THE town of Sasovo. It is in the very center of Russia, the former Ryazan Province. They were what is called serednyaks, peasants of average means: a single horse was the sum total of their property. Of course, during the era of collectivization they were considered kulaks, well-to-do peasants, and were stripped of everything and banished from their house. Her father miraculously escaped execution—he paid them off, giving them some chickens, or plying someone with drink—and fled to Moscow, where he worked as a stoker. Motya followed him. She was twenty-nine. Peasants were forbidden from traveling freely around the country. Neither Motya nor her father had a permit for living in Moscow, so they spent days on end hiding in a dark basement. For the first few months, Motya only dared leave the basement at nighttime. Then she lucked out. The wife of an official from the City Council took her in as a nanny for her child, and her husband obtained a residence permit for Motya. At that time, many country girls who had fled to escape collectivization hired themselves out as nannies. She had never been married. She told us that she had had a husband for a week. Then he took to drink and started stealing everything from the house, and she ran away from him. Whether this was true or not, I don't know. But it seems to me that it was a fabrication— she was a typical old maid.

Acquaintances of ours told us about her. She was working for an Austrian family. When the father of the family was arrested at the beginning of the war as a foreigner, and his wife and two children were exiled from Moscow, Motya sheltered them in her house in her village and worked at a collective farm to support them. She went to the fields every day—five miles there and five back—to supply them with bread and food. There were two little boys, whom she raised and adored. At the end of the war, their father returned, and they left for some city in the Ural Mountains. Motya went to work in a factory so she could work the evenings for them.

Nevertheless, once she overheard a conversation in which they were saying that she had become too great an expense and they would have to let her go. She boarded a train and went to Moscow. She went to work in a textile factory, and for one year she lay on her bed, her face to the wall, whenever she wasn't working. That was how deeply the betrayal by that family had affected her, what a tragedy it had been for her—that they wanted to rid themselves of her after she had devoted five years of backbreaking labor to them, and they had only survived through her sacrifices.

Sima and I discussed Motya, and we went to the dormitory where she lived to persuade her to come and live with us. I was shocked by her emaciated appearance. She was just skin and bones, with sunken cheeks, terrible staring eyes, an unattractive face, and a rasping, unpleasant voice. I shuddered and thought, Maybe we don't need a nanny like this? But I wanted very much to start working, to do something with my life. And I was afraid, not knowing how to deal with a baby, and knowing next to nothing about managing a household—I learned all of that later. I was afraid to do it alone, in other words. So I tried to persuade her to come to live with us, and finally she agreed.

When she came to our house, Sima's father was suffering from cancer. She began taking care of him, selflessly, single-mindedly—as she did everything. She was something of a fanatic.

In those years Motya didn't go to church. It was only at the end of her life that she turned religious, and went to church all the time. At that time, her fanaticism took the form of devotion to labor. For example, she wouldn't allow a floor polisher into our apartment. She herself would boil wax by some special method and then polish the entire parquet floor herself. She wouldn't permit the bed linen to be sent to the laundry. (Later, I called the shots, but in those years, she decided everything.) The sheets were of the finest quality linen, enormous in size, and had been made by a firm that provided linens to the Czar. Motya found a brass tub somewhere—a huge thing, even thinking about picking it up scared me—and boiled all the linen in it at night. The next night she would press it. She starched

and ironed all the sheets. After her labors, the linen was like it had come from the best pre-Revolutionary laundry. So that's how Motya came into our lives—despotic, strict, with a strong opinion about everything—and proceeded to take charge.

Then Pavel was born. Sima's father died when Pavel was only three months old. Motya was also absolutely devoted to Pavel. She wouldn't let me near him unless I had to breastfeed him. I couldn't change his diapers; I wasn't allowed. Still, all of this might have been tolerable if she hadn't declared war on our way of life. She railed against our friends, about the fact that we fed everyone. To quote her, it wasn't a home, but a vile flophouse. Very much according to peasant custom, she only recognized blood relatives. She was not polite or gracious to the guests, and made it clear to them that they were not welcome here. She took a particular dislike to Leonid Pinsky. After he returned from the camps, he lived with us for weeks at a time. He worked here, writing his first book. She made scenes in my absence: "Why are you loafing about here? Who invited you?" I was still young and didn't know how to deal with this, how to resist her onslaughts.

Only for Elka did Motya make an exception, since he and Sima worked together. But she couldn't keep herself in check and went about grumbling all the time. Sima would lie sprawled out on the divan, or he would act out roles of characters in scenes he was inventing. The scenes were often very funny, and Sima and Elka would roll on the floor laughing. Motya was indignant: "Other people take work seriously, but these fellows . . . They're just layabouts, they cackle like crazy and call it work! At least that one bangs away at the typewriter; but our own man, over there . . . No Mrs. Lungina, no matter what you say, he's a slacker. A slacker, that's all there is to it!"

She couldn't stand it when Sima and I would say sweet things to each other in her presence, or express our feelings for each other. "You'll never grow up," she said. "You just bill and coo like little doves. Grown people don't act that way. They force hanky-panky on a groom and bride, that's one thing—but you've been married for ages! It's shameful! I don't want to see it . . ."

Motya had never gone to school, but thanks to her persistent nature she taught herself how to read. I remember with some satisfaction how she—letter by letter, sounding out the words—read "about love" in large print books. Her favorite reading was a slim little pamphlet, a paraphrase of the story of Cosette from Victor Hugo's *Les Miserables*. She read it countless times, and each time tears would stream down her face. Motya and Cosette were inseparable. Later, however she spurned all impious books and spent all her free time reading the Holy Scriptures.

She had her own opinions, her own interpretations, of everything. About collectivization, she said that it was when the laziest and most muddle-headed people settled accounts with those who got up at dawn and worked till nightfall. "In our village the most impoverished turned masters and started bossing everybody around. But don't think that they got away with it, Mrs. Lungina. It all ended badly. The most brutal of them, the one they called 'The Cursed,' drowned in a swamp. And the others were killed or jailed." She called Stalin a cur; about Khrushchev, she said he was an ordinary peasant; and about Brezhnev, that he was an idiot, who didn't understand a thing, and that she could do a better job of running things than he did.

There was another story she told me many times. One of her friends became a nun when she was still a girl. They destroyed the convent, but she made a vow to live as though the Soviet authorities didn't exist. When the first Stalinist elections were announced, she grew confused. What was she to do? She couldn't think of breaking her vow, but it was equally terrifying not to vote—she would be denounced. In the end, she didn't go back on her word. She didn't vote, but she lost her mind and ended up in an insane asylum.

Later it came out that Motya had had very disturbing conversations with Pavel since he was five or six. She told him that his papa and mama didn't love him, that they loved only their friends, they would be ruined finally, they would be thrown into debtor's prison and then she and he would go begging, and none of his parents' friends would lift a finger to help them or give them so much as a crust of bread. I believe this double vision of the world—Sima's and mine, and Motya's—has laid its imprint on Pavel's worldview, or rather, on his faith in the world and in people.

Over the years, Motya gained more and more power in our family. At a certain moment, I knew I couldn't tolerate this anymore. I said, "You know, Motya, I've found you a good position with a professor's family. You can manage the household there. Let's try to part ways."

She agreed. She held out for two or three weeks at the new place, but she would come over to see us, and I could tell that she was terribly unhappy, that it just wasn't working out for her there, that her world had collapsed. She couldn't live without Pavel, and was generally miserable. Sima and I faltered in our resolve, took pity on her, and said, "Fine, you can come back."

From time to time she made huge scenes, on one or another pretext. She always found something. One of her favorite subjects was that she had lived for thirty years in this horrible Moscow of ours, still hadn't earned the right to have a room. All the intellectuals got rooms, but working people didn't get them.

Motya also had a habit of provoking people whenever she could. She would say, for example, "Of course I can't expect you to go through any trouble to help me get a room. It wouldn't benefit you at all. It's better for you when I'm living here." Which wasn't at all true—I was longing for her to leave. She said, "It's convenient for you to have a servant girl right by your side. You wouldn't think of causing any inconvenience to yourself."

She had an idée fixe about being buried in her native village. She constantly talked about death and began preparing for it with plenty of time to spare, as though for a celebration or a holiday. She picked out her garments and all the accouterments for the funeral: a long white and blue floral dress made of shiny satin, three white headscarves, a cross, cheap rings, and plush slippers. She made ready forty black headscarves for the women who would accompany her to the graveyard, forty black armbands for the left arm for the men, and forty wooden spoons for the funeral repast. But to me she always made these comments when the subject came up: "As though you're really going to take me to my papa and mama. You'd never take me there in a million years, you're just pretending you will. You're fooling me, just sweet-talking me. You'll never do it." That's the way she usually talked to me. At the same time, she was absolutely devoted to the children; and to us, too. She liked me least of all, but she did like me, because I resolved all the conflicts with her.

Back to the room. What I had expected to be terribly difficult, impossible to realize, turned out to be very easy. I went to our house manager and said—frightened and trembling, for we were always afraid of everything—that I needed a room for Motya. Motya was getting old, she wanted to live on her own. I spoke timidly and babbled something vague to her. "A room? That's the easiest thing in the world. Are you prepared to pay eighty rubles?" said the house manager. I said, "Eighty?" just to make sure—it sounded like such a paltry sum. She said, "For eighty rubles I'll take you to the District Executive Committee." I was stunned. Strangely enough, everything worked out. Very smoothly. True, later this woman to whom I had given eighty rubles was arrested. I was very much afraid that they would hold me accountable, but they didn't. Motya got a room in a three-room apartment in a building across the street from us, and became somewhat calmer, and more reconciled to her life.

Yet she still had this violent intensity about her, which later turned into religious fervor. For example, during the Easter Fast she wouldn't take into her hands a knife that had been used to slice butter. Before Easter, and before Christmas, she wouldn't sleep for five days. She scrubbed the house clean, boiled her special wax, polished the floors, ironed. Five months beforehand she would fetch pig's legs from her village. They were black, and she soaked them for a month on the balcony, then dried them out and scraped them off. When I see these little white feet in the store nowadays! . . . She boiled meat jelly. It was a very long process, a ritual. She turned everything into a ritual. After staying awake for five days in a row, keeling over and falling down, she went to the midnight

mass at the church. This atmosphere of fanatical intensity perme-
ated the house.

At the same time . . . how do I put this? In a strange way, though
her nature, her character, was diametrically opposed to mine in so
many ways, she was very close to me. She was like a relative, like
family. The boys, Pavel and Zhenya, loved her very much. She stood
with us through thick and thin. When Sima had no work, she refused to take money from us. She would have gone through fire and
water for the sake of Pavel. Right up until her death, until her illness—she died of cancer—though she lived right across the street,
she would come to us early in the morning and go home in the
evening to sleep. Even on Sundays, although she could easily have
stayed at home, she came over.

She died on the tenth of January. The winter that year was
bitterly cold. We had no idea how to fulfill our promise to her. I
couldn't allow myself to become the person she had always suspected I would be after her death. I had to keep my word to her. It
turned out that there was no service that would transport her body

back to her home Sasovo. At a certain moment, Pavel suggested that he would put the coffin in the trunk of his little Lada, but we decided that was out of the question. We were at our wit's end. Finally, Pavel found a truck somewhere. The driver agreed to take on the task, for a large sum; but the coffin kept sliding around on the floor of the truck. We had to nail it down. A horrible task.

Motya's cousins, who had come to Moscow from the village for this purpose, gave us a list of what should be served at the funeral repast, without fail; otherwise, they would judge us harshly and say that Motya's masters were terrible skinflints. Among these mandatory items were oranges. For some reason it just had to be winter, when they were next to impossible to find. I remember running from one store to the other—back then, they distributed special ration cards for weddings and funerals, which allowed one to buy food that was otherwise impossible to come by or afford—in the grocery store on the Lubyanka, for example. There were simply no oranges to be had. There were no oranges in Moscow. Then, somehow, in some closed distribution center, at twice the normal price, we managed to get hold of some, thank god, and set out for Sasovo.

The trip took a whole day. The road was slippery and terrifying. We arrived in Sasovo at about eleven at night. It was silent, it was dark. Of the fifty cottages, only about fifteen were still occupied. The others were abandoned. The windows were boarded up. We were told that the coffin had to stay for one night in the church. We went to get the priest. It took a long time and proceeded in fits and starts. We went from one cottage to another, accumulating a crowd of old women. Finally, one of them knocked boldly on the door of the priest. Very reluctantly he came out, and gave us the key to the church. We opened the doors with great difficulty, put down the coffin, and went on to the village of Nizhnee Maltsevo, where Motya's first cousin lived, and where the funeral was to take place.

Because there was only one priest for the entire county, and he wasn't able to carry out all the rites in all the villages, brigades of widows were formed for carrying out the wake service. This was a means of generating extra earnings. Four or five people, widows, all dressed in black, were paid to sing the whole night, above—not above the coffin, because Motya's coffin remained in the church—

but above chairs arranged to hold the coffin the following day. They sang psalms. And burned incense. They burned the incense in an empty sardine can. They burned incense in this empty sardine can, and sang psalms. Until morning.

In the morning, we went back to Sasovo, and there we finished the funeral service. Now we had to dig the grave. The ground was frozen solid—hard to dig. The graveyard was two miles away. Four or five people volunteered to dig. They told us that there must be vodka in large quantities, but that we couldn't give it to them while they were digging. They'd drink it all up and get smashed right away. We had to keep the vodka at home. We had to have them come every hour or hour and a half, pour them one glass each, not more, and have them go back and dig some more. That was the way it was done. While they were digging, they would run back and forth these two miles, five or six times, and drink a glass of vodka each.

When we returned to Maltsevo after the funeral service and went to the cemetery—they carried the coffin to the cemetery on towels, and all the women had donned the black headscarves Motya had made, and the men wore the armbands—we noticed that although the grave was dug, it was covered with boards and shovels. It had to be ransomed. They needed more vodka. A "quarter" of vodka, three liters. They drank it then and there, and fell down drunk next to the grave. Others helped lower the coffin into the grave, because the diggers were too drunk to move.

They lowered the coffin into the ground and filled it up the best they could. We went to the house where the funeral repast would be held. A funeral repast unfolds according to a strict ritual—there is a certain order in which dishes must be served. First the kutya in tea saucers—rice topped with a cross made of raisins. Then came millet pancakes followed by borsch with corned beef, soup with noodles, various appetizers, and, finally, buckwheat porridge and kissel.

Two tables were placed parallel to one another, and on each table was a wooden bowl with oranges. That meant that the funeral repast was up to the mark. We, the outsiders and the old women, were seated at one table. The few men who still lived in the village sat at the other table. The hostess of the meal seated us in such a way that they couldn't see us. It was especially important that they not see Pavel—she was afraid that quarrels would start up, anti-Semitic remarks. Something of the sort did get started—but she made a comment that I've never forgotten: "What are you blathering about? Don't you go spoiling my conversation." This drawn-out ritual she called a "conversation." "If you spoil my conversation, I'll throw you out."

Finally, the whole thing came to an end without a scandal. It turned out that of the men sitting at the other table—there were seven or eight altogether—not a single one had managed to avoid prison. All of them at one time or another had done time.

Thus, we committed Motya to the ground, having fulfilled, in the face of much difficulty, her last request.

67

I'D LIKE TO SAY THAT I REALIZED, FINALLY, THAT LIFE IS ABOUT LOSS. GRADually people died, and the space around us grew steadily emptier.

Elka died in such a terrible way, so unexpectedly, because he hadn't been ill before that, and it was a terrible blow of fate. Noam Naumov died, too—he was an extraordinary person, someone of exceptional goodness. He had a unique quality about him: although we were all friends together, he was also friends with each member of the family individually. He had a one sort of relationship with Sima, another kind with me. We were connected through our work, and if there was something I didn't know, something I had doubts about, or vacillated about, he was my first advisor. He was an absolutely brilliant translator. He translated a plethora of books from Spanish, from Italian. He had his own relationship with Pavel and Zhenya. He loved them dearly, and brought warmth into our lives. Without him, the lives of each of us became poorer, and colder.

Then Leonid Pinsky died of cancer. This was also a great loss for us.

Then Vika. He also had cancer. It has already been ten years. We couldn't even attend the funeral.

Nevertheless, while Sima and I were together, this life that had grown emptier, this world . . . You know what it felt like? It was like black holes were forming all around us. All of a sudden there's just nothing there. The space people leave behind doesn't fill up again. It remains empty, and it's very strange and difficult to try to live with these black holes surrounding you. But while we were together, we lived a very happy life. We somehow maintained that rhythm, that tonality, that sound of our life that had begun on the first day, and had never changed. It was the perpetual sound of the joy we felt as we passed through life together.

There's a legend that the old Renaissance masters always made two cameos. That authentic cameos, which were carved from the

most expensive, most valuable ivory, were always made in pairs. Then they were released into the world and sold at opposite ends of it. If they came back and met on the same hand, it was a guarantee of happiness. In a similar way, Sima and I felt that we were two cameos that had been released into the world, on opposite sides of it; and then we met. And this is happiness—that's what our happiness consists of. Because love, happy marriages—I don't know many of them, I won't try to pretend. Unfortunately, most marriages around me I would call—not exactly unhappy, but complicated and difficult. But I know happy marriages, too. Our dear friends the Zolotukhins, for example, are happy. Dusya Kaminskaya and Konstantin Simis —that's a happy marriage; and Boris and Galya Levinson, too. But, let me see, those are serious happy marriages. My marriage with Sima was happy, and not serious. It was light, it was cheerful, it was weightless. At any given moment, it was fun. It was a game we played together; there was a holiday feeling about it. Every day was a holiday. While daily life could be severe, and we were sometimes flat broke, and all the rest of it, still, our life together was never dreary and mundane.

That was because Sima was such a wonderful person. Very talented, both as a playwright and as a director; although he had not been given the opportunity to develop his gifts as a director, unfortunately. But I think he was most talented at life. He knew how to love life, to turn it into something extraordinary. Like a diamond, all its rays would begin to glitter and shine. We had forty-nine years of this kind of life together. Not only did the sense of wonder that filled us not fade with each year, but, on the contrary, it grew stronger.

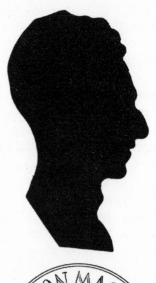

I never saw another marriage quite like ours—one that wasn't deep and serious, but fun and happy at any given moment. For instance, on our last trip together, when I was going out for bread, Sima always wanted to tag along. I said, "I'll be back in ten minutes. I'm going to the corner to buy some French bread." He said, "Who knows how much longer we have to be together? It's more fun to walk together, too." And it's true; it was more fun together. I said, "Well, all right. Let's go together, then." This word, "fun," was also always on Vic's lips. When he wanted to praise someone or express his fondness, he would say, "We have fun together, it's easy and fun to be with him." He was also one of those people who loved light-hearted joy and fun. That's why he was so unbelievably attached to Sima. They got along beautifully together, acting silly, performing scenes and playing various roles, puffing out their chests in the mirror like strongmen, acting out little dialogues; in short, it was a game.

Vic was very artistic, very creative. So was Sima. I am not. But together, Vic and Sima, or Sima just by himself, could draw me into this game, too. We would pretend we were, I don't know, French counts, or jobless Italians. We would perform scenes from another kind of life. Then, when the three of us were in France together, we also used to pretend. It was a game. And this game, juxtaposed with our own demanding and pitiless existence, resulted in something completely existential, to use a high-flown word, a sense of exceptional fullness. When I think of the life I have lived, I feel there was not an inch, not even a sixteenth of an inch, of emptiness. Everything was overflowing—with feelings, thoughts, acts and actions, events. It had content. Though I know that people often say that life is somehow empty for them.

What delighted me most of all was Sima's ability to see into the things he witnessed. Things seemed to come to life under his gaze. I'll never forget when we went to Vilnius for the first time. Next to the station there is a beautiful red brick church. Gothic style. Suddenly, Sima—he was always a man of inspiration, a person of the spoken word—suddenly he was carried away by this church, and began to analyze its construction. He spoke with such enthusiasm, and so convincingly, about its divine longing and aspiration, about how the church itself led us to God—it was a kind of disquisition that was both aesthetic and theological, and I was absolutely stunned.

Sima had always had a religious bent. He loved all kinds of churches and temples. He was, of course, an ecumenist by temperament, but he somehow taught me to share his vision, and I loved being with him and sitting in these holy places together. We would always stop in all the churches, and Sima would light a candle. In the places where it wasn't customary to light candles, we would just sit. For me, it was a time for meditation, I suppose. Nothing religious. Unfortunately, any sense of religion devotion is absent in me. Although I understand that religion is a source of comfort and support for those who are devout.

To be completely honest, I must admit that these questions have only now become profound and important for me, now that Sima is no longer with us, and I am alone. From time to time I feel some glimmer of something opening up in me—but it is a very weak glimmer. I have been reading books related to these matters, but to say that I have truly arrived at religious belief, that I believe in some Other World—I can't see my way through to that. I am seeking some entrance there, I am wandering in the dark, something is pulling me in that direction, but I haven't found the door, to be perfectly honest about it.

We lived together for many years, and I was familiar with Sima's gift of achieving that state; and, still, I was astonished. When we got to the hotel in Vilnius, I said, "Sima, write it down. Write about it, it will be a remarkable article." He said, "I don't remember it. I don't remember anything I said to you." And that was true. He never remembered afterward what opened up in him during these moments of improvisation. He said, "It's like what Mandelstam described, that someone whispers the poetry in his ear—that's the feeling I have when I can suddenly enlarge upon a subject like that. It's like I'm hearing a voice."

He didn't remember a thing, and he wrote nothing down. Of course, it was my fault. Although we lived a wonderful and happy and fun life together, I am guilty in many ways. I never recorded what Sima said, never even saved the notes he kept, papers he jot-

ted things down on—always scraps of paper, never in a journal
or notebook, never. Thousands of scraps of paper that have all
gone missing, for the most part. Now they're scattered to the
winds. Many wonderful pieces of writing have just disappeared. I
should have recorded what he said, what he jotted down. His students still remember things he said in his moments of improvisation. He told me about "moments of illumination" that came
upon him all of a sudden, when the essence of some phenomenon
or matter opened up to him, like a picture in an art album. There
is an example of this in Sima's book *Wide-Awake Visions*—an
analysis of the Mona Lisa.

Apart from all of this, besides his brilliant talent, his ability to
bring even a stone to life, Sima was an exceptionally sensitive and
tactful human being. I've never met anyone quite like him in this
respect. He was terribly concerned about not burdening anyone
else with trouble. He related to people of the highest standing, and,
say, Motya's relatives, from Lukyanovo in the Sasovo province, in
the same way, making no distinction between them. He would simply choose a more down-to-earth topic of discussion with them.
He spoke to them with the same amount of consideration, but he
spared them more intellectually wrenching or ponderous issues.

This was surprising to me, and I tried to learn this art from
him. From birth I was prone to a kind of haughtiness. I considered
myself to be a French mademoiselle, a smart lass. People would
praise my intelligence, saying "she's a bright one," and I heard this
so often that I began to think—maybe I really am? Sima taught me
that one shouldn't think about this, that it isn't even your affair; it's
for other people to decide whether you are smart or not. Every
human being, each one without exception, deserves to be treated
with attention and respect.

Sima was drawn to people in the way people who love flowers
are drawn to flowers. They know that even the tiniest, most common wildflower has its own beauty and charm, its own scent, it own
architectonics—that's how Sima related to people. This was a lesson
for me, and it astonished me and captivated me time and again. He
possessed in abundance those qualities that I most appreciate: a
prodigious imagination, the ability to see everything in the re-

fracted light of wonder, and sensitivity toward the ones he loved. Toward everyone.

I witnessed good people from good families arguing about whose turn it was to put the kettle on. In our family, the arguing went in the opposite direction: it was about who would get to be the first to do it. Each one wanted to take it upon himself. When your companion wants to take more of the burden, it inspires you to want to do the same. It's a curious dynamic, and I've tried to figure it out. The less your companion wants to do, the less you want to do yourself. And vice versa. There's feedback. We would wrest the household duties from each other's hands—unpleasant tasks, difficult chores. We each wanted to do it for the other.

Sima, of course, enveloped me in a kind of cloud of love, at the same time protecting me from the outside world with its crudeness and cruelty. Now, without this enveloping love, I find it very hard to live. Above all, life is dull without him; but I have also come into contact with a world that I both knew and did not know, did not experience firsthand, because Sima's love cushioned me from it, absorbed it. Of course, it turned my life into something wondrous and unreal. I worked and interacted with many other people. Lucy Tovalev and her son were always with us until she was given a room in Moscow, and then an apartment. There were many other people who needed our help for many years, people whom we loved, people who were our friends and relied on us to help them go through life. Nevertheless, my life was easier, especially compared to the lives of people around me, because Sima always stood between me and hardship, and tried to take all the hardship upon himself.

He was a strong person in the sense that if he said yes, he meant it, and if he said no, then no was exactly what he meant. People he found unacceptable, situations that he felt were unworthy or beneath his dignity, he swept aside. I remember when our Pavel became a student in a screenwriting program, after a few weeks of spending time in these circles he told Sima, "You know, Dad, it's amazing, no one says bad things about you and Nusinov. They criticize everyone else, but I haven't heard a single bad word about you." He was very moved. I said, "Maybe it's awkward for them to talk in front of you?" "No, that's not it . . . They criticized everyone without mercy. It was just faultfinding and pestering for its own sake."

I think that Sima did actually make it through these difficult times without compromising himself or others. He passed through the official system, when he couldn't avoid coming into contact with it, almost without a hitch. His unwillingness to compromise or be compromised was not even so much out of moral consider-ations, but because of some organic underpinning of his nature. It was simply the way he was.

It's hard for me to talk about Sima. I wanted to share everything with him. Every line that I read, if it was something I liked, I wanted to read aloud. Even if it disturbed me, I also wanted to read it aloud, so that I could share my indignation with him.

There was one thing in our lives that was not right, besides the fact that I didn't record him and wasn't careful enough about pre-serving his papers and conversations. It wasn't right that we spent so much time with other people, that we socialized so much. This was partially my fault. I am a very extroverted, sociable person, and I don't know how to stay aloof, to refuse someone. We always had company, and Sima and I were seldom completely alone. When Pavel grew up, we were always accompanied by a foursome of his friends, no matter where we went: in the summer—to the moun-tains; in the winter—skiing. We also went canoeing every year. Al-ways with a bunch of kids. Very rarely were we by ourselves. That is, we were always together, we almost never parted—but we weren't alone. Not enough of the time.

Summing up my life, I would say that, besides Sima, my sons were the most important thing to me. Sima and I have two won-derful boys. One of them, Pavel, will be forty-eight this year. If peo-ple used to refer to Pavel as "the son of Sima Lungin," now they say—said, rather, while Sima was still alive—that he was "the father of Pavel Lungin." He became, almost overnight, in some strange and wonderful way, a film director, although he had been seeking his own path for a long time before that. Our sons are late bloomers, in the sense that it has taken them a long time to find their footing in the world. It took them a long time to make up their minds about who and what they wanted to be.

Pavel studied in the Department of Mathematical Linguistics. Those were the years when it became fashionable to study a completely idiotic profession, which, in fact, doesn't really exist. Linguistics as linguistics, yes; and mathematics as mathematics; but there is no such thing as mathematical linguistics. Pavel was very proud to graduate from this department; then he took a job in the Institute of Concrete Sociology. There used to be an institute by that name in Moscow. A year and a half later he was kicked out of the institute when a new director arrived, who said, "I don't like young people with beards who walk through the hallways, looking askance at things with an ironic expression. Get rid of the beard." To which Pavel replied, without a moment's hesitation, "When can I submit my resignation?" And Pavel, who already had a wife, Tanya, and a young son, Sasha, ended up unemployed. They lived with us. Then the "struggle against parasitism" intensified. We were terrified that he would be arrested, like Brodsky, and that they would send him away somewhere. Brodsky's trial received a great deal of publicity, but trials like this, and the exile of young people who were borderline dissidents—and Pavel was one of them—were not uncommon at the time.

Trying to find a way out of this problem, we thought he might enter the Advanced Screenwriting and Directorial Program, where Sima had taught for many years. Pavel did enter the program, and began to write screenplays. The scripts were quite nice, but they were never turned into great films. Those years were very different from the years when his father had made his debut as screenwriter. The directors were very weak; and, overall, the middle of the Brezhnev years were like some sort of Middle Ages. They were years of slow, but steady decay, a swamp in which things would move forward slightly, then lose ground again. Society began to rot from the inside. We were all convinced—I've already mentioned this—that we were destined to die in this swamp, that we would stagnate in it until the end of our days. A good film was very rare during those days—there was no real foundation to nurture it.

Pavel wanted to make his own films. He was not permitted to do so, since he didn't have training as a director. Perestroika changed it all, though. It freed something up inside him, relaxed him, in a sense. He wrote a screenplay that was bolder than anything he had written before; in other words, he stopped censoring himself. Indeed, we were all guilty of self censorship over the course of many years. Everyone who wrote and wanted to see his work on the stage or on the screen estimated how much freedom he could claim, and where the boundary of possibility lay. Now, Pavel began to write very freely, and he succeeded so well at it that a foreign producer who was interested in auteur film offered to let him make the film himself. Pavel was happy, and to the great alarm of Sima and myself, he plunged into this adventure, though he admitted to the producer that he had never in his life filmed a single shot.

When he was already forty years old, he made the film *Taxi Blues*, which received the Best Director award in Cannes. This was an incredible honor and thrill, and Sima and I ascended those famous carpeted steps in Cannes, and the radio blared on all the Cannes street-crossings that the parents of director Pavel Lungin were coming . . . It was a very moving, solemn, and wonderful occasion. Pavel is still active in this profession, and we, of course, are exceedingly proud of him. We think the world of him and his work.

There is an eleven-year age difference between our sons. They are both similar and different from each other. Zhenya has been interested in theater since childhood. He wanted to be an actor. Inna Tumanian wanted him to take the lead in the film *The Boy and the Elk*, based on Sima's screenplay. The main character was Zhenya's age at the time, and Zhenya had a very sweet face; he was chomping at the bit to act in the film. Everyone considered the issue to have been decided already, including, of course, Inna. But the Arts Council, which approves the casting decisions, vetoed it. They said it wasn't advisable, his Jewishness was too apparent. That was a signal for Zhenya that he couldn't be an actor in this country: his Jewishness would, most likely, always be apparent. So Zhenya attended the theater arts program in the GITIS to become a theater critic and historian. But the wound remained.

Children experience injury and insults far more deeply than adults do. I think an adult would have reasoned: well, they didn't take me this time—maybe next time they will, who knows what will happen. For Zhenya, however, it constituted a rejection. Then, having understood the impossibility of getting work due to the "fifth paragraph," he decided to leave at any cost. He began to meet all kinds of foreign girls, thinking that he was in love with them—primarily so he could get married and leave, I think.

Finally, it did happen. He married an Italian girl, and moved to Padua; but it was clear that the marriage was fictitious, that he wasn't in love at all, and had contrived the whole thing. Three weeks later, they began to fight, and separated. He left her in the middle of the night and never returned. Thus began his years of wandering abroad. At last, he ended up with my friends the Vernants. They invited him to visit them, and Zhenya has lived in Paris ever since. He also became infatuated with film. He made a film on Russian and French money, *Angels in Heaven*. He's now thirty-six, and he's trying to make another film. He is still seeking his own path, and I am certain that sooner or later he'll find it.

That is probably the real culmination of my life.

We also have grandchildren. One of them is already grown—Sasha, Pavel's twenty-four-year-old. There are two other grandchildren in Paris, because Zhenya married a French woman. There is a boy named Antoine, who is six and a half, and a girl of three and a half named Anna. Zhenya is very insistent that people not call her

"Ani," in the French manner, but "Anna." "No," he said, "she has a Russian name, Anna." Unfortunately, they don't know a word of Russian. Maybe "hello" and "goodbye" . . . They live in Paris with their mother, and Zhenya lived with them until the moment he lost his head over film and became obsessed with directing himself. Of course, films like that he can only make here; that is to say, one can't

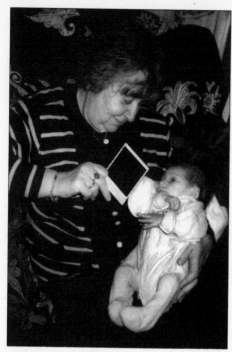

make the films here, because there is no funding for it, but in France it's all the more impossible. So Zhenya has been living here in Moscow with me for a year and a half, hoping that something will work out for him.

I talk to Antoine on the phone, and he asks me, "Can you please explain to me why all the other fathers work in Paris, and my dad works in a place called Moscow?" I have a hard time explaining to him why. I say, "You know, that's just how it is for grownups. Things are complicated and hard." And he says to me, "Then I don't want to be a grownup."

There are students, too, Sima's and mine. It's obvious why Sima would have them—he taught screenwriting together with our close friend Mila Golubkina in the Advanced Screenwriting Courses. His students were very loyal to him. I realized this at the terrible point in my life when Sima died. I received letters of condolence from people who had graduated from his class many years before, and I saw how very much alive Sima still was in their memories. That meant, for me, that he was somehow still alive. Through them. They told me that before they began writing, they would still always ask his advice, discussing their ideas with him in their imaginations. It couldn't offer me comfort, but it did give me joy.

Strangely enough, I have students, too. Fifteen years ago, Pavel started urging me: "Mama, you always translate things that are generally accessible. Translate a book that can't be translated, and get it published." After setting me such a task, he also told me which book it should be. There was a French writer, long since dead, named Boris Vian. He could not be published, not for political reasons, but for aesthetic ones, because of his artistic conceptions and methods. I decided to undertake this task, and I translated a small novel, *Foam of the Days*. At that moment, I was asked to teach a seminar for young translators from the French, graduates of the University of Foreign Languages. I asked Noam Naumov to co-teach it with me, and together we decided (which was very bold of us) to assign each of our students a story by Vian.

There is no prose writer more difficult to translate than Vian, in my opinion. It's like translating poetry. Vian is all about word-play, associations, and idioms for which equivalents can't be found in Russian—every language has its own idiomatic expressions, and the wordplay is based on French phraseology. To tackle this problem, one must find one's own, completely different idiom or pun—often miles away from the original French, but able to convey the same feeling, the same associations. This is an extremely difficult task, as hard as rendering a line of poetry, a poetic metaphor, in another language. It took me a long time to translate *Foam of the Days*. It took me almost two years. I translated half a page or a page; and then not every day.

Altogether, the Vian collection took three years to complete. The editor in charge of the project, a very nice man, told me, "Lilya, take your time. Someone's going to go on vacation, someone's bound to get sick, someone else will find a new job." The book would have to go through all the necessary channels, steering clear of all kinds of dangers. Vian writes in the introduction that there is nothing on earth worth living for except pretty women and jazz. Would it really be possible to translate a book like that and publish it in the Soviet Union? Unfortunately, the editor himself didn't live to see the book to fruition. But the book, wonder of wonders, was published. Was it successful? That's putting it mildly. It sold like hotcakes.

We worked together beautifully. Every story had one translator and two reader-translators. But it wasn't just about translation. Just as in Sima's classes, I spent a great deal of time talking to my students about many other things. We discussed everything. I think that Noam and I helped to train and educate these young people somewhat, but we also sent them out into the world armed with some of our own ideas. Three of them became superb translators—the best of their generation, I believe: Natalia Mavlevich, Irina Istratova and Nina Khotinskaya. It's been ten years now since the seminar was held, but our friendship continues. It is very heartening to me that now Natalia Mavlevich runs a similar seminar, and will pass on the baton. She has ten people studying and practicing translation under her, and their working method is still the one that Noam and I devised.

Life, which portended so much difficulty for us, turned out to be full of dreams-come-true. The most diverse kinds of dreams came true in our lives. The last time we were abroad, we traveled around half of Europe. We took a wonderful trip through Italy. We visited Venice, and parts of Spain. We went to Barcelona and saw the work of Gaudi, which Vic had taught us to love. He adored Gaudi, and had a book with photographs of his work before anyone else knew who he was. So we were already familiar with these improbably curious structures before we saw them in person. We were in Amsterdam, and in Bruges. We heard the first performance of *The Mystery of St. Paul the Apostle*, which Sima wrote with our friend, the composer Nikolay Karetnikov.

These wonderful trips were a continuation and an amplification of the journeys we made when traveling abroad was still virtually impossible. Three times we traveled through the mountain passes of Svaneti in Georgia. In the spring we would go canoeing with entire gangs of Pavel's friends.

Our final trip abroad lasted eleven months. We returned to Moscow on the twentieth of December. Sima had a third heart attack on the twenty-ninth of January 1996, and an hour and a half later, he was gone.

Left alone without him, I live quite a different life. It doesn't resemble the life we lived together at all. I think I know now what grief is. It is the absence of desire. In fact, there's really nothing I want. Virtually nothing. Very little. Well, I do want Zhenya to find his true calling, of course. I want Sima's book, which I mentioned earlier, to be reissued. It came out at the very beginning of Perestroika, and for that reason wasn't given the proper attention. It is called *Wide-Awake Visions*, and it sums up his thoughts on the specific nature of writing for the cinema and theater.

I would very much wish for a book that I translated ten years ago to be published. It is called *The Neverending Story*, by Michael Ende. My friend, the translator Alexandra Isaeva, who unfortunately died this year, also wanted to translate it, and we worked on it together. Each of us translated half of the book. In the meantime, Perestroika got underway, and Detgiz, the children's publishing house, almost ceased to exist. The book languished with them, since it was necessary to pay hard currency to the foreign publisher who owned the rights. And there was no money.

I decided that I would write to Michael Ende myself. I loved him for the way he viewed the world, for his understanding of its multifaceted nature, for his exceptional kindness, and his incredible imagination. I hoped that if I wrote a good enough letter, perhaps he would let us publish the book for free. The only thing I knew about him was that he was a very private, secretive writer, that he had a villa near Rome, where he lived with his wife, that he had little interaction with the world, and that he had theosophical ideas and sympathies. This is apparent in some of the ideas in his books, as well. His address, I was told, was impossible to get hold of. I wrote to the publisher. The gist of my letter was as follows.

> Since you devote yourself to contemplating such serious and thorny questions in your works, I would ask you please to consider what I have to say to you, as well . . . Our children need spiritual guidance no less than material assistance. Your book, which so clearly delineates the boundary between good and evil, is absolutely essential for Russian children. I beg you, help us publish it. We have no money for it, it is very hard for us to come by hard currency—but this could be a form of humanitarian aid from you.

I was crushed when I didn't receive an answer. I wrote a second letter.

> Dear Michael,
> Please allow me to call you "dear"—this is not a formality, not an empty phrase, not a polite form of address. You have truly become dear to me. I beg you, please answer my letter . . .

He didn't. But his publisher did. It turned out that he had no rights to the book himself. He had signed them over completely to the publisher in Stuttgart. They conducted all the financial negotiations. I wrote them a third letter, and they named a price for the author's rights of five thousand Deutschmarks. That wasn't much, but it was still more than we had, which was nothing.

Suddenly, I received a letter from the publisher saying that Michael Ende had put forth my candidature for a stipend in Munich. They assumed that since Michael Ende had proposed this, it would most likely be awarded to me. I thought, well, that means he read my letter; so I didn't write it in vain after all, then, did I?

Indeed, two weeks later I got word that I had been given a two-month stipend and the opportunity to travel to Munich to work. Three people were allowed to come on this stipend, to stay in a castle—Villa Bertha, it was called, and there was an apartment for us there. So Sima and I went. Villa Bertha was surrounded by a divine park and a lake, but I could only think about one thing, naturally. How could I meet Ende? I kept asking everyone. Yes, they said, he lives in Munich, but it is forbidden to give out his telephone number or his address—he is inaccessible.

I called his editor, and said, "Please, I must see Ende, somehow. It's silly—we live in the same city." "I'll tell him." Or rather, we— "we will pass on your message, but it's doubtful anything will come of it." I was terribly disappointed. Suddenly, three days later, the telephone rang and an unfamiliar voice on the end of the line said, "Das ist Michael Ende . . ."

I was dumbstruck. He said, "You know, they gave me your telephone number, I want very much to see you!" I said, "I want to see you, too!"

I was nervous and afraid. He had invited us to meet him in a strange place—on the Rathaus Square. At three in the afternoon on a Sunday. I assumed that he would take us to a café for fifteen minutes and treat us to a cup of coffee, and that would be that. Wracked with doubts, we made our way to the square at the appointed time, but it turned out to be Shrove Sunday. How would we ever find him? On the square there were five orchestras and throngs of people wearing costumes, everyone dancing and singing . . .

We stood under the clock that we had agreed on as our meeting place. I was thinking, Well, he'll never find us at this rate. Then I looked around and saw a man standing some distance away from us. His appearance was extraordinarily appealing to me. He looked somewhat like Vic Nekrasov, a similar type: sunken cheeks, tall, and lean. A very attractive countenance. I said, "Sima, if only that were him!" I had told him what I would be wearing (black jacket, and so on). The man looked, and made a beeline for us. It was Ende, of course. What's going to happen now? I wondered.

He took us to his home. His dear wife, with whom he had lived near Rome, had died, and after that he had married a Japanese woman. She was not a young, beautiful Japanese girl, however, but an old translator. It was strange—this elderly Japanese woman. Next to her he still looked very young and handsome. Imagine what he had done—he had an enormous living room, one corner of which he had set up in a Japanese style. So that she wouldn't feel homesick, as he explained. It had a raised floor covered with tatami mats, some decorations—a real Japanese interior within his own living room. There were remarkable paintings hanging on the walls. I remembered that his father had been an avant-garde painter, who had been persecuted by the Nazis (the Nazis, like the Soviet authorities, did not like avant-garde art). After the defeat of Hitler, he had achieved recognition.

We began to talk, and, you know the way it sometimes happens, within the first few minutes we felt we had known each other our whole lives, and that we understood each other without even saying anything. Sima took part in the conversation, and I translated. We discovered a remarkable coincidence of tastes, interests, and so on; and it seemed that this person we had just met was family. "But why did you never answer my letters?" I said. He said, "Didn't I?" He laughed. "I thought I had."

At five o'clock we had tea. It was a beautiful tea ceremony, heavenly tea, sweets that his wife had prepared—this house was alive with Japanese tradition, it seemed. It was all very, very interesting for us. After tea I stood up, thinking it was time to leave, but he said, "Where are you going? I've booked a table at a restaurant for us, we're going there for dinner this evening." And so we spent the whole day and evening together. We talked until one o'clock in the morning, and still it seemed there was so much more to talk about. I said, "Now what? I want to see you again." He said, "I do, too. I will call you. If you need anything urgently, call me. This is how you do it. You call me, and hang up. Then immediately dial again. I'll pick up. But don't worry, I'll call you."

One day passed, then another, five, six days—no call. I was perplexed again—it wasn't all put on, it wasn't just pretend—we really did have a meeting of the minds. At last we heard from him: "I'm calling you from the hospital, but I'm feeling a bit better now. You can come visit me." We went to see him in the hospital, and left when the nurse made us go. We had had another effusive conversation. He said, "The day after tomorrow, when I am released, I'll call you, and you will come and visit me at home." And there was another curious coincidence, a *komischer Zufall*, as they say in Germany.

There was a very nice woman who was also living at Villa Bertha. She had once been a well-known photographer. When she heard that I was going to visit Ende, she said that she had a unique photograph of Ende's father, which she had taken when she was just a girl, at the beginning of her career. I told him in the hospital, and he was very excited about it. "I don't have these photographs, but I have heard that they exist. I want very much to get hold of them."

She gave me a large print, and I waited for him to call, but he never called again. On the eve of our departure, Sima and I went over to his house, but we didn't dare ring the doorbell. I deposited yet another letter—and the photograph, which I had put into a large envelope—in his mailbox. I left our telephone number in Paris, and we set out for Paris. Three weeks later, I received a letter from the editor in Germany, with whom I had become friends. She wrote, "I am sorry to have to give you the tragic news that Mr. Ende died in the hospital." Apparently, he had not been released.

During our conversation, I told him that we would publish his book without fail. He wanted very much for people in Russia to read it. Now it is even more important to me that the book be published here, not only because of my wish that our children be able to read the book, but also because of the promise I made to him. It is not a luxury. It is as necessary as our daily bread.

In this book, one of the main ideas is that the most important thing is to want something very deeply. And then to do what it is that you wish. This is an ancient formula, it is expressed in Rabelais: *fais ce que voudras*—"do what you will." Human beings have long contemplated what this might mean. Whether one needs this absolute freedom, and how it should be understood. Everyone, even Rabelais, who had a bent for extremes and boundlessness in everything, also came to the conclusion that what was important was what you wanted. Perhaps Ende was quoting Rabelais. I cannot call this a children's book. It is universal. At the end of the book, a great question is posed—whether to stay in the world of Fantastica or to return to the real world, with its good and evil, its cruelty, its injustice. It is absolutely clear what this boy will choose. Bastian, the main character, categorically chooses life. In this book there is an abundance of optimism. Affirmation of life—the affirmation of the living, of what is alive—is the good. That is what you arrive at if you put it into simple words.

I want people to be able to read this book.

All in all, grief, I think, is the absence of desire. I don't want to go to France. I talk to my grandson on the phone, and I say, "Antoine, do you remember me?" Because we left on the twentieth of December of last year. He hasn't seen me for a year, and for a five-year-old, that is a long time. I ask him, "Do you remember me?" He says, "How can you ask me a question like that? Of course I remember you! And I remember Sima. I often look at the pictures of him, and I miss you both a lot. But you I'll see again, and I won't see him." In other words, he understands. I was struck by this phrase. I asked little Anna, "Do you remember me?" She said, "No, I don't remember you at all. I forgot about you, but I still love you and send you a kiss." I think I need to go see her.

But I have no desires left. That's like a black hole, too. I do want to remember the past, though. I want to remember it in the sense that my life with Sima was not just ours alone; it absorbed the life of our whole generation, it was some sort of small part in a strange mosaic made of all those who are passing away at the end of the twentieth century. We are among them. In choosing certain episodes, now these, now others, I have probably told everything very clumsily, very unsystematically. It's hard to tell things otherwise,

and in particular for me. I'm not blessed with the gift of logical thought. Still, I wanted these little shards of our life to help the reader, perhaps, to understand not only how we lived (ours was a special case, we found a lucky ticket for a joyous life, lived against a somber and terrible background) but how and why our whole generation lived, what we responded to, what moved and motivated us.

Life is senseless, but it's beautiful, all the same. It's senseless, terrible, horrifying; but it's also beautiful, and I still think that the good prevails over the bad. Look at how many wonderful people crossed our paths! You have to take the time to look closely at people around you. You might not notice how remarkable they are at first—you have to take the trouble to discern what a person carries inside. Perhaps it will turn out to be a small footpath leading to some sort of joy.

That's all, I suppose. I think I've said what I wanted to say.

Acknowledgments

I WOULD LIKE TO OFFER MY GRATITUDE TO THE FOLLOWING FOR invaluable assistance during the production of this book:

The Lungin family; Ludmila Golubkina; Boris and Marina Zolo-tukhin; Natalia Mavlevich; Inna Tumanian; Roman Rudnitsky; Mark Aronov; Felix Dektor; Irina Martynova; Arina Istratova; Ksenia Staroselskaya; Anatoly Chernyaev; Lev Bezymensky; the Lindgren family; Jean-Pierre Vernant; Christine Lutz; Lyalya, Nata, and Zina Minor; Anna Grishina; Nina Rubashova; Georgy Knabe; Beatrice Olkina; Natalia Musienko; Tatiana Solovyova; Vara and Kirill Arbuzov; Isai Kuznetsov; Inna Barsova; Alla Chernova; Juliana Ilsen; Noemi Grebneva; Yevgeny Agranovich; Yelena Rzhevskaya; Galina Medvedeva; Alexander Kaufman; Alexander and Galina Braginsky; Dmitry Gutov; Irina Sirotinskaya; Flora Litvinova; Galina and Vladimir Novohatko; Alla and Igor Zolotov; Boris Levinson; Natalia Tsoi; Julia Aronova; Dmitry Shevarov; Julia Lurie; Andrei Khrzhanovsky; Margarita Shaburova; Maria Bubnova; Dmitry and Maxim Golland; Freya Van Saun; Gennady Fadeev; Svetlana Novikova; Rene Yalovetskaya; Anna and Ivan Kuzin.

The French embassy in Russia, and, personally, Christine Vergeade, Igor Sokologorsky; and Darya Apollonova; The German embassy in Russia, and, personally, Sabina Hoffman; The Swedish embassy in Russia, and, personally, Marianne Hultberg; Kristine Johansen; and Maria Vedenyapina; Lycée Victor-Duruy in Paris; Saint-Jean-de-Luz city council; Poltava Museum of Local Lore, and, personally, Ludmila Nikolayenko; Naberezhnye Chelny History Museum, and, personally, Zulfira and Mansur Safin, and also Leonid Gorbunov; Moscow City Archives, and, personally, Lidia Naumova; Memorial, and, personally, Alena Kozlova and Alexander

Daniel; Andrei Sakharov Museum and Community Center, and, personally, Tatiana Gromova and Peter Redway; Marina Tsvetaeva Memorial Flat and Museum Cultural Center, and, personally, Nadezhda Kataeva-Lytkina, Natalia Gromova, and Esther Krasovskaya; Moscow's Gorky School Number 204, and, personally, Galina Klimenko; Azbuka publishing house, and, personally, Denis Veselov; National Library of Russia, and, personally, Ivan Serbin; *Izvestia*, and, personally, Ludmila Komleva and Boris Pasternak; The friends and students of Lilianna Lungina and Simon Lungin; Varya Gornostaeva, Sergei Parkhomenko; Grigory Chkhartishvili, Leonid Parfenov, Oleg Dobrodeev, and Sergei Shumakov, without whose enthusiasm and help the film *Word for Word* would not have been shown; and equally to Ludmila and Inna Birchansky and Yekaterina Dorman.

Oleg Dorman

Illustrations

Lungin family archive: 11, 14, 15, 16, 18, 19, 20, 21, 22, 26, 27, 28, 30, 37 (*top*), 39, 41 (*center and bottom*), 43, 45 (*top and center*), 48, 49, 51, 69, 71, 82, 92, 93, 94 (*top, center right*), 97 (*bottom*), 105, 124, 135 (top), 139, 143, 155, 156, 157 (*bottom*), 172, 173, 174 (*drawing by Viktor Nekrasov*), 211, 215, 217 (*bottom*), 219, 225, 239, 240 (*center*), 264, 267, 275, 276, 302, 307, 308 (*drawings by Viktor Nekrasov*), 314, 317, 318, 326

Oleg Dorman: 41 (*top*), 46, 56, 62, 157 (*top*)

Minor family archive (Paris): 37 (*bottom*), 45 (*bottom*)

Vernant family archive (Paris): 240 (*center*)

N.S. Musienko: 58, 59, 61

T.G. and M.V. Korolev: 94 (*center left*), 95 (*bottom*), 112 (*right*), 113

A.D. Davidov: 64

N.A. Ilsen: 84

I.O. Barsovoi: 152

G.S. Knabe: 96

T.A. Troynovsky: 101

R.A. Bezymensky: 63, 141

N.A. Gromovoy: 135 (*bottom*)

N.M. Grebnevoy: 169

L.D. Mazur: 98, 99, 188, 203 (*right*)

K.A. Arbuzova: 114

I.K. Kuznetsova: 115

N.G. Asmolovoy: 186

I.P. Sirotinsky: 229

T.V. Gavrikova-Marshankina: 298

A.M. Pichikyan: 228

Goldin family archive: 134

Naberezhnye Chelny History Museum: 126, 128, 132

Index